BL
1/11

THE REVELS PLAYS

General Editor: Clifford Leech

A WOMAN
KILLED WITH KINDNESS

A
WOMAN
KILDE
with Kindneſſe.

Written by Tho: Heywood.

LONDON
Printed by William Iaggard dwelling in Barbican, and
are to be ſold in Paules Church-yard.
by Iohn Hodgets. 1 6 o 7.

Title page of the 1607 edition, reproduced from the unique copy
in the British Museum

A Woman
Killed with Kindness

THOMAS HEYWOOD

EDITED BY

R. W. VAN FOSSEN

THE REVELS PLAYS

METHUEN & CO LTD
LONDON

This edition first published 1961

Introduction, Apparatus Criticus, etc.
© 1961 Methuen & Co Ltd
Printed in Great Britain by
The Broadwater Press Ltd, Welwyn Garden City, Herts
Catalogue No. (Methuen) 2/6702/10

TO MY MOTHER

AND THE MEMORY OF MY FATHER

General Editor's Preface

The aim of this series is to apply to plays by Shakespeare's predecessors, contemporaries, and successors the methods that are now used in Shakespeare editing. It is indeed out of the success of the New Arden Shakespeare that the idea of the present series has emerged, and Professor Una Ellis-Fermor and Dr Harold F. Brooks have most generously given advice on its planning.

There is neither the hope nor the intention of making each volume in the series conform in every particular to one pattern. Each author, each individual play, is likely to present special problems—of text, of density of collation and commentary, of critical and historical judgment. Moreover, any scholar engaged in the task of editing a sixteenth- or seventeenth-century play will recognize that wholly acceptable editorial principles are only gradually becoming plain. There will, therefore, be no hesitation in modifying the practice of this series, either in the light of the peculiarities of any one play or in the light of growing editorial experience. Nevertheless, in certain basic matters the plan of the series is likely to remain constant.

The introductions will include discussions of the provenance of the text, the play's stage-history and reputation, its significance as a contribution to dramatic literature, and its place within the work of its author. The text will be based on a fresh examination of the early editions. Modern spelling will be used, and the original punctuation will be modified where it is likely to cause obscurity; editorial stage-directions will be enclosed in square brackets. The collation will aim at making clear the grounds for an editor's choice in every instance where the original or a frequently accepted modern reading has been departed from. The annotations will attempt to explain difficult passages and to provide such comments and illustrations of usage as the editor considers desirable. Each volume will include either a glossary or an index to annotations: it is the hope of the editors that in this way the series will ultimately provide some assistance to lexicographers of sixteenth- and seventeenth-century English.

But the series will be inadequately performing its task if it proves acceptable only to readers. The special needs of actors and producers will be borne in mind, particularly in the comments on staging and stage-history. Moreover, in one matter a rigorous uniformity may be expected: no editorial indications of locality will be introduced into the scene-headings. This should emphasize the kind of staging for which the plays were originally intended, and may perhaps suggest the advantage of achieving in a modern theatre some approach to the fluidity of scene and the neutrality of acting-space that Shakespeare's fellows knew. In this connection, it will be observed that the indications of act- and scene-division, except where they derive from the copy-text, are given unobtrusively in square brackets.

A small innovation in line-numbering is being introduced. Stage-directions which occur on separate lines from the text are given the number of the immediately preceding line followed by a decimal point and 1, 2, 3, etc. Thus the line 163.5 indicates the fifth line of a stage-direction following line 163 of the scene. At the beginning of a scene the lines of a stage-direction are numbered 0.1, 0.2, etc.

'The Revels' was a general name for entertainments at court in the late sixteenth and seventeenth centuries, and it was from the Master of the Revels that a licence had to be obtained before any play could be performed in London. The plays to be included in this series therefore found their way to the Revels Office. For a body of dramatic literature that reached its fullest growth in the field of tragedy, the term 'Revels' may appear strange. But perhaps the actor at least will judge it fitting.

CLIFFORD LEECH

Durham, 1958

Contents

Contents

Preface

This edition attempts to present an accurate text of *A Woman Killed with Kindness*, based on the 1607 quarto, to set forth the unsolved problems about the relationship of the two early editions, and, in Introduction and Commentary, to provide such critical and explanatory information as may help towards an understanding of the play. The edition is a revised version of my Harvard University doctoral dissertation, written under the supervision of Mr Alfred Harbage and the late Mr Hyder Rollins, to whom I am grateful for help and encouragement, especially for an introduction to editorial methods without which I could hardly have undertaken my task.

I should like to thank the authorities of the libraries that have permitted me to collate copies of the early editions: the Houghton Library at Harvard, the Folger Shakespeare Library, the Library of Congress, and the Boston Public Library. I am also grateful to the libraries that have provided me with microfilms and photostats: the Houghton Library, the Folger Shakespeare Library, the Henry E. Huntington Library, the Yale University Library, the University of Texas Library, the University of Illinois Library, the Newberry Library, the British Museum, the Bodleian Library, the Victoria and Albert Museum, the University of Edinburgh Library, and the University of Glasgow Library. I owe a particular debt to the staffs at the Houghton, the Folger, the Duke University Library, the Library of the State University of Iowa, and the Cornell College Library for kindnesses extended to me as a reader. Research for the edition was materially aided by a grant from the Duke University Research Council.

Miss Dorothy Cohen, Mr Charles Forker, and Mr Joseph Pequigney, friends at Harvard, were generous with advice and assistance during the early stages of my work. Mr John Fisher, Mr Oliver Ferguson, Mr George Williams, Mr Charles McDonald, and Mr

Barnet Kottler, colleagues at Duke, have given freely of their time and their learning. Mr John Shackford, my colleague at Cornell, has kindly read and commented on the Introduction, as did Mr Kottler and Mr McDonald at an earlier stage. Mr Arthur Brown, of the University of London, kindly responded to questions about the text of the play. Mrs Eleanor McDonald and Miss Luella Snyder provided valuable secretarial assistance.

My greatest debts, however, are to my wife and to the General Editor. My wife, who was responsible for the careful typing of an extremely difficult manuscript, whose keen eye has caught many errors that escaped me, whose sense of style has eliminated the worst of my crudities, has also lived cheerfully through the whole experience. The General Editor has contributed far more than any general editor could be expected to do. Preparing the edition under his supervision has been an education in itself.

R. W. VAN FOSSEN

Cornell College, Mount Vernon, Iowa
January, 1960

Abbreviations

(excluding texts, for which see p. lxxi)

(A) WORKS OF REFERENCE, ETC.

Abbott
E. A. Abbott, *A Shakespearian Grammar*, 1929.

Brereton
J. Le G. Brereton, 'Notes on the Text of Thomas Heywood', *Beiblatt zur Anglia*, XVII (April 1906), 108–23.

Chappell
W. Chappell, ed., *Old English Popular Music*, revised by H. Ellis Wooldridge. 2 vols., 1893.

Daniel
P. A. Daniel, MS. notes in a set of the Pearson edition of Heywood's *Dramatic Works* at the Folger Shakespeare Library.

Deighton
K. Deighton, *The Old Dramatists: Conjectural Readings on the Texts*, 1896.

D.N.B.
Dictionary of National Biography.

E.E.T.S.
Early English Text Society.

Farmer and Henley
J. S. Farmer and W. E. Henley, eds., *Slang and Its Analogues*. 7 vols., 1890–1904.

Griffiths
A. Griffiths, *Chronicles of Newgate*. 2 vols., 1884.

Kökeritz
H. Kökeritz, *Shakespeare's Pronunciation*, 1953.

McK.
R. B. McKerrow, *Printers' & Publishers' Devices in England & Scotland 1485–1640*, 1913.

Nares	R. Nares, *A Glossary*, ed. J. O. Halliwell [-Phillipps] and T. Wright. 2 vols., 1882.
O.E.D.	*Oxford English Dictionary.*
Oxford	*Oxford Dictionary of English Proverbs.*
Shakespeare's England	*Shakespeare's England: An Account of the Life & Manners of His Age.* 2 vols., 1916.
Sykes	H. D. Sykes, 'Elizabethan and Jacobean Plays: Suggested Textual Emendations', *N. & Q.*, cxxxv (October 1917), 441–2.
Tilley	M. P. Tilley, *A Dictionary of the Proverbs in England in the Sixteenth and Seventeenth Centuries*, 1950.

(B) PERIODICALS

J.E.G.P.	*Journal of English and Germanic Philology.*
M.L.N.	*Modern Language Notes.*
M.L.Q.	*Modern Language Quarterly.*
M.L.R.	*Modern Language Review.*
N. & Q.	*Notes and Queries.*
P.M.L.A.	*Publications of the Modern Language Association of America.*
P.Q.	*Philological Quarterly.*
R.E.S.	*Review of English Studies.*
S.B.	*Studies in Bibliography.*
S.P.	*Studies in Philology.*
Sh.S.	*Shakespeare Survey.*
T.L.S.	*Times Literary Supplement.*

Quotations and line-numbers for Shakespeare are from W. J. Craig's one-volume Oxford edition (1925); for the Bible from a 1589 printing of the Geneva Bible. The titles of Shakespeare's plays are abbreviated as in C. T. Onions, *A Shakespeare Glossary*, 2nd ed., 1946 (1919), p. x.

Introduction

I. THE AUTHOR AND THE PLAY

A Woman Killed with Kindness, Thomas Heywood's acknowledged masterpiece and probably the finest example of Elizabethan 'domestic' tragedy, was first produced in 1603 and published in 1607. Reprinted once (perhaps twice) during the next ten years, it was not again in print until it appeared in Dodsley's *Select Collection of Old Plays* in 1744. It has since then taken its place as one of the landmarks of dramatic literature.

Little is known of the author except what he tells us himself and what may be surmised from his writings. He was born in Lincolnshire about 1574, probably studied at Cambridge, and by 1596 was at work writing plays, as is attested by a reference in Henslowe's *Diary*.[1] He wrote for several dramatic companies, chiefly for the company (later Queen Anne's) sponsored by Edward Somerset, Earl of Worcester, of which he was a member. He was a prolific writer of both dramatic and non-dramatic works, though apparently only a small portion of his output has come down to us. Of his work for the stage, he says in the 'Address to the Reader' in *The English Traveller* (1633) that he has 'had either an entire hand, or at the least a maine finger', in 220 plays.[2] Of these, only some twenty-odd survive. He attempted plays of all types: chronicle history (such as *Edward IV* and *If You Know Not Me You Know Nobody*); domestic tragedy (*A Woman Killed with Kindness* and *The English Traveller*); romantic drama (*The Royal King and the Loyal Subject*); comedy of adventure (*The Fair Maid of the West*, *The Captives*, and *Fortune by Land and Sea*); comedy of low life (*The Wise Woman of Hogsdon*); dramatized legend and mythology (*The Four Ages* and

[1] W. W. Greg, ed., *Henslowe's Diary* (1904–8), I, 45.
[2] Thomas Heywood, *The English Traveller*, in [? R. H. Shepherd, ed.] *The Dramatic Works of Thomas Heywood* (1874), IV, 5. The publisher was John Pearson, and this edition will be referred to subsequently as 'Pearson'.

The Rape of Lucrece); and many city pageants and masques. His chief non-dramatic works include *An Apology for Actors, Troia Britannica, Gunaikeion; or Nine Books of Various History concerning Women*, and *The Hierarchy of the Blessed Angels*. Writing almost to the end, Heywood died in 1641.[1]

A Woman Killed with Kindness is first referred to in a series of entries in the diary of Philip Henslowe, the famous theatre manager under whose auspices Worcester's men first produced the play in March 1603, probably at the Rose, a popular public theatre built about 1587 and refurbished in 1592. At one time or another, a number of Elizabethan companies gave plays there.[2] Henslowe's entries run as follows:

pd at the apoyntment of the companye the 4 of
febreary 1602 [N.S. 1603] vnto the tayller for velluet &   } xxij[s]
satten for the womon gowne of blacke velluet
wth the other lynenges belonginge to yt the some of

pd vnto Thomas hewode the 5 of febreary 1602
for a womones gowne of blacke velluett for   } vj[ll] 13[s]
the playe of a womon kylld wth kyndnes some of

* * *

pd at the a poyntment of the company
the 12 of febreary 1602 [*in*] vnto thomas Hewwod in   } iij[ll]
p*a*rt of payment for his playe called a womon
kylled wth kindnes the some of . . . .

* * *

pd at the apoyntment of the company the 6 of
marche 1602 vnto Thomas Hewode in fulle ⟨p⟩   } iij[ll]
payment for his playe called a womon kyld
wth kindness the some of . . . .

* * *

---

[1] The standard biography of Heywood is that by A. M. Clark, *Thomas Heywood: Playwright and Miscellanist* (1931), from which the unattributed information in the two preceding paragraphs has been taken. The best brief account of the life is in G. E. Bentley, *The Jacobean and Caroline Stage* (1941–56), IV, 554–7. The classification of plays above is adapted from that in the *D.N.B.*

[2] See Greg, *Henslowe's Diary*, II, 55, E. K. Chambers, *The Elizabethan Stage* (1923), II, 225–7, and J. Q. Adams, *Shakespearean Playhouses* (1917), pp. 142–60.

pd at the apoyntmente of Thomas blackwode
the 7 of marche 1602 vnto the tayller wch made
the blacke satten sewt for the woman kyld wth kyndnes
the some of . . . .[1] } x^s

The six pounds paid Heywood seem meagre enough, but the sum was apparently a standard one. The tailors' fees, by comparison, seem excessively high, but clothing was expensive at the time, and the amounts, again, are typical.[2]

Four years later, in 1607, appeared the first known edition of the play: '*A Woman Kilde with Kindnesse*. Written by Tho: Heywood. London Printed by William Iaggard dwelling in Barbican, and are to be sold in Paules Church-yard. by Iohn Hodgets. 1607.'[3] We can assume that the publication was unauthorized, for in the preface to his *Rape of Lucrece*, published in 1609, Heywood writes as follows: 'Since some of my plaies haue (vnknown to me, and without any of my direction) accidentally come into the Printers handes, and therfore so corrupt and mangled, (coppied onely by the eare) that I haue bene as vnable to know them as ashamde to chalenge them. This therefore I was the willinger to furnish out in his natiue habit: first beeing by consent, next because the rest haue beene so wronged in beeing publisht in such sauadge and ragged ornaments ...'[4]

2. SOURCES

It has long been recognized that Heywood drew the sub-plot for his play from an Italian story frequently adapted and translated during the Renaissance. In 1884 Symonds pointed out that the Acton-Mountford plot comes from Illicini's Sienese novella about the courteous Salimbene, and Koeppel traced the story through

[1] Greg, *Henslowe's Diary*, I, fos. 119v–120v.

[2] For useful tables of comparative monetary values, see G. B. Harrison, ed., *William Shakespeare, Twenty-three Plays and the Sonnets* (1948), pp. 1084–5, and A. Harbage, *Shakespeare's Audience* (1941), p. 59.

[3] A bibliographical description of both seventeenth-century editions may be found on p.lxv. See also A. M. Clark, 'A Bibliography of Thomas Heywood's Works', *Oxford Bibliographical Society Proceedings*, I (1927), 97–153, and W. W. Greg, *A Bibliography of the English Printed Drama to the Restoration* (1939–57), I, 390 (no. 258).

[4] Greg, *Bibliography*, III, 1207.

B

Bandello and Belleforest to Painter's *Palace of Pleasure* (1566), a popular collection of stories translated from various writers and the source for many plots in Elizabethan and Jacobean drama.[1] Painter's prolix version of the story in question is a fairly literal translation of the twenty-first of Belleforest's *Histoires Tragiques*,[2] which is itself an expansion of the forty-ninth novella in the first part of Bandello's work. Painter gives it an appropriately lengthy heading: 'A Gentleman of *SIENA*, called *ANSELMO SALIMBENE*, curteously and gently deliuereth his enemy from death. The condemned party seeing the kinde parte of *SALIMBENE*, rendreth into his hands his sister *ANGELICA*, with whom he was in loue, which gratitude and curtesie, *SALIMBENE* well markinge, moued in Conscience, woulde not abuse hir, but for recompence tooke hir to his VVyfe'. The story may be summarized as follows:

> After a quarrel stemming from a debate about the relative merits of hounds on a boar hunt, the prominent Salimbene and Montanine families of Siena began a prolonged feud that ended in the near-extinction of the Montanines, leaving only Charles and his sister Angelica, both now poverty-stricken, to sustain the 'whole Bloude and Name of the Montanines'. So attractive was Angelica that Anselmo Salimbene fell hopelessly in love with her. Had it not been for the irreconcilable differences between the two families, he would have sought her hand in marriage. Meantime, Charles had been thrown into prison and condemned to death on default of paying a fine on a trumped-up charge by a vicious neighbour who wanted to secure to himself the one small farm—which Charles had refused to sell—remaining from the Montanine possessions.

[1] J. A. Symonds, *Shakspere's Predecessors in the English Drama* (1884), p. 462; E. Koeppel, *Quellen-Studien zu den Dramen Ben Jonson's, John Marston's, und Beaumont und Fletcher's*, Münchener Beiträge zur Romanischen und Englischen Philologie, XI (1895), 137; William Painter, *The Palace of Pleasure*, ed. J. Jacobs, 3 vols. (1890). The story by Illicini (who is known variously as Ollicino, Licinio, Ilicini, Glicino, and Lapini) appears in *Raccolta de' novellieri italiani*, XV (1815), 3–63; there is a translation in the second volume of Thomas Roscoe, *Italian Novelists*, 2nd ed. (1836), pp. 82–104, and Symonds provides a summary in *The Renaissance in Italy*, Pt IV, II, 2nd ed. (1898), V, 85–6. Jacobs (I, XC) gives Gentile Sermini as the origin of Bandello's story. Symonds (*Renaissance*, p. 85) mentions both versions.

[2] See F. S. Hook, ed., *The French Bandello*, University of Missouri Studies, Vol. XXII (1948), No. 1, pp. 36–8; the French text is conveniently reprinted in this volume.

When Anselmo heard of Charles's misfortune, out of his great love for Angelica and fear for her prospects if her brother died, he paid the fine anonymously and Charles was released. Charles, astonished to learn that his deliverer was his mortal enemy, finally decided that Anselmo must be in love with Angelica and resolved, therefore, to offer his sister to him in payment. Angelica was so vehement in her refusal of this proposal that Charles fainted, and she, in turn, berated herself for her unkindness and resolved to submit to the plan, intending to kill herself rather than sacrifice her chastity. Charles then took her to Anselmo, who, once he had overcome his astonishment, received her gratefully and honourably as his wife. 'You see what is the force of a gentle heart well trained vp, that would not be vanquished in curtesye and Lyberality.'[1]

Fenton's translation of Belleforest's version,[2] 'A wonderful Vertue in a gentleman of Syenna on the behalf of his ennemye, whom he delivered from Death; and the other, to retorne his courtesye with equall frendshyp, presented him with his Sister, whom he knew hee loved entierlye', is quite similar to Painter's, but even more prolix. Fenton expands on Belleforest considerably, elaborating descriptions and adding moralizing comments, but the basic outline of the story is identical in Bandello, Belleforest, Painter, and Fenton.[3] Neither English version provides convincing verbal parallels, but since Heywood elsewhere shows close familiarity with Painter, *The Palace of Pleasure* is perhaps the more likely source.[4] At any rate, one version or the other obviously provides the main outline for Heywood's plot. The chief difference between the novella and the play, aside from the inevitable dramatic condensation of the long-winded laments and reflections in Painter and the toning down in the play of the theme of genteel courtesy, lies in the characters of Salimbene and his counterpart Sir Francis Acton: Sir Francis's evil designs on Susan are altered by love at first sight;

[1] Summarized from Jacobs, III, 288–328. Excerpts from Painter's translation are printed in the Appendix, pp. 103–15 below.

[2] Geffraie Fenton, *Certaine Tragicall Discourses* . . . (1567), as reprinted in Volume XIX of the Tudor Translations, *Certain Tragical Discourses of Bandello translated into English by Geffraie Fenton* (1898), I, 18–83.

[3] See Hook, pp. 21–32.

[4] Koeppel, *Quellen-Studien*, pp. 133–7. In the annotations to the play, attention is called to a few possible reminiscences from Painter.

Salimbene had earlier conceived an entirely honourable love for
Angelica and has, in fact, had Charles released from prison because
of it. Heywood's alteration in making Sir Francis a vindictive an-
tagonist who plans Susan's seduction only as a final cruelty to Sir
Charles has left him open to the charge, as we shall see, of creating
an inconsistent and unbelievable character. The playwright was
wise, however, in omitting a pair of fainting spells that are perhaps
even less credible than Sir Francis's transformation. Angelica
swoons, following a long and tearful lamentation delivered on hearing Charles's proposal; moved and unnerved, Charles faints too;
Angelica revives, only with great difficulty succeeds in rousing
Charles, and accedes to his proposal. Susan's horrified response
and subsequent submission, on the other hand, seem much less
artificial.

To turn to the main plot is to turn to a much more complicated
problem, since no single obvious source has as yet been identified.
Various scholars, however, have pointed out a number of sources
from which Heywood may well have taken suggestions. Koeppel
was the first to suggest that Painter provided the hint for the main
plot just as he had provided the entire structure for the sub-plot.[1]
The fifty-eighth story of Painter's first book, 'A President of Grenoble aduertised of the ill gouernement of his wife, took such order,
that his honestie was not diminished, and yet reuenged the facte',[2]
may be summarized as follows:

> The aging president's fair young wife took advantage of her hus-
> band's absence to go to bed with his 'very propre and handsome
> clerk', but their intrigue was witnessed by a trusty servant, who
> reported it to his master. Though the president was reluctant to
> believe the story, he agreed to wait for a repetition of the offence
> and witness it himself. One morning the servant called him back
> from Court to see for himself. Entering the chamber alone, the
> president found his wife and the clerk in bed together, but, for
> honour's sake, concealed the clerk in a closet, called in the servant
> to show him his error, and discharged him—but with 'five or six
> yeares wages' and other preferment. He ordered the guilty couple

[1] *Quellen-Studien*, p. 136.
[2] In Jacobs, II, 101–3. Painter derives his story from novel 36 in the
Heptameron of Queen Margaret of Navarre, trans. and ed. E. A. Vizetelly
(1894), IV, 63–72.

to say nothing of the affair. At one of a series of feasts given later, he commanded the clerk to dance with his wife and then ordered him to leave the town for ever. 'Afterwardes when the President had made all his frendes and kinsfolkes, and all the countrey, beleue what great loue he bare to his wife, vppon a faire day in the moneth of May, he went to gather a sallade in his garden, the herbes whereof after she had eaten, she liued not aboue xxiiii. houres after, whereof he counterfaited suche sorrowe, as no man could suspect the occasion of her death. And by that meanes he was re-uenged of his enemy, and saued the honour of his house.'

Though the outcome of the story is totally unlike that of the main plot in *A Woman Killed with Kindness*, there are a number of similarities in plot: in both it is a trusted servant who informs the husband of his wife's infidelity; in both the husband is incredulous; in both he surprises the guilty couple alone and allows the lover to escape; in both he reproaches the wife for the dishonour she has brought upon him and their children. The clerk in the story, more-over, is named 'Nicholas', as is the faithful servant in Heywood's play. Even when these similarities have been considered, important differences remain. Apart from the completely different endings, the general effect of the two is quite unlike, because of the rather barren tone in which the story is told, because of the president's cruel treatment of his loyal servant, and because of his dominating concern for the appearance of honour, a concern so totally foreign to Heywood's hero.

There are, however, other close correspondences, suggested by R. G. Martin, between the play and Painter's forty-third novel in Book I, 'Wantones and pleasaunt life being guides of insolencie, doth bring a miserable end to a faire ladie of Thurin, whom a noble man aduanced to high estate: as appereth by this historie, wherein he executeth great crueltie vpon his sayde ladie, taken in adulterie'.[1] The following summary is adapted from Martin's:

A great lord of Piedmont, almost fifty years old, married a young girl of Turin and brought her to live at his country estate. At first a model wife, she soon tired 'of to muche reste and quiet, and began to be inamoured of a Gentleman her neighbor'. She confessed her love to the gentleman, who accepted her favours with alacrity, and

---

[1] 'A New Source for *A Woman Killed with Kindness*', *Englische Studien*, XLIII (1911), 229–33.

it was not long before the servants began to suspect. Finally, the lord himself came to distrust his wife's altered demeanour, grew suspicious of his neighbour's frequent passing before the castle gates, and at length invited him to come frequently to visit, 'vsing the thinges of my house, as they were your owne'. In hiding, he observed the untoward behaviour of his wife and the gentleman. Some days later, he prepared and had brought to him a letter purportedly from the Duke of Savoy, ordering him on an embassy to France. Shortly after his departure, the lady sent for her lover, who hastened to the castle. The lord returned, made his way to the bedchamber, surprised the lovers, and forced his wife and the old female go-between to hang the gentleman from a beam in the chamber. The lord then 'caused the bedde, the clothes, and other furnitures (wherupon they had taken their pleasures past) to be burned' and his wife to be shut up in the chamber with her lover's body. 'And wheu [sic] shee had continued a certaine space in that stinking Dongeon, without aire or comfort, ouercome with sorrow and extreme paine, she yelded her soule to God'.[1]

The lover is, like Wendoll, a person of some social standing; in both versions the husband invites the lover to be his guest; in both, the servants become suspicious; the husband feigns an illness, parallel to Frankford's in the cardplaying scene. Most striking, a forged letter is used in both versions to call the husband away and allay the suspicions of the lovers. The circumstances of the discovery are similar, and, finally, there is a parallel between the lord's ordering the furniture to be burned and Frankford's sending away all his wife's belongings. The differences are equally obvious: in the story, the lord invites the neighbour in order to trap him, whereas Frankford invites Wendoll out of pure magnanimity and thereby himself provides the opportunity for the liaison; the wife in the story makes the overtures, but it is Wendoll in *A Woman Killed with Kindness* who seduces Anne. In the play, Nicholas, one of the servants, conveys his suspicions to his master; in Painter the master becomes suspicious for himself. It is difficult to be sure that Frankford's illness is feigned, but the lord's explicitly is. Finally, the ending of this story is even less similar to the end of the play than is that of Painter's fifty-eighth novel, and the tone of the whole is again vastly different.

[1] In Jacobs, I, 240–8, who gives Boaistuau, 1559, No. 5, as Painter's source and Bandello, Part i, novel 42, as the ultimate origin of the story.

Two additional stories in Painter have been suggested by McEvoy Patterson,[1] but the similarities between them and Heywood's play are remote. The fifty-seventh novel of Book I[2] is the story of a woman who committed adultery with a gentleman 'brought vp' in her husband's house. The plot includes a feigned journey, the repentance of the wife, and her eventual forgiveness by her husband. The fifty-ninth novel of Book I,[3] again a story of adultery, treats of two close friends, one of whom married. The single man continued to live harmoniously with the friend and his wife until the married man groundlessly began to suspect an illicit liaison. His lack of trust eventually led the bachelor to cuckold his erstwhile friend. Little more than the close friendship of the two men provides a link with Heywood's plot.

Even though the resemblances pointed out by Patterson are slight, it is possible, as he suggests, that Heywood put together the main plot of his play by drawing details from all four of the stories in Painter examined above. Recently, however, W. F. McNeir has suggested a different line of descent for the plot.[4] According to his thesis, Heywood found his material in Robert Greene's 'The Conuersion of an English Courtizan' (1592), itself an adaptation of a tale inserted in George Gascoigne's 'The Adventures of Master F. J.' (1573).[5] Greene's story can be summarized as follows:

> An English gentleman, married to a fair young woman, had as his bosom friend a gentleman who fell in love with the former's wife

---

[1] 'Origin of the Main Plot of *A Woman Killed with Kindness*', in *University of Texas Studies in English*, No. 17 (1937), pp. 75–87.

[2] In Jacobs, II, 97–100. Painter's story comes from Queen Margaret's *Heptameron*, novel 32, in Vizetelly, IV, 17–28. W. Creizenach, *The English Drama in the Age of Shakespeare*, trans. C. Hergon (1916), p. 231, suggested that in *A Woman Killed with Kindness* Heywood 'placed on English soil one of the Queen of Navarre's French tales'.

[3] In Jacobs, II, 104–6. Painter's story has its origin in Queen Margaret's *Heptameron*, novel 47, in Vizetelly, IV, 203–11.

[4] 'Heywood's Sources for the Main Plot of *A Woman Killed with Kindness*', in J. W. Bennett, O. Cargill, and V. Hall, Jr, eds., *Studies in the English Renaissance Drama* (1959), pp. 189–211.

[5] Greene's version is most readily available in G. B. Harrison, ed., *Robert Greene, The Thirde & Last Part of Conny-catching*, together with *A Disputation Betweene a Hee Conny-catcher and a Shee Conny-catcher* (1923), pp. 60–9. For Gascoigne's story see *A Hundreth Sundrie Flowres*, ed. C. T. Prouty, *University of Missouri Studies*, XVII (1942), 96–100.

and fairly easily succeeded in making her his mistress. Their relationship continued for some time until a maid 'who had been an old seruant in the house, began to grow suspitious'. Having her suspicions confirmed, she revealed the state of affairs to her master, who was so reluctant to believe what she told him that she suggested that he pretend to go away from home in order to lay a trap for the lovers. The master therefore announced, within a day or two, that he would go hunting, but returned with the maid to spy on the love-making of his wife and friend. Swearing the maid to silence, he resolved to 'reserue his honour inuiolate, reclaime his wife, and keep his friend'. In pursuance of this aim, he began the practice of leaving a counterfeit coin in the window each time he had intercourse with his wife. When, her curiosity aroused, she inquired about these coins, he replied that 'I giue thee hyer, which is for euerie time a slip, a counterfeet coyne, which is good inough for such a slipperie wanton'. The wife immediately confessed all, begged pardon, and promised reform. At the next interview with her lover, she, weeping, made him swear on a Bible to grant her a request. She then made known her remorse and asked him to forgo any 'vnlawfull pleasure' in the future. He too repented their folly and gave his promise. The wife told her husband 'what had past betweene her and his friend'. The husband expressed his pleasure and thus 'reclaimed with silence a wanton wife, and retained an assured friend'.

There are certainly resemblances between Greene's narrative and Heywood's plot, and the differences between Greene and Gascoigne, as McNeir shows, bring the former considerably closer to Heywood. Nevertheless, the similarities seem no closer than those between the novellas and Heywood. The verdict must remain 'not proven'.[1]

Even more indefinite, but of the first importance, is the relationship of *A Woman Killed with Kindness* to earlier middle-class tragedies and to the didactic tradition on which they in part rely.[2]

---

[1] It may also be noted that P. Niemeyer, *Das bürgerliche Drama in England im Zeitalter Shakespeares* (1930), p. 66, has suggested that a forerunner of the plot is to be found in certain medieval miracle plays, and O. Cromwell, *Thomas Heywood: A Study in the Elizabethan Drama of Everyday Life*, Yale Studies in English, LXXVIII (1928), 55, finds a link with a tale in the *Gesta Romanorum*.

[2] The most useful book on this subject, though it exaggerates homiletic considerations at the expense of artistic ones, is H. H. Adams, *English Domestic or Homiletic Tragedy*, Columbia University Studies in English

Most Elizabethan and Jacobean tragedies, including all up to the time of Marlowe and all of Shakespeare (with the possible exception of *Othello*), treat the lives of great men, usually kings and noblemen, persons from the lower classes being considered fit subjects for comedy or for comic material in serious plays. But beginning in the 1590's it is possible to distinguish a group of tragedies quite unlike those dealing with persons of high estate. H. H. Adams defines this new genre, the so-called 'domestic tragedy', as 'a tragedy of the common people, ordinarily set in the domestic scene, dealing with personal and family relationships rather than with large affairs of state, presented in a realistic fashion, and ending in a tragic or otherwise serious manner'.[1] As Adams points out, this group of plays owes something in subject-matter and in tone to the fifteenth-century morality plays, in which 'the plain citizen . . . first became recognized as a character suitable for serious drama'.[2] *Everyman*, the most famous of these morality plays, is typical of them in that its protagonist is an allegorical representative rather than an individual, but, again typically, he is clearly representative of all men rather than those of royal lineage, and the play has a homely realism not unlike that of the Elizabethan domestic tragedies. The didacticism explicit in the moralities, moreover, can be found, to a greater or lesser degree, in the later plays.

Aside from Heywood's two contributions to the genre, *The English Traveller* and *A Woman Killed with Kindness*, most of the extant domestic tragedies, including the fairly well-known *Arden of Feversham*, *A Yorkshire Tragedy*, and *A Warning for Fair Women*, all anonymous, are murder plays. The earliest is *Arden of Feversham*, produced about 1591 and published in 1592, which shares with the other plays mentioned the characteristics in Adams's definition. Certainly Heywood wrote *A Woman Killed with Kindness* in the

---

and Comparative Literature, No. 159 (1943). See also the books by Niemeyer and Cromwell referred to on p. xxiv, n. 1; H. W. Singer, *Das bürgerliche Trauerspiel in England* (1891); A. Winkler, *Thomas Heywood's 'A Woman Killed with Kindness' und das Ehebruchsdrama seiner Zeit* (1915); F. M. Velte, *The Bourgeois Elements in the Dramas of Thomas Heywood* (1924); and M. Doran, *Endeavors of Art: A Study of Form in Elizabethan Drama* (1954).

[1] pp. 1–2; compare Doran, p. 143.   [2] Adams, p. 55.

tradition established by *Arden*;[1] similar domestic subject-matter, in many respects anticipating the relationship of Anne and Frankford, can be found in the Jane Shore plot of Heywood's *First and Second Parts of King Edward the Fourth* (1599).[2] Winkler, who discusses the similarities between *A Warning for Fair Women* and *A Woman Killed with Kindness*, decides that the later play owes far more to the earlier one than to any novella.[3] A more considered view would perhaps be that, on the one hand, through Painter, Heywood owes much to the Italian novella writers and, on the other, much to his predecessors in domestic tragedy, but that the debts are different in kind rather than in degree. In the Italians (and perhaps in Greene) he found the outline for his plots; in the earlier plays (which here share common ground with Greene) he found precedent for the middle-class English setting to which he could shift his material and, concomitant with this setting, the realistic treatment of everyday life and domestic activity that contributes so much to the success of his play.

Finally, no discussion of Heywood's sources would be complete without a reference to the title of the play. *Joan as Good as My Lady* and *The Blind Eats Many a Fly*, both lost plays, are evidence that Heywood had a fondness for proverbial titles, and in '*A Woman Killed with Kindness*' he found one of good standing and wide dissemination. In its more primitive form it has been traced back as far as *An enterlude of Welth and Helth*, of about 1557: 'Then let vs go hence, with kindnes my her[t?] ye do kyll'.[4] In 1582 it appears with much the same connotation that it carries in Heywood:

> I wish my selfe no worse bestowed, then marrie an to [*sic*] old welthy Widdow. I doo not thinke, but by good vsage, to continue her first affction [*sic*] geeuen, euen vnto hir verie Graue.
>
> You will kill her with kindnesse, (quoth Maria Belochye.
>
> Yea, Madam, (ϕ Soranso) if her nature be so froward, as to die with good vsage.[5]

---

[1] *A Warning for Fair Women* (1599) and *A Yorkshire Tragedy* (1606) have, indeed, been attributed to Heywood; see Clark, *Thomas Heywood*, pp. 301–28, 337–8.

[2] Pearson, I, 1–187.   [3] pp. 15, 46.

[4] Reproduced in Tudor Facsimile Texts, No. 167 (privately printed, 1907), D1v, 1.1. The proverb is No. K51 in Tilley.

[5] George Whetstone, *An Heptameron of Ciuill Discourses* (1582), sig. T4v.

But its most famous occurrence is in *The Taming of the Shrew* (c. 1594):

> This is a way to kill a wife with kindness;
> And thus I'll curb her mad and headstrong humour.
> He that knows better how to tame a shrew,
> Now let him speak: 'tis charity to show.
>
> (IV. i. 211–14).

3. THEME

The chief consideration, of course, must be not where Heywood got his material, but what he did with it, and critical opinion on the merits of the play has varied widely. Heywood has, on the one hand, been attacked on various grounds. The play is made up of two hypothetical situations. It has no internal consistency. The entire situation is naively unreal. The lack of unity deprives the characters of any verisimilitude they might have had.[1] *A Woman Killed with Kindness* 'distinctly lacks elevation of thought or feeling. An ever-popular sentimentality vitiates its scenes'.[2] There is no purgation; Frankford is 'a most dreadful cad'; the love-at-first-sight motive in the sub-plot is not convincingly handled; the whole is no more than 'Elizabethan hokum'; it 'lacks character delineation, it lacks unity'. The play is 'childish and primitive'.[3] On the other hand—and that the critics can be talking about the same play is difficult to believe—this splendid tragedy is a consummate masterpiece in plan and execution.[4] It is 'absolutely the best Elizabethan drama of its kind'. It has conviction, power.[5] In fact, to overpraise the play, 'or to regard it other than as one of the choicest of Elizabethan plays', is impossible.[6] These comments, though obviously extreme, are representative of the varied critical reception the play has met with. Two so widely separated views can hardly be reconciled, but a careful consideration of the theme, the structure, the characters, and the style

[1] W. J. Courthope, *A History of English Poetry* (1895–1910), IV, 215–16.

[2] H. W. Wells, *Elizabethan and Jacobean Playwrights* (1939), p. 71.

[3] W. P. Eaton, *The Drama in English* (1930), pp. 127–30.

[4] Singer, p. 41 ('Diese herrliche "tragödie des hausfreundes" ist ein vollendetes meisterstück in anlage und durchführung').

[5] Velte, pp. 100, 111.

[6] F. E. Schelling, *Elizabethan Drama* (1925), p. 337.

may at least make it possible to understand what in the play has elicited such disparate opinions.

First of all, Heywood has domesticated the material of his play in every sense. The romantic and courtly Italian stories borrowed from Painter have been transformed to something inherently English, unadorned, imbued with the spirit of contemporary country life. Such assertions are of course subjective, but many features of the play can be adduced to support them. In the main plot, the emphasis is on the relationship between husband and wife, not on the somewhat sensational events of the seduction, and on Frankford's friendly nature as exemplified in all his dealings in the play—with Wendoll, with Nicholas, with Cranwell, with Sir Francis and Sir Charles. A country wedding, a family dinner, an evening of cards— these events in the lives of ordinary men transferred to the stage are largely responsible for the simplicity and homeliness that pervade the action. The sub-plot, less successful in achieving verisimilitude to everyday life because of the inherent improbability of its central action, is nevertheless at least partially integrated into the country scene: it opens with the gentlemanly banter among Sir Francis, Sir Charles, Cranwell, and Wendoll that ends in the fatal wager; the hawking scene which follows was probably as appropriate to the class involved and as familiar, at least by reputation, to the heterogeneous audience of the Elizabethan theatre as is the ubiquitous nightclub scene to the American or English cinema-goer today. The succeeding scenes involving litigation and imprisonment reflected matters that were distressingly common in the vicarious experiences of the theatre-goers, if not in their personal affairs.

A number of lesser considerations, in addition to matters of characterization and style to be discussed later, contribute to the 'ordinary' quality of the play. There is first of all Heywood's statement in the Prologue, with its implicit but clear indication that he was striving for a kind of effect at least comparatively unusual in the contemporary theatre:

> Look for no glorious state, our Muse is bent
> Upon a barren subject, a bare scene. (ll. 3–4).

With such an announcement audience and reader are better prepared to accept and interpret the setting, personages, and events
that follow.[1]

Further, as Robert Louis Stevenson noted,[2] Heywood has a remarkable facility for names, names which characterize as skilfully
as Dickens's, but without Dickens's grotesquerie. Sharpe goes too
far when he says that the play 'probably contains in its Actons, its
Mountfords, Frankfords, Wendolls, Malbys, Cranwells, and Shaf-
tons a good number of more-or-less well concealed personal identi-
fications',[3] but his reaction is testimony to Heywood's skill in no-
menclature. It may be added that even the given names, what few
there are, have the ring of common usage about them—John,
Charles, Francis, Anne, Susan. The servants contribute not only
another group of common names, including in Spiggot the Butler,
Roger Brickbat, Jack Slime, Sisly Milk-pail, Joan Miniver, Jane
Trubkin, and Isbel Motley some rather feeble attempts at humour,
but much of the country feeling that dominates the early part of the
play. Scene ii, the servants' version of the wedding party, even more
than the opening scene itself helps establish an aura of rural festivity
and domestic happiness.

Domesticity pervades the play. From Sir Charles's encomium on
Anne (i. 13–24) to Frankford's final speech of forgiveness (xvii.
114–20), the theme of the blessings of family life dominates, no-
where more clearly than in Frankford's soliloquy opening scene iv
(ll. 1–14). These lines serve other functions: they help to characterize Frankford and to make the tragic conclusion more terrible by
building up its antithesis early in the play; they also contribute to
the insistent domestic theme. Even the sub-plot, chiefly concerned
with other matters, extols the joys of domestic bliss (vii. 1–8). Thus
in both plots, and in the main plot throughout, the common, the
everyday, the domestic, is emphasized. Indeed, as Yves Bescou has
astutely observed, Frankford's house assumes a symbolic value—

---

[1] Similar apologetic matter appears in the epilogue to *Arden of Feversham*
and in the choruses of *A Warning for Fair Women*.

[2] Letter to W. E. Henley, April 1882, in *Letters*, ed. S. Colvin (1899), I,
239.

[3] R. B. Sharpe, *The Real War of the Theaters* (1935), p. 230.

'en verité la maison est ici l'un des personnages principaux'; and
the punishment Frankford imposes upon Anne is familial—she is
excluded for ever from 'home'.[1]

More than mere setting or atmosphere, this domesticity is itself
a theme of the play, the main plot of which is, after all, concerned
with the relationship between the loving husband and the erring
wife, with adultery and the penalty exacted for it, with remorse and
repentance, with forgiveness and reconciliation. In order to understand exactly what Heywood is trying to say about this theme, we
must first know something of the beliefs and practices of the time
concerning adultery. The usual punishment for adultery, not an
offence under the civil law, but subject only to ecclesiastical prosecution, was public penance in one form or another, whether in the
church, in the pillory, or with the sinner wrapped in a sheet exposed
to the jeers of passers-by. There is on record, for example, the
punishment of one Margaret Orton, who 'accordinge to her ap-
pointement hathe done her pennance, in the parishe Churche of
Barkinge, in Essex, before yᵉ seconde Lesson at morninge prayer,
vpon Sonday the xviiith day of March aᵒ 1575; and ther was redd
the firste parte of the homilie againste whoredome & adulterie, the
people ther present exorted to refraine from soche wickednes wher-
by the[y] might incurre the displesure of Almightie God for vio-
lating his holy lawe'.[2]

The wife's real ordeal came after her public penance had been
completed, for, as a social outcast and a woman, she would have
had a most difficult time. We have, for example, Elizabeth Shuttle-
worth's statement at her hearing, 9 October 1561, on charges of
adultery: 'beynge askid "howe she will lyve hereafter, sins she cannot mary, and her husband hath refusid her"; she sais "she knowis

---

[1] 'Thomas Heywood et le problème de l'adultère dans *Une femme tuée
par la bonté*, *Revue Anglo-Américaine*, IX (1931), 139.

[2] The 484th case (1576) in *Series of Precedents of the Archdeacon's Court
of Essex* (1847), p. 160. Only a year later, William Harrison, in his 'Description of England' that forms a part of Holinshed's *Chronicles*, advocated
more severe treatment for adulterers which 'would prove more bitter to
them than half-an-hour's hanging, or than standing in a sheet, though the
weather be never so cold' (in William Harrison, *Elizabethan England*, ed.
L. Withington [1902], p. 242).

not, but as God will provide for her" '.[1] Thus by one interpretation
Frankford's real kindness to Anne consists not 'in sparing her life
but rather in his continuing to shelter her from an unfeeling world
after she has forfeited all right to such protection'.[2] If we turn to the
play, however, we see that Anne expects only death to follow upon
her husband's discovery of her infidelity:

> Though I deserve a thousand thousand fold
> More than you can inflict, yet, once my husband,
> For womanhood—to which I am a shame,
> Though once an ornament—even for His sake
> That hath redeem'd our souls, mark not my face
> Nor hack me with your sword, but let me go
> Perfect and undeformed to my tomb.   (xiii. 94–100).

It would, indeed, be dishonourable of him to consider any other
course: 'He cannot be so base as to forgive me, / Nor I so shameless
to accept his pardon' (xiii. 139–40). Anne's opinion is substantiated
by the tradition of revenge in the drama and in contemporary practice: short shrift was given the unfaithful woman, whose husband
had the right to kill her.[3] In the world of the play, and by inference
in life, Heywood shows his audience that the more gentle course,
the Christian course, brings satisfactions impossible to vindictive
punishment of any kind. For Anne's true contrition leads to the
moving scene first of her reunion with her sorrowful but still loving
husband, then of her death, a death inevitable for the whole atmosphere and development in the main plot of the play. The pattern of
sin, repentance, atonement, and forgiveness is complete. Heywood
has, furthermore, the distinction of being the first to 'put into dramatic form ... the punishment which arises from the erring characters' consciousness of their guilt in the place of the punishment of
an exterior physical revenge'.[4]

---

[1] In F. J. Furnivall, ed., *Child Marriages, Divorces, and Ratifications*,
E.E.T.S., No. 108 (1897), p. 80.

[2] W. Thorp, *The Triumph of Realism in Elizabethan Drama 1558–1612*
(1928), p. 113.

[3] See H. H. Adams, p. 151; F. S. Boas, *Thomas Heywood* (1950), p. 39;
and C. L. Powell, *English Domestic Relations, 1487–1653* (1917), p. 204.

[4] F. T. Bowers, *Elizabethan Revenge Tragedy, 1587–1642* (1940), p. 225.
M. Grivelet, *Thomas Heywood et le Drame Domestique Élizabéthain* (1957),
p. 84, has pointed out the similarity between the attitude expressed in the

The Christian overtones in this situation and its development are further accentuated by frequent Biblical and theological allusions. When Wendoll is introduced into the Frankford household, for example, Nicholas comments that 'The Devil and he are all one in mine eye' (iv. 88). Wendoll is later referred to as a Judas (xiii. 76) and likens himself to Cain (xvi. 126). Anne, moreover, draws an equation between her faithfulness to her husband and her soul's health: 'The love I bear my husband is as precious / As my soul's health' (vi. 141–2), and, at the point of yielding to Wendoll's persuasiveness, admits in an aside, 'My soul is wand'ring and hath lost her way (vi. 151). When, finally, she resolves to starve herself to death, it is with salvation as a goal: 'But when my tears have wash'd my black soul white, / Sweet Saviour, to Thy hands I yield my sprite' (xvi. 105–6).[1]

L. B. Wright has shown that this redemptive process is by no means Heywood's only thematic concern in the main plot;[2] *A Woman Killed with Kindness* is only one among several of Heywood's plays that exemplify, whether positively or negatively, the ideal of unwavering friendship between two men. Thus Wendoll is but little troubled about the immorality of seducing Anne; his real concern is for the violation of his friendship with Frankford, who has been both friend and benefactor:

> And shall I wrong this man ? Base man ! Ingrate !
> Hast thou the power straight with thy gory hands
> To rip thy image from his bleeding heart ?
> To scratch thy name from out the holy book
> Of his remembrance, and to wound his name
> That holds thy name so dear, or rend his heart
> To whom thy heart was join'd and knit together ?
>
> (vi. 44–50).

When Frankford reproaches Nicholas for accusing Anne and Wen-

---

play and that in Heywood's prose treatise *Gunaikeion* (1624), p. 179: 'But much is that inhumane rashness to bee auoided by which men haue vndertooke to be their owne justicers, and haue mingled the pollution of their bdes [*sic*] with the blood of the delinquents. . . '

[1] I owe much of this analysis to Professor Harold Jenkins; compare Grivelet, pp. 218–19, 226.

[2] 'The Male-friendship Cult in Thomas Heywood's Plays', *M.L.N.*, XLII (1927), 510–14.

doll, it is his friend that he thinks of first (viii. 61–4). When, with sword drawn, Frankford is restrained by the maid from pursuing Wendoll, his imprecations are directed not at his having seduced Anne, but at his having betrayed their friendship: 'Go, to thy friend / A Judas' (xiii. 75–6). When Wendoll repents, he repents his treachery to a friend (xvi. 37–41). In connexion with these clear indications of Heywood's concern with the theme of friendship, however, we must remember that the play begins and ends with, and devotes most of its attention to, the relationship between husband and wife. Beside the speeches cited above, we must place such important utterances as Frankford's soliloquy that follows Nicholas's accusation:

> She is well born, descended nobly;
> Virtuous her education; her repute
> Is in the general voice of all the country
> Honest and fair; her carriage, her demeanour
> In all her actions that concern the love
> To me her husband, modest, chaste, and godly.
>
> (viii. 95–100).

Frankford's chief concern in these lines, despite another reference to Wendoll as Judas in line 102, is clearly his wife, not his friend. Similarly, his moving speeches to Anne in scene xiii—such as 'Did I not lodge thee in my bosom? / Wear thee here in my heart?' (xiii. 113–14)—emphasize the love that had existed between them, not the fact that she had chosen his friend to betray him with. And Wendoll in his speech of self-condemnation does more than accuse himself of playing false to a friend: 'O God, I have divorc'd the truest turtles / That ever liv'd together' (xvi. 47–8). We can, then, accept the presence and significance of the friendship theme in *A Woman Killed with Kindness* without allowing it to usurp the place of principal interest.

The more serious problems of interpretation arise in connexion with the sub-plot, which has provoked condemnation and even ridicule on practically all counts, most notably for its lack of connexion with the main plot.[1] Freda L. Townsend made the first con-

---

[1] See, for example, T. S. Eliot, 'Thomas Heywood', *Selected Essays*, 2nd ed. (1934), p. 177. The essay originally appeared in *T.L.S.*, 30 July

siderable attempt to discern a unity in the play.[1] She finds a key in Clark's recognition of several basic similarities between the two plots that tie them together thematically: 'Heywood retains the same atmosphere, conventions, kinds of characters, manner of speech, and general accessories in the romantic tragi-comic plot as in the domestic drama.'[2] These similarities, she thinks, are not accidental, but are indicative of a more basic unity, for virtue and honour are inextricably tied together in both plots: Sir Charles's honour can be vindicated only by the sacrifice of Susan's virtue. Susan agrees, but, equating virtue and honour, she tells her brother, 'But here's a knife, / To save mine honour, shall slice out my life' (xiv. 84–5). Similarly, in the main plot Frankford speaks of his wife's loss of her virtue in terms of honour: 'thou art wounded in thy honour'd name' (xvii. 118); and Wendoll's sin is one of broken faith. Miss Townsend also sees 'the contrast and thematic unity' brought out in dialogue and in 'the juxtaposition of the climactic scenes in each action'. Charles feels a 'surcharge of kindness' on his soul as the result of the payment of his debts by Sir Francis; Frankford will 'surcharge his wife with kindness'. Anne and Susan both speak of sacrificing their hands and breasts and compare the value of honour with that of the soul's redemption. Heywood 'could not have failed to intend the dramatic contrast between the chaste Susan and the unchaste Anne, between the honourable Sir Charles and the dishonourable Wendoll, between the rewards of virtue and the wages of sin'.[3]

In a subtle and sympathetic analysis of *A Woman Killed with Kindness*, Peter Ure suggestively elaborates Miss Townsend's thesis about the virtue–honour relationship and the surcharge of kindness:[4]

1931, pp. 589–90, and was also reprinted in *Elizabethan Essays* (1934), pp. 101–16.

[1] 'The Artistry of Thomas Heywood's Double Plots', *P.Q.*, xxv (1946), 97–119; compare Winkler, p. 13, and Bescou, pp. 136–7.

[2] Clark, *Thomas Heywood*, p. 230, cited in Townsend, p. 100.

[3] pp. 101–2.

[4] 'Marriage and the Domestic Drama in Heywood and Ford', *English Studies*, XXXII (1951), 200–16.

Even more striking than this play upon Honour is the way the underplot takes up the paradox of the drama's title. Sir Charles must discharge the burden of moral debt which his enemy's kindness has laid upon him; similarly, Mistress Frankford must find a way to repay with interest the kindness of Frankford after his discovery of her adultery. Cheated of her rightful punishment, in which she expects to suffer the part of a Tamyra or a Penthea . . . she must herself inflict upon herself the appropriate penalty in order to discharge the mounting debt to husband and conscience. Frankford's improper kindness has surcharged her and in the end kills her—it is the paradox at the heart of the play, suitably pointed by the concluding lines of the fifth Act. Both plots thus explore this strange paradox and run a concurrent course: Sir Charles suffers under the monstrous burden of being forgiven by a bitter enemy and is driven to an immorality (the prostitution of his sister) in order to free himself of it; Mistress Frankford, pardoned by a deeply injured husband, has to rid herself of the debt by an act of contrition that proceeds far beyond Christian penitence. She starves herself to death. In the conclusion, Acton's magnanimity to Susan is balanced by Frankford's passionate compassion as his wife dies. Both men have been consistently kind and these final mercies are a consummation of their virtuous Magnificence.[1]

This convincing thesis effectively answers the oft-repeated objections to the yoking of two supposedly heterogeneous plots for the sake of filling out two hours' traffic. It substantiates by analysis the contribution of the sub-plot to 'the victory of loftier over lower motives which constitutes the supreme effect of the play'.[2] Grivelet has recently called attention to the pun on 'match' that links the two plots here: 'C'est le thème de l'union et de l'affrontement qui s'expriment en anglais par un même mot.'[3] Sir Charles says of the newly married Frankfords, 'You both adorn each other, and your hands / Methinks are matches' (i. 65–6). Only a few lines further on, he speaks to Sir Francis: 'I'll make a match with you: meet me to-morrow / At Chevy Chase, I'll fly my hawk with yours' (93–4). And Sir Francis replies, ' 'Tis a match, 'tis done' (98). The same conjoining of themes appears again in the cardplaying scene, where

[1] p. 204.
[2] A. W. Ward, ed., *A Woman Killed with Kindness* (1897), p. xvii. The introduction, from which this quotation is taken, is reprinted in Ward's *Collected Papers* (1921), III, 367–83.
[3] pp. 207–8.

the 'match' symbolizes the rivalry between Frankford and Wendoll:

> *Anne.* Come, Master Frankford, who shall take my part?
> *Frank.* Marry, that will I, sweet wife.
> *Wen.* No, by my faith, sir, when you are together I sit out;
>   it must be Mistress Frankford and I, or else it is no
>   match.
> *Frank.* I do not like that match.   (viii. 124-9).

Conversely, 'la longue inimitié qui avait dressé Sir Francis Acton contre les Mountford finira par se transmuer en un mariage.'[1] This is not to say that the sub-plot is entirely successful or that it can necessarily be defended against the charge of sentimentality, a charge which we shall examine later. It is to say, however, that Heywood saw a common theme in the two plots that has eluded too many of his critics, who, put off perhaps by the comparative woodenness of the characters, perhaps by the 'distasteful' transaction arranged by Sir Charles, perhaps by what they consider preposterous in the basic action, have thrown out the baby with the bath-water.[2]

4. STRUCTURE

It can be shown, furthermore, despite criticism to the contrary, that Heywood put his two plots together with considerable dramatic skill. A careful examination of the structure of the play reveals a principle of dramatic construction that could be of great effectiveness theatrically; and it is important to keep the theatre in mind, to remember that what may in the study seem to be inconsistencies in characterization or absurdities in plot development might cause no difficulty to the spectators in the pit. One does not wish to belabour the obvious, but so much earlier criticism has wasted itself on minutiae irrelevant to dramatic presentation that premises must be made clear.

The external connexion between the plots is simple but skilful: they begin simultaneously, the discussion of married life that sets

---

[1] Grivelet, p. 208.

[2] In 'Honor and Perception in "A Woman Killed with Kindness"', *M.L.Q.*, xx (1959), 321–32 (which appeared after my typescript had gone to the printer), Patricia Meyer Spacks argues that the world of the play 'is not a world of true and significant moral standards—it is rather a world of appearance'.

the stage for the main plot and the wager that initiates the events of the sub-plot occupying practically the whole of the first scene. Sir Francis, who is to become one of the three central figures in the sub-plot, is brother to Anne Frankford, the woman who is killed with kindness. Sir Charles, shortly to be Sir Francis's bitter enemy, praises Anne's virtues and accomplishments, and, in a speech that becomes ironic in retrospect, both for speaker and for subject, comments with feeling on the happiness that he sees before him. Wendoll, soon to be taken into Frankford's house and to betray his trust by seducing Anne, participates in the wager by making a side bet with Cranwell; the latter is a slightly sketched figure who, as a guest of Frankford's, participates as an unwitting witness of the card-playing scene when Frankford's suspicions are deepened and as a sad spectator of the discovery, banishment, and reconciliation that follow. Wendoll continues the superficial connexions of the plots as the witness of the fight in scene iii and the bearer of tidings to Frankford in scene iv.

The other interrelationships that follow are more subtle and, at the same time, more important dramatically. They can best be seen in a chronological analysis. Scene ii, the servants' frolic in the yard, provides a comic counterpart of the festivities that have preceded, and builds, in the dancing that closes the scene, to a height of gaiety that continues the mood established by the first scene, a mood contrasting sharply with all to follow in the play. Similarly, the argument over the merits of hawks and hounds is reflected in comic vein in the bickering among the rustics over the tune and dance to be chosen for their celebration. Up to this point, both spectator and reader might logically expect the play to be a comedy.

With scene iii we are in a world of more ominous happenings. The spirit and excitement of the hawking scene erupt into bitter argument, violence, and killing, and the scene closes only after Sir Charles's remorse and his affectionate relationship with his sister have been carefully set forth.[1] The transition from these dire events

[1] W. L. Ustick, 'A Note on *A Woman Killed with Kindness*', *M.L.N.*, XLV (1930), 514–15, quotes from James I, *Basilikon Doron*, to show the typicality of this scene—that it is not lugged in merely to further the plot: 'hawking . . . is . . . subject to mischances; & (which is worste of al) is ther through an extreame stirrer vp of passions'. Grivelet goes too far in sug-

is skilfully managed by Wendoll's bringing the news of the combat, manslaughter, and arrest to the Frankfords; his arrival interrupts the equanimity of the happy household set forth in Frankford's opening soliloquy. Again the technique is one of dramatic contrast, from the violence of the hunting scene to the peacefulness of domesticity. This scene, depicting Frankford's friendly invitation to Wendoll to become his companion and dependent, is largely expository,[1] but a hint of the ominous events to follow is presented in Nicholas's refusal to wait on Wendoll, a refusal based on a strong, if unexplainable, dislike (iv. 85–8).

Thus far, as Miss Townsend has seen, there has been no indication that two separate actions are being developed, but, beginning with the next two scenes, 'each action is set firmly on its feet, and now Heywood is careful not to let one intrude upon the other. Instead he sets them in contrast to each other, and makes the events in one complement and bear out the mood of the other'.[2] Scene v introduces the false Shafton, whose apparently generous loan to Sir Charles brings on the worst of the latter's troubles. Thus Shafton's 'generosity' here, with its deadly consequence, follows directly after Frankford's kindness to Wendoll,[3] and Shafton's villainy is immediately paralleled in the main plot by Wendoll's plan, set forth and executed in scene vi, to repay Frankford by seducing Anne: he calls himself 'A villain and a traitor to his friend' (vi. 25). Most of this scene is devoted to Wendoll's conquest of Anne, but it carries along the suggestion of a counteraction in the words of Nicholas (ll. 180–3), who has heard the final colloquy of the guilty lovers.

In scene vii, Shafton brings his villainy to fruition by demanding from Sir Charles either the payment he knows Sir Charles cannot make or the land he has set his heart on; the next stage of the action

---

gesting that the scene echoes the ballad of Chevy Chase, but it is perhaps true that the choice of locale was not mere whim: 'Le nom seul suffit à évoquer la lutte sanglante et chevaleresque que chante la fameuse ballade' (p. 203).

[1] Grivelet, p. 216, finds a parallel between Frankford's impulsive installing of Wendoll in his home and Sir Charles's impulsive murder of the huntsmen.

[2] p. 117.   [3] Grivelet, p. 206.

is initiated in this same scene when Sir Francis falls in love with Susan at first sight. Thus in these adjacent scenes, vi and vii, the threat to stability is fully stated in each plot; the working out of these threats begins in the next pair of scenes. That the turning points of the two plots thus occur in close juxtaposition makes for an effective parallelism in subject-matter and in tone, though complications of various sorts take place in both plots before they reach a similar resolution in the final scene. In scene viii, Nicholas tells the incredulous Frankford of the treachery perpetrated by his wife and friend; the *double entendre* of the cardplaying scene determines Frankford to take immediate steps to learn the truth; and the scene ends with Frankford's plan to surprise the lovers 'when they think they may securely play' (viii. 218). This strangely contrived and artificial scene serves to give a symbolic and yet highly dramatic life to the tensions growing among the main characters.[1] Scene ix, devoted to the sub-plot, shows Susan's inability to find a benefactor for her brother and Sir Francis's unsuccessful attempt to offer her money, and ends, like scene viii, with a resolution that alters the course of action (ll. 73-5).

From this point on, the regular alternation of scenes between the two plots is replaced by a new pattern: the rapid resolution of the sub-plot is set forth in two brief scenes that separate blocks of scenes leading up to the emotional climaxes of the main plot. The brief scenes devoted to the sub-plot, however, are paired with the blocks devoted to the main plot in much the same fashion as the alternating scenes that have preceded. Thus scene x and scenes xi, xii, and xiii portray a discovery and a decision, by Sir Charles and Frankford, in their respective plots. In x, Sir Charles is released from prison, learns to his astonishment that Sir Francis is his benefactor, and resolves on a plan to give his sister to Sir Francis in payment for the kindness done him. Similarly, in the main plot, scene xi presents the ruse of the false letter by which Frankford is enabled to surprise Anne and Wendoll in each other's arms; scene xiii presents the act of surprising itself, followed by Wendoll's flight and Frankford's banishing of Anne; and scene xii, a brief colloquy among the servants, serves to build suspense and to make

[1] See *ibid.*, p. 210.

more probable by separation on the stage two events that require a lapse of time between them.

The emotional climax of scene xiii is followed in scene xiv by the final climax in the sub-plot. Sir Charles tells Susan of his decision to give her to his benefactor-enemy, she acquiesces at last, but with the understanding that she will commit suicide rather than lose her honour, and Sir Francis, finally, brings complete reconciliation in his crowning magnanimous act of taking Susan to wife (ll. 153–6).

Heywood uses the last three scenes, xv, xvi, and xvii, for the slower dénouement of the main plot. Once again he employs the dramatic technique of contrast, juxtaposing to the happy union of scene xiv the touching scene xv, which shows the discovery of Anne's lute, and through this discovery the complete isolation felt by Frankford: 'Now nothing's left; / Of her and hers I am at once bereft' (xv. 23–4). In the closing speeches of the scene, Heywood prepares for the juncture of the two plots in scene xvii and re-emphasizes in the minds of the audience the contrast between the rejoicing group of Sir Francis, Sir Charles, and Susan and the forlorn isolation of Frankford. Scene xvi presents the other side of the coin—Anne in sad solitude, separated for ever from her husband and children—and aligns itself even more closely as a complement to scene xv in the repeated use of the effective symbolism of the lute (ll. 71–4).[1] The scene continues with the confrontation of Anne and Wendoll, included to show her complete reformation, and concludes with a final insight into Wendoll's character.

Scene xvii is a triumphant justification of the dramatic structure which Heywood has worked out. It continues the tragic mood of the two scenes that have preceded, but at the same time ends the play with the reunion between husband and wife that Frankford's character has all along made inevitable. The reunion is thus parallel to that in the sub-plot (scene xiv), but with a difference, for it is a reunion only at the moment of death. All three principals of the sub-plot, it should be noted, are present for this final scene; except for Wendoll, once Frankford's intimate friend, all those who attended

---

[1] There is here also an effective contrast with Sir Charles's characterization of Anne in scene i: 'her own hand / Can teach all strings to speak in their best grace, / From the shrill treble, to the hoarsest bass' (ll. 19–21).

the wedding party that opened the play are here. Aside from the servants, only one character appears who was not present in scene i,
and it is significant that that one character is Susan. Thus the figure
who has most strikingly stood for the side of honour and virtue, in
whom no blemish can be found, has taken the place of the figure
whose lack of honour and virtue has brought about the unhappiness
that makes this final ironic reunion so poignant and, in a sense, so
incomplete. We must not miss the neatness with which Heywood
points this contrast between the theme and mood of the first scene
and the theme and mood of the last. The play opened with a wedding. It closes with a wedding that is also a funeral. The contrast
appears most clearly in Frankford's final conversation with Anne:

> And with this kiss I wed thee once again.
> Though thou art wounded in thy honour'd name,
> And with that grief upon thy deathbed liest,
> Honest in heart, upon my soul, thou diest.
>
> *Anne.* Pardon'd on earth, soul, thou in Heaven art free;
> Once more thy wife, dies thus embracing thee. [*Dies.*]
> *Frank.* New marry'd and new widowed; O, she's dead,
> And a cold grave must be our nuptial bed.
>
> (xvii. 117–24).

Ure has pointed out the 'firmness of structure' that Heywood's
treatment of the marriage theme gives to the play: 'happiness (the
wedding prologue), grief (the discovery of the broken contract),
happiness (the re-marriage in death)'; this structure 'allows him to
define the second happiness as something new in kind, wrested
from sorrow and penitence'.[1] We can add that the sub-plot shows
the same structure, from the cordial, bantering friendship of Sir
Francis and Sir Charles, through the sorrow caused by altercation
and recrimination, to a new friendship based on love and an appre-
ciation of the value of other human beings. As we have seen, one
threefold structure parallels and reinforces the other.

5. CHARACTERS

Thus the two plots are firmly welded together by theme and by
structure. Even when conditions of dramatic presentation have
been allowed for, however, certain difficulties in characterization

[1] p. 210.

remain, at least by modern standards, though it is doubtful that
Heywood's portraits are deserving of such blanket condemnation
as they have sometimes received.[1] Frankford, the character to
whose emotions and motivations Heywood devoted the greatest
care, has for the most part received favourable treatment from the
critics.[2] We see him from the beginning of the play as the Christian
gentleman—but not Adams's 'theological prig'. In the opening
scene he banters half-ashamedly with his friends, quite a convincing portrait of the bridegroom. His soliloquy that opens scene iv
shows him as the contented family man, perhaps a trifle self-satis-
fied, but almost too typical of the middle-class hero he is supposed
to represent. The chief function of this scene, so far as Frankford
is concerned, is to present him in his normal state, to show him in the
full bliss of domesticity before he is plagued by doubts or cast down
by tragic certainties. The soliloquy contributes to this portrait; his
generous treatment of Wendoll later in the scene adds a further
touch. Reacting to the fight in a very natural fashion, he shows chief
concern for his new brother-in-law Sir Francis. Thus he replies to
the news of Sir Charles's crime with the words, 'Now trust me I
am sorry for the knight; / But is my brother safe?' (iv. 53–4). In
his next speech, he again expresses his sympathy for Sir Charles,
but without maudlin moralizing, and turns immediately to a subject closer to hand—a case of more modest hardship, but one in
which Frankford can do a good turn:

> Sir Charles will find hard friends; his case is heinous
> And will be most severely censur'd on.
> I am sorry for him. Sir, a word with you:
> I know you, sir, to be a gentleman
> In all things, your possibilities but mean;

---

[1] See, for example, E. C. Dunn, introduction to *Eight Famous Elizabethan Plays* (1932), p. xii, and H. H. Adams, pp. 156–7.

[2] See, for example, J. A. Symonds's review of Pearson's edition of *The
Dramatic Works of Thomas Heywood*, in *The Academy*, VI (25 July 1874),
87–8, reprinted in Symonds's preface to A. W. Verity, ed., *The Best Plays
of Thomas Heywood*, Mermaid Edition (1888), pp. xxviii–xxx; J. Copeau,
'La première tragédie domestique: Une femme tuée avec douceur, par
Thomas Heywood', *Revue d'art dramatique*, Nouvelle Série, XIII (1902),
432, 435; and Velte, p. 107. Contrast H. H. Adams, p. 156, and Bescou,
pp. 130–1.

> Please you to use my table and my purse—
> They are yours.   (iv. 60–6).

He sees what appears to him desert and rewards it, but he is blind
to the weaknesses in Wendoll's character that Nicholas has somehow seen intuitively (iv. 85–8).

Frankford does not speak again until scene viii, in which Nicholas informs him of his wife's infidelity and the cardplaying sequence
confirms the suspicions that have been raised. In the conversation
between Nicholas and his master, Frankford's generosity is re-
emphasized in the unsolicited offer of an advance on wages followed
by Nicholas's tribute in an aside: 'By this hand, an honourable
gentleman. I will not see him wrong'd' (viii. 31–2). When, however,
Nicholas begins to impugn Anne and Wendoll, Frankford reacts in
a perfectly normal fashion: passion overcoming his usual kindliness, he speaks angrily to Nicholas and finally strikes him. He
simply cannot believe evil of his wife and close friend, yet second
thoughts and Nicholas's obvious earnestness lead him to inquire
further. Nicholas's argument that he has nothing to gain by his
revelations seems convincing. Frankford's confidence has at least
been shaken, though in the soliloquy that follows his dismissing
Nicholas (viii. 95–111) he refuses to act hastily. He must have time
to think. But time for thought is denied him by the conclusions he
is forced to draw from the *double entendres* of the cardplaying scene.
From the lines spoken, it is impossible to tell whether Wendoll and
Anne are innocently betrayed by their own words or are exchanging
glances and enjoying a joke between themselves; a producer could
have it either way. To Frankford, at any rate, the exchange is
damning. Unable to bear more, sick at heart, he brings the game
to an end, but plots with Nicholas to expose the lovers absolutely.
Through this carefully developed series of reactions to Nicholas's
report and to the card game, Frankford is provided with credible
motivation for believing Anne guilty. The almost miraculous testimony of the cardplaying dialogue, even without his reasoned consideration of Nicholas's motives, is enough.[1]

---

[1] An opposing view is expressed by F. Marshall, review of 8 March 1887
Dramatic Students Society production of *A Woman Killed with Kindness*,
in *The Theatre*, XVIII (1887), 211, and E. H. C. Oliphant, *Shakespeare and
his Fellow Dramatists* (1929), I, 853.

Scene xi adds little to our knowledge of Frankford's character, but the commentators are unanimous in their praise of his appearance in the discovery scene (xiii), where his grief, his anger, and his kindness are so convincingly blended. As he and Nicholas enter the house, Frankford is still hoping against hope that his wife may be innocent; yet, knowing somehow that he will find what he fears to find, he prays also that he may restrain himself from violence (ll. 26–33). He finds the worst, and only his Christian belief keeps him from exacting a bloody revenge on the guilty pair. Before returning to the bedroom to wake them, Frankford utters the most moving speech in the play:

> O God, O God, that it were possible
> To undo things done, to call back yesterday;
> That Time could turn up his swift sandy glass,
> To untell the days, and to redeem these hours;
> Or that the Sun
> Could, rising from the west, draw his coach backward,
> Take from the account of time so many minutes,
> Till he had all these seasons call'd again,
> Those minutes and those actions done in them,
> Even from her first offence; that I might take her
> As spotless as an angel in my arms.
> But O! I talk of things impossible,
> And cast beyond the moon. God give me patience,
> For I will in to wake them.   (xiii. 52–65).

The poignancy of these lines is heightened not only by the falling off in tone at the end, but by their setting, inserted as they are between two homely speeches by Nicholas. They contrast as well with Frankford's outburst of anger, from which he is saved by the restraining hand of the Maid, as he pursues Wendoll across the stage. This moment alone is enough to give Frankford flesh and blood. Not superhumanly good, he is simply better than most of us, as befits the hero of a play that is, after all, still a tragedy, even if it ignores some of the 'rules' of the classical drama. His humanness is further revealed in his debate with Anne: he does not preach at her or revile her; rather he asks her how she could possibly have done such a thing. Horror and incredulity are mixed. Frankford's words to Anne after he has decided on a course of action imply an apparent vindictiveness, but they must be seen in a seventeenth-century light; Anne's view that he could not be so *base* as to forgive her makes his behaviour seem more creditable:

> I'll not martyr thee
> Nor mark thee for a strumpet, but with usage
> Of more humility torment thy soul
> And kill thee even with kindness.   (xiii. 153–6).

These words might also be regarded as a symptom of Frankford's distraught condition, certainly evident in the uncharacteristic manner in which he discourteously brushes Cranwell aside when the latter tries to interrupt his pronouncement of sentence.

His behaviour in the last scene is in keeping with what we have learned of him before—he is still the noble, compassionate Christian gentleman. Again, moreover, the nobility is compelling because Heywood has tempered it with human failings. The Frankford who enters the room speaks with the half-pompous, half-self-satisfied air of the man embarrassed by the situation in which he finds himself, a public meeting with his unfaithful wife:

> Good morrow, brother; good morrow, gentlemen.
> God, that hath laid this cross upon our heads,
> Might had He pleas'd have made our cause of meeting
> On a more fair and a more contented ground;
> But He that made us, made us to this woe.   (xvii. 68–72).

His greeting to his wife is cold—'How do you, woman?' (74)—but in his next speech he has begun to soften. Only a touch of reproach remains:

> That hand once held my heart in faster bonds
> Than now 'tis gripp'd by me. God pardon them
> That made us first break hold.   (79–81).

Anne's illness and her obviously genuine repentance end his discomfort and his coldness. The rest of his speeches to her assure her of his forgiveness and seek to re-establish the relationship that had been theirs before the unfortunate affair with Wendoll. His final speech, the closing lines of the play, alludes to the title in a tone different from that in scene xiii. There is once again the predominating feeling of grief, this time tinged with regret for what might have been:

on her grave
I will bestow this funeral epitaph,
Which on her marble tomb shall be engrav'd.
In golden letters shall these words be fill'd:
'Here lies she whom her husband's kindness kill'd.'

(136–40).

If Frankford is, on the whole, a consistent and believable character, the working of whose mind we can understand, not quite so much can be said for Anne, whose easy yielding to Wendoll's overtures has been the one event in the play that the critics almost unanimously condemn.[1] At least part of the explanation for her behaviour lies in the beliefs and practices of Heywood's time. As Alfred Harbage has indicated, one of the points of contrast between plays written for the private and for the public stages is that the latter maintain the 'old decorum'. Thus, 'in both comedy and tragedy, the popular school of dramatists not only failed to cultivate chances for erotic treatment but took considerable pains to avoid it', and any 'comment on "lack of motivation" ' in the seduction scene in *A Woman Killed with Kindness* 'is somewhat beside the point'.[2] Secondly, noting the behaviour of Lady Anne and Queen Elizabeth in Shakespeare's *Richard III*—also a play for the public stage—A. M. Clark reminds us that suddenness of perversion and conversion is one of the conventions of the Elizabethan theatre.[3] Thirdly, Hallett Smith contends that Anne is related to the erring women in the popular poems setting forth the complaints of royal mistresses. 'Heywood followed the tradition when he was making his play. He knew that his audience was interested in the type of woman he was presenting; the success of his fellow-poets proved that. And he knew that the audience would not require a psychological analysis of the sinning woman, because she would be immediately recognized as belonging to a familiar type'.[4]

Peter Ure defends the seduction scene as we have it on structural grounds: 'The three great incidents of the Frankford story, the

---

[1] In a long article in defence of Anne, '*A Woman Killed with Kindness*' *P.M.L.A.*, LIII (1938), 138–47, H. D. Smith provides a convenient summary of earlier opinion about her.

[2] *Shakespeare and the Rival Traditions* (1952), pp. 205–6.

[3] *Thomas Heywood*, p. 234.   [4] p. 147.

seduction, the discovery, and the death, to all of which the wedding-scene is an important prologue, are three blocks of time drama-turgically handled. To the first naturally belong the struggle of conscience, the seduction, the yielding... Heywood could not de-lay with the early effect without disrupting the structure.' He achieves a shape for the marriage theme by allotting each of the main incidents 'only that share of stage time proportionate to its importance in the total scheme'.[1] Grivelet notes these three divi-sions into which the action of the main plot falls, 'la faute, la sen-tence, l'expiation', and observes that this structure is emphasized by the fact that Wendoll is accorded fullest attention in the first, Frankford in the second, and Anne in the third.[2] To have devoted full treatment to Anne's motivation in the seduction would have been to destroy this thematic and dramatic pattern.

Playing with dramatic patterns rather than presenting the study of character that would be expected of a modern novelist, Heywood takes care to include in his portrait of the perfect wife in the first scene a series of qualities every one of which becomes ironic in retrospect. Frankford himself twice emphasizes, in his soliloquy in scene iv, those characteristics in Anne that she so strikingly lacks after her fall. That fall is not wholly preposterous. One would not wish to push the suggestion too far, but in Anne's interruption of Wendoll's account of the fight at hawking there is an impulsiveness that would make her yielding more credible.[3] Perhaps, after all, she is a woman capable of being 'swept off her feet by a wind of passion which she has no power to resist'.[4]

When Wendoll declares his love to her, her first reaction is the fully appropriate one of any wife in similar circumstances, a com-pound of surprise, horror, and righteous indignation: 'The host of Heaven forbid / Wendoll should hatch such a disloyal thought' (vi. 110–11). Here and throughout her protests she accuses Wendoll

[1] pp. 206–7.

[2] pp. 205, 212. Only Winkler (p. 17) and Eliot (p. 176) find it unneces-sary to provide excuse or explanation for Anne's behaviour.

[3] This assumes it is a mistake for Baskervill, Heltzel, and Nethercot to assign this speech to Wendoll.

[4] T. M. Parrott and R. H. Ball, *A Short View of Elizabethan Drama* (1943), p. 122.

of betraying Frankford's friendship and generosity. Not once does she indicate that she feels any loathing or even dislike for her seducer. Thus the aside that indicates her surrender is by no means so inappropriate to what has gone before as it might at first appear: 'What shall I say? / My soul is wand'ring and hath lost her way' (vi. 150–1). She yields, aware that she has been 'enchanted' by Wendoll's wily persuasiveness, fearful that this maze may 'prove the labyrinth of sin', but not without some inner struggle, and not without some motivation.

By the time we next see Anne and Wendoll on the stage together alone, loathing and fear have replaced whatever pleasurable emotions she may have felt earlier. Here Anne's own analysis of her situation is a revealing one:

> You have tempted me to mischief, Master Wendoll;
> I have done I know not what. Well, you plead custom;
> That which for want of wit I granted erst
> I now must yield through fear. Come, come, let's in.
> Once o'er shoes, we are straight o'er head in sin.
>
> (xi. 110–14).

'Want of wit', as Marshall says, accurately characterizes a woman who fell less from any desire to sin than from a lack of prudence and courage.[1] Swept away by the moment, she did not think clearly; now she sees the evil of what she has done, but she can find no way out.

Her repentance when Frankford discovers her with her lover is moving and unfeigned, a moment of remorse and humiliation made the more human by her one request of her husband:

> even for His sake
> That hath redeem'd our souls, mark not my face
> Nor hack me with your sword, but let me go
> Perfect and undeformed to my tomb.   (xiii. 97–100).

Scene xvi, as we have seen, portrays the confrontation between Anne and Wendoll that reveals the completeness of her repentance. The meeting between Anne and Nicholas earlier in that scene has much the same effect. Nicholas enters, hands her the lute with a curt 'There' (17), and replies to her sorrowful recognition of it in

[1] p. 209.

a cold speech that opens with a bawdy and unkind pun (20–5). The genuineness of Anne's repentance, her obvious grief, her vow to starve herself to death—these affect Nicholas strongly:

> I'll say you wept; I'll swear you made me sad.
> Why how now, eyes ? what now ? what's here to do ?
> I am gone, or I shall straight turn baby too.   (xvi. 66–8).

A skilful touch on Heywood's part, this alteration shows Frankford's strongest partisan, the man who reported the criminals to his master, now deeply moved by the woman he had earlier called a whore.

In the last scene Anne's behaviour needs little comment; it merely carries forward to death the sincerity of her repentance. She is allowed to die happy, reunited with her husband, and we cannot but feel that she has earned her happiness. A final objection remains to be disposed of: the sentimentality of death from a broken heart.[1] As Hallett Smith points out, Anne quite specifically does not die of a broken heart, but of starvation. She has told Nicholas in scene xvi that she has resolved to take no more nourishment, and Jenkin confirms the carrying out of this resolution in the final scene (ll. 34–7). 'Mrs. Frankford is fasting for penance and she actually dies of starvation, which is surely a method of suicide as valid as poison or the dagger or serpents at the breast.'[2]

Wendoll is perhaps the most ambiguous of the members of the triangle. After his contribution to the opening banter about married life, he remains silent until Sir Francis and Sir Charles have agreed on their wager. Then, quite gratuitously, he offers, 'Ten angels on Sir Francis Acton's hawk; / As much upon his dogs' (i. 103–4). The sum is modest compared to the two hundred pounds put at stake by the principals, but enough to give pause when in scene iv Frankford comments on Wendoll's impoverishment. Wendoll himself hints at second thoughts on the subject of gambling after Sir Francis's hawk fails: 'She hath stroke ten angels out of my way' (iii. 4). A gentleman 'somewhat press'd by want' (iv. 33) has no business indulging in such extravagances; one so careless in these matters is just the man to succumb to greater temptations when they present themselves.

---

[1] Eliot, p. 176.   [2] p. 141.

D

Wendoll's surprise and gratitude when Frankford offers him his maintenance seem genuine enough; doubtless they are, but something in the man has, as we have seen, caught the keen eye of the servant, Nicholas, who earlier in the scene has reported Wendoll's hasty arrival in uncomplimentary terms: 'Sure he rid in fear / Or for a wager' (iv. 23–4). No higher motive, he seems to say, could be attributed to this fellow.

The mixture of good and evil in Wendoll is most evident in the seduction scene, where his better and worse selves quarrel for domination. The first fifty-two lines of this scene are really one long soliloquy, twice broken—by the appearance of Anne and Frankford crossing the stage and by Jenkin's counterpointed commentary on Wendoll's lines. The first section finds Wendoll attempting to stifle a passion that rises within him. Not until the second section, after Anne and her husband have crossed the stage, does spectator or reader know the identity of the object of his love. The nine lines of that section, in fact, make the startling identification only to follow it with a desperate plea that acknowledges his realization of the sin inherent in his wishes. The conflict of emotions comes through the rapid sweep of the lines:

> Thou God of thunder,
> Stay in Thy thoughts of vengeance and of wrath
> Thy great almighty and all-judging hand
> From speedy execution on a villain,
> A villain and a traitor to his friend.   (vi. 21–5).

His sense both of sin and of gratitude is strong, but, his reason overcome by passion, not strong enough. He concludes by throwing the burden of his transgression on Fate (ll. 45–52). Even after he has thus resolved on his course of action, further doubts occur, but he perseveres in his attempts to persuade Anne to take him as a lover, and at last he succeeds in eliciting from her the pity that is only one step from a stronger emotion. The assurance of secrecy tips the balance, and, half reluctantly, she consents.

In scenes viii and xi he successfully maintains the appearance of continued friendship and concern for Frankford's welfare, even joining with apparent relish in Anne's suggestion that he accompany Frankford on the way to York (xi. 77). Frankford's refusal of his offer, of course, he accepts with concealed delight; for he is too overwhelmed by his pleasures with Anne to suspect a trap. That caution has flown is evidenced by his rude proposal that he and Anne eat in her chamber, leaving Cranwell to his own devices.

Although Wendoll participates in the discovery scene only by fleeing across the stage pursued by Frankford and thus living up to Nicholas's taunting enumeration of the causes for which he might be expected to hasten (iv. 23-4), his two long speeches in scene xvi give us a further, and final, insight into his ambivalent character. According to stage convention we must accept the repentance expressed in his soliloquy (xvi. 32-4). He continues to blame Fate for his present position, but, still in soliloquy, expresses remorse for the separation he has brought to the Frankfords. Anne's sad plight moves him so deeply that he resolves to do what he can for her: 'I'll do my best good will / To work a cure on her whom I did kill' (xvi. 98-9). Anne's instant rebuff and Jenkin's taunts, however, succeed in bringing out the less attractive side of his character. We need feel no surprise at his attempt to assuage his pride (xvi. 129-36). Although Heywood has been criticized for allowing Wendoll to go scot-free,[1] the end he meets is sound: Heywood does *not* indulge himself in poetic justice; instead, he uses this scene both to reinforce what he has already shown us of good and of evil in Wendoll and to set forth the inescapable reality that evil does get away unpunished.

By way of final comment on the characters in the main plot, we should notice that Heywood has attempted, in varying degree, to gain sympathy for all three members of the triangle: the cuckolded husband retains his dignity, the unfaithful wife dies repentant, the false friend is shown to have some sense of his evildoing.

The characters in the sub-plot, Sir Francis Acton, Sir Charles Mountford, and his sister Susan chief among them, are not so satisfactory as those in the main plot.[2] Susan, as the soul of virtue, lacks

---

[1] F. J. Cox, introduction to his edition of *A Woman Killed with Kindness* (1907), p. 6.

[2] Even Grivelet, whose thorough and sensitive analysis attempts to defend practically every aspect of the play, is forced to fall back on dramatic pattern as his chief justification for the minor action: 'Dans la seconde,

the complexity and unpredictability of Anne; hence her interest as
a character suffers. From our first meeting with her, when she discovers her brother 'wounded among the dead' (iii. 57), to her last
words of any significance ('Alas that she should bear so hard a fate; /
Pity it is repentance comes too late' [xvii. 31–2]), she is always ready
with the sententious remark, the proper moralizing observation.
Only once, in the scene where her brother tells of his plan to deliver
her to Sir Francis, does she rise above the commonplace, and there
it is a thrilling bit of theatricality that moves us rather than any
penetrating revelation of character:[1]

> Susan. I see your resolution and assent;
>   So Charles will have me, and I am content.
> Sir Cha. For this I trick'd you up.
> Susan.   But here's a knife,
>   To save mine honour, shall slice out my life.
>   (xiv. 82–5).

Her brother Charles is little better, though the contrast between
the carefree gentleman of scene i and the embittered prisoner of
scene x at least provides an opportunity for a skilful actor to show
the progressive deterioration of the character. But, unlike Frankford, Sir Charles shows little real feeling for the events that have
occurred, develops a monomania for repaying Sir Francis, and
simply uses his sister, preposterously, as a final piece of negotiable
property. Only once, and that immediately following the killing,
does he show any remorse for his crime or any realization that he
has brought his troubles upon himself (iii. 42–5). Hereafter he does
not once allude to his crime. This reticence may be necessary for
an ending to the plot that will contrast neatly with the outcome of
the main action, but it is neither natural nor affecting.

---

l'auteur a schématisé à dessein. On a l'esquisse sans les couleurs, ou le
reflet estompé de la réalité. Ni Acton, ni Sir Charles, ni Suzanne n'in-
téressent par eux-mêmes mais en tant seulement qu'ils servent de support
à la réflexion' (p. 210).

  [1] Grivelet's defence of her abrupt about-face in acceding to Sir Francis's
offer of marriage will hardly do as an explanation of her psychology: 'Par
là, en effet, Heywood fait valoir—et tout son théâtre est subordonné à cette
conviction—que l'honneur doit s'incliner devant l'amour vrai, c'est-à-dire
l'amour conjugal' (p. 209).

Sir Francis, if possible, is worse still. Though his falling in love at first sight may be intended to make Anne's equally sudden reversal less incredible, there is for him no persuasive Wendoll; there is, moreover, no trace elsewhere in the play of the kind of susceptibility here revealed, unless it be in his reaction to Anne's pathetic situation in the final scene. Nothing, in fact, can satisfactorily account for a transformation from insatiable hunger for revenge to weak-kneed infatuation in the space of twenty lines. Yet he comes upon the scene with the words, 'Again to prison! Malby, hast thou seen / A poor slave better tortur'd?' (vii. 75–6), and in his next speech can reveal, 'I am enchanted, all my spirits are fled, / And with one glance my envious spleen stroke dead' (ll. 93–4).

The minor characters, for the most part, are mere types, filling a function in the plot and no more. Cranwell and Malby, in main plot and sub-plot respectively, provide a kind of objective frame of reference. Both are in attendance at the wedding party; both participate in the quarrel at the hawking match; they appear together in scene v to inform the audience how Sir Charles has fared at his trial. Then in scene vii, Malby gently attempts to get Sir Francis to listen to reason: 'Methinks, Sir Francis, you are full reveng'd / For greater wrongs than he can proffer you' (ll. 85–6). His later appearances, in scenes xiv and xvii, are of little significance. Cranwell's analogous rôle is most clearly evident in scenes xi and xiii. In scene viii he has done no more than provide the equivalent of a fourth for bridge, but in scene xi his excusing himself from supper after Frankford has left on his supposed journey has the ring of knowing more than it professes, as if, in disgust, Cranwell wishes to avoid the love-making of Anne and Wendoll. In scene xiii he speaks only two words, interrupting Frankford's announcement of Anne's punishment with 'Master Frankford—' (l. 156). But Frankford will not let him proceed, and we cannot tell what sort of reaction the brief phrase is meant to convey. We can see only that for some reason he wishes Frankford to reconsider his course of action. Slightly enigmatic, speaking rarely and tersely, he is present at all the crises between Anne and Frankford. His portrait is too slight to be highly significant, but he seems to cast a brooding shadow over the already sombre play, reacting almost as a member of the audience might be expected to react. One thinks of him as comparatively old.

Like Malby and Cranwell, the servants are sketchily drawn, but also like them, and unlike the other minor characters, they are of some interest in themselves—partially because they go beyond the usual 'comic relief' given to such supernumeraries. Nicholas, the soul of loyalty, is the most interesting of the group. We have seen already how his intuitions about Wendoll are used in scene iv and how he reacts so sympathetically to Anne's grief in scene xvi. He is notable throughout the play for his frankness and forthrightness, particularly when he risks his livelihood to tell Frankford what he knows of Anne and Wendoll (scene viii). In the last scene, when Anne's grieving friends, understandably but extravagantly, second Frankford's 'I'll wish to die with thee' (l. 97), Nicholas undercuts the extravagance with a typically homely observation: 'So will not I; / I'll sigh and sob, but, by my faith, not die' (ll. 99–100). This same down-to-earth quality is revealed to a lesser degree by the other servants, especially by Sisly and Jenkin in scene xii, when they pray fervently that God's grace may keep their mistress pure. The inherently sentimental is again undercut by the earthily realistic: 'When the cat's away the mouse may play' (ll. 5–6).

This undercutting of sentimentality is the most important function of the servant scenes, but that they are, whether in themselves or taken in connexion with other elements in the play, in some way less than effective is evident from the many charges of sentimentality that have been hurled at both plots. 'Sentimental validity', says Hallett Smith of T. S. Eliot's charge that Anne's death is sentimental, 'is substituted for moral validity in drama when the character's will is made irrelevant or impotent. Of this substitution Heywood is not guilty.'[1] This statement also replies, in anticipation, to Madeleine Doran's charge that 'an easily achieved divine mercy takes the curse off original sin'.[2] Such may be true of the other plays that Miss Doran discusses, but, as we have seen, Mistress Frankford does not achieve divine mercy easily. Miss Doran's second objection, that the sentimental leads to the double ending in which only the guilty die,[3] can be answered by pointing to the

[1] p. 147.   [2] p. 146.   [3] *Ibid.*

guilty Wendoll's escape and to the innocent Frankford's suffering, which is as great as Anne's. She escapes, into what, we know not; he must remain behind, and it is notable that he does not reply to Sir Charles's invitation, seconded by Cranwell, that he divide his sorrow equally among his friends (xvii. 125–9).[1]

The most cogent attack on the sentimentality of the play is that of L. C. Knights: 'In Heywood's general dramatic technique statement takes the place of evocation: Mrs. Frankford is *stated* to be the model wife, and the moral of the play is stated, not implicit; in other words Heywood's drama is sentimental rather than ethical. And sentimental drama is made by exploiting situations provided by conventional morality rather than by exploring the full significance of those situations.'[2] Though it would be foolish to try to deny the truth in the first part of this quotation—Heywood does lean too heavily on statement—one might suggest that the moral is *both* explicit and implicit. Heywood is adventurous in so far as he does explore what a Christian should do in a situation where the revenge impulse can most easily disguise itself as justice. Yet, having made his decision, he seems content with it: no problem, or the possibility of one, remains. He lacks the sense of a permanent difficulty that, e.g., Ford seems to keep in *The Lady's Trial*.[3] Because of this feeling of a too great ease in the manner of Heywood's thinking, the word 'sentimental' is not altogether inappropriate.

To this deficiency must be added another, most fully discussed by M. E. Prior: 'Frankford is the flower of his class, an admirable civilized type, but his limitation as the main figure of a great action can be seen in the very definition of his virtues, and particularly in his assertion that he is happy among other men because in his mean estate he embraces content. This may be the goal of all true philosophy, but it is not enough for the tragic hero. . . He loses his con-

[1] E. Bernbaum, *The Drama of Sensibility: A Sketch of the History of English Sentimental Comedy and Domestic Tragedy, 1696–1780* (1915), p. 36, provides an effective reply to this group of charges; compare Bescou, p. 127.

[2] *Drama & Society in the Age of Jonson* (1937), p. 249. With the statement about Anne compare Eliot, p. 176: 'What is perhaps clumsy is the beginning superfluously by a scene directly after the marriage of the Frankfords, instead of by a scene marking the happiness of the pair up to the moment of Wendoll's declaration'.

[3] I owe this comparison to the General Editor.

tent, but he does not lose himself—his tolerance (at least by contemporary standards), his capable mind, his ability to act humanely.'[1] Prior goes on to contrast the play with *Othello*. Such a contrast, he feels, shows one of the principal differences between tragedy and 'drame'—'plays in which the main characters face a trying situation and confront a difficult problem, any solution to which seems to involve them in possibly unhappy consequences. In tragedy, the course of the action involves the character essentially . . . [Frankford's] basic qualities remain in large part unthreatened by the action. *Othello* is tragic; *A Woman Killed with Kindness* is sad and pathetic.'[2] One can agree with this distinction without losing sight of the merits of the play. Sadness and pathos lend themselves all too readily to sentimentality, but they are not synonymous with it. Here sentimentality is largely avoided by Heywood's firm sense of dramatic structure, by the contrasts in tone set up in the comments of the servants, by the fact that reunion comes only at death, and, most of all, by the creation of characters showing some degree of complexity.

The failure of complexity of characterization in the sub-plot makes it impossible to defend that part of the play against the charge of sentimentality. The skilful structure is operative here as in the main plot, but the realism provided by the servants is lacking, events lead capriciously to a 'happily-ever-after' ending, and the characters lack dimension.

6. STYLE

One cause of difficulty in interpretation of both plots has been the style, Heywood's admittedly 'dull and earthy Muse' (Prologue, 11). Almost all the critics agree with the author that the diction and versification are, for the most part, unadorned, representative of a normal conversational tone. Most of them find this plainness generally commendable, appropriate for the realism of middle-class life with which the drama deals. Lamb's famous 'prose Shakespeare' contains something of both praise and blame, but Hazlitt

---

[1] *The Language of Tragedy* (1947), p. 96. Compare Ure, p. 210, and Thorp, p. 113.

[2] p. 96.

is less equivocal: 'The dialogue (bating the verse), is such as might be uttered in ordinary conversation. It is beautiful prose put into heroic measure.'[1] He goes on to praise three of the 'scattered exceptions' to this general rule, including two that have not found favour with later critics, Wendoll's 'red-leav'd table of my heart' (vi. 127) and Frankford's 'Cold drops of sweat sit dangling on my hairs, / Like morning dew upon the golden flow'rs' (viii. 58–9).[2] Those later critics who are favourably impressed with Heywood's style speak in much the same terms.[3] Prior, writing about the language of tragedy, discriminates somewhat more carefully. He attributes the 'verisimilitude' of the diction to the importance of establishing a particular social environment in the play, but notes that verisimilitude is abandoned for emphasis and instances the frequent couplets and the artifice of wordplay in the cardplaying scene. Of the small amounts of figurative language, reserved for moments of emotional strain, he finds that the more elaborate (such as Frankford's speech on the lute) seem thrust into an inappropriate context, the more simple (such as Anne on the lute) seem not to destroy the norm of conversational speech.[4] T. S. Eliot (appropriately, as a distinguished poet, dramatist, and critic) has written what is at once the most perceptive comment on a specific passage and the most useful generalization about Heywood's poetic practice as a whole. His remarks deserve to be quoted at length:

> Heywood's versification is never on a very high poetic level, but at its best is often on a high dramatic level. This can be illustrated by one of the best known of quotations from *A Woman Killed with Kindness*:
>
> O speak no more!
> For more than this I know, and have recorded
> Within the red-leaved table of my heart.
> Fair, and of all beloved, I was not fearful
> Bluntly to give my life into your hand,

---

[1] Charles Lamb, *Specimens of English Dramatic Poets* (1808), p. 112; William Hazlitt, *Lectures Chiefly on the Dramatic Literature of the Age of Elizabeth* (1820), p. 73.

[2] Hazlitt's misquotation of the second passage is reproduced here.

[3] See, for example, Velte, pp. 132–4, Clark, *Thomas Heywood*, p. 248, and Boas, p. 158.

[4] pp. 97–9.

> And at one hazard all my earthly means.
> Go, tell your husband; he will turn me off,
> And I am then undone. I care not, I;
> 'Twas for your sake. Perchance in rage he'll kill me,
> I care not, 'twas for you. Say I incur
> The general name of villain through the world,
> Of traitor to my friend; I care not, I.
> Beggary, shame, death, scandal, and reproach,
> For you I'll hazard all: why, what care I?
> For you I'll live, and in your love I'll die.

The image at the beginning of this passage does not, it is true, deserve its fame. "Table of my heart" is a legitimate, though hardly striking, metaphor; but to call it *red-leaved* is to press the anatomical aspect into a ridiculous figure. It is not a conceit, as when Crashaw deliberately telescopes one image into another, but merely the irreflective grasping after a fine trope. But in the lines that follow the most skilful use is made of regular blank verse to emphasize the argument; and it is, even to the judicious couplet at the end, a speech which any actor should be happy to declaim. The speech is perfect for the situation; the most persuasive that Wendoll could have made to Mrs. Frankford; and it persuades us into accepting her surrender. And this instance of verse which is only moderately poetical but very highly dramatic is by no means singular in Heywood's work.[1]

'Only moderately poetical but very highly dramatic'. This is precisely the point. Given his subject-matter and characters, Heywood, like Arthur Miller, dares not be poetical. His elaborately rhetorical passages, like Miller's, run the risk of seeming outrageously out of place. Most of his verse does, however, fill its dramatic function unobtrusively and effectively, if on occasion flatly and monotonously. One might justifiably complain that there is no attempt to differentiate among speaking voices, except between the middle-class characters and the servants, but, in general, to look with favour on what Heywood is doing in the play is to approve of the spareness of the verse. To object to the very nature of the material is to find fault also with Heywood's prosiness and lack of imagination.

---

[1] pp. 175–6. The most interesting adverse comments on Heywood's imagery and poetic manner may be found in Knights, p. 249, and Grivelet, pp. 242–4.

7. STAGE HISTORY

The theatre-goers of the early seventeenth century, unconcerned
with such fine points, apparently liked the play enough to make it
a resounding success. The two (or possibly three) editions within
the space of a few years are evidence that it had a fairly healthy and
continuing popularity. It was, at any rate, popular enough to make
possible a familiar allusion to it in 1604 in a passage explaining the
ways and means of cuckolding: 'And being set out of the shop,
with her man afore her, to quench the jealousy of her husband, she,
by thy instructions, shall turn the honest, simple fellow off at the
next turning, and give him leave to see *The Merry Devil of Edmon-
ton*, or *A Woman Killed with Kindness*, when his mistress is going
herself, to the same murder'.[1] Heywood himself, probably in the
same year, took the opportunity of advertising his masterpiece in
another of his plays: 'Here's such wetting of Hand-kerchers, hee
weepes to thinke of his Wife, shee weepes to see her Father cry!
Peace foole, wee shall else have thee claime kindred of the Woman
kill'd with kindnesse.'[2] Although positive evidence is lacking and
one cannot interpret precisely the 'oftentimes Acted' on the title
page of the 1617 quarto, the play probably remained in the repertory of the Queen's Men for a number of years, with performances
at both the Curtain and the Red Bull.[3]

The play almost certainly had an effect on the drama of its day,
though hardly so extensive an effect as Winkler, who traces practically all later plays involving adultery back to *A Woman Killed
with Kindness*, would suggest.[4] Heywood himself did make capital

[1] Thomas Middleton (?), *The Blacke Booke* (1604), in A. H. Bullen, ed.,
The Works of Thomas Middleton (1886), VIII, 35–6.

[2] *The Wise-woman of Hogsdon*, Act III, in Pearson, V, 316. Other contemporary and later allusions that have been suggested refer much more
probably to the proverb ('kill with kindness') than to the play. See A. W.
Ward, *A History of English Dramatic Literature to the Death of Queen Anne*,
new and rev. ed. (1899), II, 587, and Clark, *Thomas Heywood*, p. 37.

[3] See G. F. Reynolds, *The Staging of Elizabethan Plays at the Red Bull
Theatre 1605–1625*, Modern Language Association of America, General
Series, IX (1940), 17.

[4] pp. 18–66. He says, p. 18, 'fast alle Dichter, die das Thema bearbeitet
haben, von Heywood beeinflusst worden sind'. Grivelet's suggestion that
the sub-plot of Dekker's *The Honest Whore, Part I*, is a parody of Hey-

of his success by introducing into *The English Traveller* (*c.* 1620–33) a plot similar to the main plot in *A Woman Killed with Kindness*, and Andrews has pointed out that 'the treatment of the erring wife by her husband (Act IV, p. 228) [of *The Late Lancashire Witches*] strongly suggests the *Woman Killed with Kindness*'.[1] Forsythe thinks that 'Shirley worked over Heywood's play' for his *Love's Cruelty* (1631), but, Forsythe to the contrary, Shirley's play is much closer to Painter's translation of 'A President of Grenoble' (Part I, Novel 58) than it is to *A Woman Killed with Kindness*. It is not at all unlikely, of course, that Shirley knew Heywood's play and drew suggestions from it.[2]

There were no productions of *A Woman Killed with Kindness*, so far as is known, from Heywood's time until the late nineteenth century, but two adaptations, neither, presumably, ever staged, appeared during the intervening years.[3] The events of the play were perhaps too strong for some eighteenth-century stomachs. Benjamin Victor, at any rate, found it necessary to alter the play drastically. His 'Advertisement' describes his procedure in writing what he calls *The Fatal Error*:

> In the year 1743 [actually 1744], the late Mr. Dodsley publish'd his collection of old Plays, in twelve volumes, to which I was a subscriber—Among them I read a Tragedy with a strange title, call'd *A Woman kill'd with kindness*, in which were several fine strokes of nature, on matrimonial distress, brought in by female infidelity—But where the seducer brings the wife to consent, who is happily situated with a young, fond, accomplish'd husband approved for his excessive tenderness, and forgiveness to such a criminal—I was, therefore, led to invent the following fable; and

---

wood's main plot also seems doubtful, but his treatment of later adultery plays such as *The Malcontent* and *Bussy D'Ambois* as intentional antitheses of *A Woman Killed with Kindness* is sometimes suggestive and is at least less sweeping than Winkler's (see Grivelet, pp. 296, 299–316). Still, the connexions seem often tenuous enough.

[1] C. E. Andrews, 'The Authorship of *The Late Lancashire Witches*', *M.L.N.*, xxviii (1913), 164.

[2] R. S. Forsythe, *The Relations of Shirley's Plays to the Elizabethan Drama* (1914), pp. 164–6.

[3] L. B. Wright, in 'Notes on Thomas Heywood's Later Reputation', *R.E.S.*, iv (1928), 135–44, summarizes the early references and criticisms and notes productions up to the time of his article.

have only borrowed a few lines from the old play, in the last scene, where the husband's forgiveness, and renew'd affection, will, I hope, be thought by the reader to be founded on humanity.[1]

The result is hard to recognize. Plain John and Anne Frankford have become Sir Charles and Lady Frankford, Cranmore is the villainous friend, Lady Frankford's brother is Lord Bellgrove, Cranmore has a virtuous sister named Emeline, beloved of Lord Bellgrove, Juletta is Cranmore's accomplice, and Nicholas has undergone a transmogrification into Humphrey. By Juletta's treachery, Cranmore is admitted to Lady Frankford's bedroom, her husband being away, and rapes her. She has previously repulsed his overtures 'with a proper indignation'. Her 'fatal error', then, lies not in succumbing to seductive wiles, but in failing to inform her husband immediately of the wrong she has undergone. She feels obliged to take poison, proclaiming just before she dies, 'Thus I die free of all premiditated [sic] guilt—My only crime, I do confess it, was my shameful weakness in being prevail'd on to conceal my injury! That was my *Fatal Error*! since it was impossible for me to bring pollution to your lov'd arms!—' She has failed to speak, moreover, only for the sake of her children. Cranmore, earlier in the scene, has died at the hand of the outraged Lord Bellgrove. This ludicrous concoction borrows more of Heywood's lines than Victor admits, but the resemblance ends there.

The second adaptation, Joseph Moser's *Ingratitude; or the Adulteress*, is closer to the plot of the original than is *The Fatal Error*, but it is equally sentimental and preposterous.[2] The married couple have now been advanced to the status of Lord Frankford and Lady Anna. Wendoll is retained as the friend and seducer, Mountford is Lady Anna's brother, and the names of Cranwell, Jenkin, Nick, Maltby, Susan, and Acton show their source, though the rôles vary

---

[1] *Original Letters, Dramatic Pieces, and Poems* (1776), II, 81. The play itself appears on pp. 83–141. Bernbaum, pp. 36–7, treats the relationship between this play and Heywood's as an example of the difference between the drama of sensibility and that of the Elizabethans.

[2] The play appears in the *European Magazine*, LVIII (July–September 1810), 51–9, 104–14, 177–89. Charles Dibdin, in his *Complete History of the English Stage* (1800), V, 253, says that Kotzebue's *The Stranger* is 'evidently taken from' *A Woman Killed with Kindness*; but the only similarity is that both plays deal with forgiven adulteresses.

from the corresponding rôles in Heywood. Lady Anna is led to her crime partly out of revenge for her husband's fancied unfaithfulness with a girl whom he is protecting in a nearby cottage. This girl, Sophia, eventually turns out to be both an old school friend of Anna and an earlier prey of Wendoll, who was then going under the name of Morven. Lord Frankford, as a friend of Sophia's father, has simply been exhibiting his kindliness in protecting her and keeping the news of her plight from Anna. Anna's guilt, however, is real, and she is banished by her husband. Mountford pursues Wendoll-Morven and kills him. Finally, Anna calls Lord Frankford to her when the events have been made known, he forgives her, and she dies. Sir Charles Mountford closes the piece with a quatrain that is hard to take seriously:

> And may our *moral* teach, that treacherous arts
> Cannot be practis'd on young *matrons hearts*,
> If husbands, cautious, when abroad they roam,
> Ne'er leave a *representative* at home.

Heywood's play, albeit in a version edited by Frank Marshall, was at last staged again by the Dramatic Students Society at the Olympic Theatre on Tuesday, 8 March 1887.[1] Though only a few lines were excised and no entire scene omitted, bowdlerizing affected the main plot, for Wedmore wishes that the Students 'had been bold instead of indiscreet, and had done us the thing pretty much as it stands. . . Really, we might have braced ourselves to bear it; and the "young person", and her middle-aged relations who influence and spoil her, might have stayed away. . . Anyhow, what we had was quite worth doing; and it was, upon the whole, very well done.'

Perhaps the most significant modern production was that given in Paris to open the famed Vieux-Colombier on 23 October 1913. The play was given in a French prose translation by Jacques Copeau which eliminated the sub-plot entirely.[2] Grivelet com-

---

[1] See *The Athenaeum*, No. 3097 (5 March 1887), p. 330. Reviews appear in 'Drama: The Week', *The Athenaeum*, No. 3098 (12 March 1887), p. 362; by F. Wedmore in 'The Stage', *The Academy*, XXXI (19 March 1887), 209–10; in *The Saturday Review*, LXIII (12 March 1887), 371–2; and by F. Marshall in *The Theatre*, IX (1 April 1887), 205–12.

[2] P. de Reul, *Présentation du Théâtre Jacobéen de Marston à Beaumont et*

ments on the appropriateness of the choice for the inauguration of
this original and influential theatre:

> Il s'agissait alors de lancer un défi à la routine boulevardière, à
> sa médiocrité satisfaite, de prendre le contre-pied des éternelles
> comédies triangulaires—le mari, la femme, l'amant—et de leur
> frivolité bien parisienne. Ce n'est pas simple hasard si Copeau,
> avec son sens passionné et quasi-religieux du véritable jeu drama-
> tique, eut recours, pour porter ce défi, à l'œuvre rustique et fer-
> vente de Thomas Heywood.[1]

Copeau himself, in his *Souvenirs du Vieux-Colombier*, says that the
scenery, designed by Francis Jourdain, was in a style which 's'in-
spirait surtout d'une économie nécessaire',[2] but if the line-cut reproduced in the theatre's prospectus for 1914–15 is any sample,
the staging was remarkable, for 1913, in its adaptability and fidelity
to Elizabethan practice.[3] The production ran for twenty-nine per-

Setting for the production of *A Woman Killed with Kindness*
by Jacques Copeau at the Vieux-Colombier, Paris, 1913.

Fletcher (1600–1625), [1941 ?], p. 126. Compare Bescou, p. 137, and a review by E. Sarradin in *Journal des débats*, 24 October 1913.
   [1] p. 232.   [2] (1931), p. 21.
   [3] [J. Copeau], *Le Théâtre du Vieux Colombier*, [1914], p. 21. For further
details, see Helena Robin Slaughter, 'Jacques Copeau metteur en scène de
Shakespeare et des Élisabéthains', *Études Anglaises*, XIII (1960), 176–91,
which also reproduces an interesting photograph of the actors on stage.

formances and was revived in Switzerland in 1916. It is perhaps worth noting that Louis Jouvet was a member of the Vieux-Colombier company.[1]

Clark records a performance in New York 'under special conditions' in 1914,[2] but there is no record of it in Odell's *Annals of the New York Stage* nor, so far as I can tell, in the New York *Times Index*. In 1922 the Birmingham Repertory Company performed the play,[3] and two scenes from it were staged at the MacDowell Club in New York.[4]

At the Malvern Festival, 4 August 1931, the play was staged in a series with *Hick Scorner* (1513), *Ralph Roister Doister* (1550), *She Would if She Could* (1668), *A Trip to Scarborough* (1777—Sheridan after Vanbrugh), *Money* (Bulwer-Lytton, 1840), and *The Switchback* (James Bridie, 1931) to form a brief survey of lesser-known English drama. The cast was a notable one, including Miriam Adams, Robert Donat, and Ralph Richardson.[5]

On 13 April 1947 the play was performed by the B.B.C. with Griselda Hervey and Peter Ustinov. This production has since been rebroadcast in both England and America.[6] Lady Margaret Hall Dramatic Society and University College Players performed a version of the play at Oxford on 19 May 1959 in which the subplot was acted as Part I, the main plot as Part II, and the concluding scenes of the play, reconciling the two stories, as Part III.[7]

8. TEXT

A Woman Killed with Kindness does not appear in the Stationers' Register. The earliest extant edition, presumably the first (1607), has the following title page:

---

[1] Grivelet, p. 232.

[2] *Thomas Heywood*, p. 38. Compare Wright, 'Notes', p. 144.

[3] Clark, *Thomas Heywood*, p. 38; Wright, 'Notes', p. 144.

[4] J. T. Shipley, *Guide to Great Plays* (1956), p. 310.

[5] See A. Dukes, 'The English Scene: the Pageant of the Theatre at Malvern', *Theatre Arts Monthly*, XV (1931), 805; J. H. Schutt, 'A Woman Killed with Kindness Produced at Malvern', *English Studies*, XIII (1931), 191; and 'Malvern Festival—"A Woman Killed with Kindness"', *The Times*, No. 45,893 (5 August 1931), p. 8.

[6] Grivelet, p. 232.

[7] From a programme provided by the General Editor.

A / WOMAN / KILDE / with Kindnesse. / *Written by Tho:*
Heywood. / [device: McK. 355] / LONDON / Printed by William
Iaggard dwelling in Barbican, and / are to be sold in Paules
Church-yard. / by Iohn Hodgets. 1607.

Only one copy of this edition is known, that in the British Museum, which I have read from photographs.

The one other early edition that survives (1617) is known in at
least twenty copies. Though its title-page reads 'The third Edition',
no copy of a second edition, if there was one, is known today, and
the edition of 1617 will be referred to hereafter as Q2. It has the
following title page:

A / WOMAN / KILDE / with Kindnesse. / *As it hath beene*
oftentimes Acted by / *the Queenes Maiest. Seruants.* / *Written by*
THO. HEYWOOD. / The third Edition. / [device: McK. 283] /
LONDON, / Printed by Isaac Iaggard, 1617.

I have collated completely six copies of this edition, the Harvard,
Boston Public, Folger (copy 1), and Library of Congress copies in
the original, the Yale (copy 1) and Huntington copies on microfilm,
and have found no press variants among these copies.

Since I have not been able to determine the relationship between
these two editions, beyond establishing the hypothesis that they are
independent of each other, I shall attempt here only to mention a
few of the idiosyncrasies of each and to account for my choice of
Q1 as copy-text. The following analysis is complicated by the fact
that there may have been a second edition printed between 1607
and 1617 or that 1607 may really be the second edition, and it is
the true first edition that has disappeared.[1] The lost edition, then,
rather than a manuscript, may have been the copy-text for either
of the two extant editions.

It appears that Q2 was not set from a copy of Q1, nor, assuming
that there really was a second edition, can the three be linked biblio-
graphically. There are four principal kinds of evidence for this
assertion, none of them conclusive. First, Q1 uses thirty-two leaves
to print the play, Q2 thirty-six. Reprints were ordinarily page for
page or else shorter than the original, in order to conserve paper
on a text already shown to be popular and hence to require less

---

[1] The text in Q1 begins on A4 (and in Q2 on A3), often a sign of a reprint.

E

attractive format in order to sell. Second, there is no indication that Q1 has influenced Q2 in spelling or in the forms of speech-headings. Third, Q2 sets as prose eight passages that Q1 sets as verse, and, contrariwise, sets as verse one passage that Q1 sets as prose. There are seven passages which both quartos set as verse but with different lineation (in two of these, Q2 is dividing a line rather than let it run over). Fourth, Q1 marks exits twenty-one times, Q2 twenty-three, but only twelve of these are in common.

I assume, therefore, that the manuscript or manuscripts behind the quartos showed extreme negligence in indicating exits. Though there is no wholly convincing evidence, it seems likely that the manuscript or manuscripts were author's foul papers or a transcript thereof rather than theatrical prompt copy.[1] In addition to the careless handling of exits, there is vagueness in stage-directions that would be unlikely to stand in copy intended for production. Thus both quartos read '*countrie* [*Countrey* Q2] *wenches, and two or three Musitians*' (scene ii), '*Enter 3. or 4. seruingmen*' (scene viii), '*Enter Seruingmen*' (scene xii). Such indefiniteness would not be unusual in authorial copy. Both quartos misassign speeches or parts of speeches, but in no case do the misassignments coincide in the two editions. In Q1, Susan is called Iane throughout scene iii, in which she first appears, and once again in scene xiv. Q1 is inconsistent about the number of Sir Francis's retainers slain by Sir Charles: at iv. 50–51, it is a falconer and a huntsman, at iii. 105, 'these dead men'; elsewhere only one huntsman is killed. I infer that the compositor must have been setting from an unrevised manuscript and following it blindly.

Q2 has had some attention from a reviser, though there is no indication of authorial revision. Susan is called throughout by her proper name, and there is no inconsistency about the number of men killed by Sir Charles. In view of the fact that, despite a vast number of minor variants, the two quartos are basically very close

---

[1] One argument in favour of a scribal manuscript may be mentioned: Heywood's statement in the preface to *The Rape of Lucrece* (quoted on p. xvii above) that his earlier plays were printed without authorization, 'coppied onely by the eare'. There is, however, no indication of stenographic interference in either quarto.

to each other, especially in the wording of stage-directions, it is at
least a tenable hypothesis that both were set from the same manuscript—or, possibly, a transcript or the lost edition may intervene.

It is fairly clear from the evidence of compositor analysis[1] that
Q2 was set throughout by Jaggard's compositor B. The great
majority of the substantive variants and the variants in accidentals
in Q2 can be accounted for by the 'misdirected ingenuity, deliber-
ate tampering and plain carelessness'[2] characteristic of B. Though
nothing is known about the compositors in Jaggard's shop in 1607,
I proceed on the assumption that whoever set Q1 (and I detect the
hand of only one compositor), he was likely to be a workman more
careful in following copy than was B. This assumption is supported
by the faithfulness with which the obvious inconsistencies referred
to above are reproduced in Q1. I have therefore, despite some hesitation, chosen Q1 as copy-text, and having made this decision I
have attempted to follow its readings, wherever a defence can be
made for them, as being more likely to be closer to Heywood's
manuscript than the variant readings in Q2. Thus I have gone so
far as to reproduce Q1's indication of syllabic and non-syllabic endings for preterites and past participles in prose passages and in
verse when the resulting metre is possible. Since, however, I posit
some independent authority for Q2, I have not hesitated to accept
readings from it, including, when necessary, elision not present in
Q1—this despite compositor B's erratic practice. As in the other
Revels Plays, spelling is modernized throughout, but I have not
attempted to modernize the grammar. Constructions common in
Elizabethan English but not in ours are discussed in the Commentary. The few instances in which I depart from the lineation of the
original are recorded in the Collation; I have tried to refrain from
hunting iambs in Heywood's occasionally erratic verse. I have pre-
served the wording of the original stage-directions whenever possible, all alterations being recorded in the Collation except the
names of the characters, which are normalized throughout in both

[1] See P. Williams, Jr, 'New Approaches to Textual Problems in Shakespeare', *S.B.*, VIII (1956), 3–14, and D. F. McKenzie, 'Compositor B's
Role in *The Merchant of Venice*, Q2 (1619)', *S.B.*, XII (1959), 75–90.
[2] McKenzie, p. 76.

stage-directions and speech-headings. Added stage-directions, chiefly exits and asides (the latter never indicated in the quartos), are enclosed in square brackets. I have not attempted to indicate the source of every borrowed synonym in the Commentary, but I have occasionally quoted, with proper credit, the explanations of my predecessors.

Neither text provides a reliable guide to punctuation,[1] though Q2 is far more exact and consistent than Q1. This comparatively normalized punctuation in Q2 is in accord with what we know of B's customary practice. I have therefore modernized punctuation consistently, on generally conservative principles, always attempting to convey what I take to be the sense implied by the punctuation in Q1 where it is defensible.

The corpus of variants in the Collation is, of necessity, quite large; it includes, in addition to all substantive variants from Q2, all variants in punctuation that could conceivably change the meaning of a passage and a few spelling variants (e.g., 'murder', 'murther') possibly implying a pronunciation different from that implied by the orthography of Q1. I include also, in addition to indicating the source of all my emendations, a comparatively large number of editorial readings that I have rejected. Readings proposed but not incorporated in the text are indicated by *conj.* (conjectured). Only the first appearance of a given reading is recorded, though certain of the early editors (notably Dodsley, Reed, Collier, and Verity) have influenced later editions strongly. Q2 forms the basis for all of the later editions except those of Pearson, which is a reprint of Q1, Collier (1850), one state of which adopts a good many Q1 readings, and Morrell, which is eclectic. The excellent edition by Katharine Lee Bates has been of immeasurable help. Of the many editions of the play in anthologies of the drama, I have found three most useful: those by Hazelton Spencer; C. F. Tucker Brooke and N. B. Paradise; and C. R. Baskervill, V. B. Heltzel, and A. H. Nethercot. A list of the collections and editions in which the play has been reprinted, together with the abbreviations employed

---

[1] Though *The Captives* is a much later play, we can take for what it is worth the evidence provided by the manuscript that Heywood was very careless in matters of punctuation. See the Malone Society reprint.

in the Collation and Commentary in this edition, appears on pp. lxxi–lxxii.

Since neither quarto is divided into acts or scenes and I see no indication in the play of a five-act structure, I have simply divided the play into scenes according to the principle that a cleared stage marks a new scene. This editorial numbering is indicated in square brackets at the left-hand side of the text: '[Scene i]'. For the convenience of the reader, a table of act and scene divisions employed by previous editors is provided on p. lxxiii below.

This edition is, then, highly eclectic, and not very scientifically eclectic at that. No one can be better aware than I of the inadequacy of this procedure, but under the circumstances, since I am unable to prove conclusively anything about the provenance of either text, since the whole issue is clouded by the hypothetical second edition, and since, in the balance, the 1607 quarto seems likely to be more faithful to its copy than does 1617, it has seemed the best compromise to follow the policies outlined above. Mr Arthur Brown of the University of London is now preparing what will doubtless be the definitive edition of Heywood's plays.[1] In it, we may hope, he will solve the textual problems that have eluded me and make available a text and notes that will be more satisfactory than any yet attempted. In the meantime I may claim for the present edition that it has a text and collation more nearly accurate, with fuller annotation, than those of earlier editors.

[1] A. Brown, 'An Edition of the Plays of Thomas Heywood: A Preliminary Survey of Problems', *Renaissance Papers* (1954), pp. 71–6.

Editions

(A) EARLY EDITIONS

Q1 *A Woman Kilde with Kindnesse*. 1607.
Q2 *A Woman Kilde with Kindnesse*. The third Edition. 1617.

(B) MODERN EDITIONS

Dodsley *Select Collection of Old Plays*, 1744, Vol. IV.

Reed Dodsley's *Old Plays*, ed. Isaac Reed, 1780, Vol. VII.

Scott *The Ancient British Drama*, Sir Walter Scott, supposed ed., 1810, Vol. II.

Collier (1825) Dodsley's *Old Plays*, ed. J. P. Collier, 1825, Vol. VII.

Collier (1850) *The Dramatic Works of Thomas Heywood*, ed. J. P. Collier, 1850–1, Vol. I.

Keltie *The Works of the British Dramatists*, ed. J. S. Keltie, 1870.

Pearson *The Dramatic Works of Thomas Heywood*, [ed. R. H. Shepherd?], 1874, Vol. II.

Verity *Thomas Heywood*, ed. A. W. Verity, 1888 (*The Mermaid Series*).

Ward *A Woman Killed with Kindness*, ed. A. W. Ward, 1897 (*The Temple Dramatists*).

Cox *A Woman Killed with Kindness*, ed. F. J. Cox, 1907 (*Old English Plays No. 2*).

Neilson *The Chief Elizabethan Dramatists Excluding Shakespeare*, ed. W. A. Neilson, 1911.

Tatlock *Representative English Plays*, ed. J. S. P. Tatlock and R. G. Martin, 1916.

Bates *A Woman Killed with Kindness and The Fair Maid of the West*, ed. Katharine Lee Bates, 1917 (*The Belles-Lettres Series*).

Matthews *The Chief British Dramatists Excluding Shakespeare*, ed. B. Matthews and P. R. Lieder, 1924.

Schelling	*Typical Elizabethan Plays*, ed. F. E. Schelling, 1926.
Smith	*Types of Domestic Tragedy*, ed. R. M. Smith, 1928 (*World Drama Series*).
Oliphant	*Shakespeare and his Fellow Dramatists*, ed. E. H. C. Oliphant, 1929, Vol. 1.
Walley	*Early Seventeenth-Century Plays*, ed. H. R. Walley and J. H. Wilson, 1930.
Dunn	*Eight Famous Elizabethan Plays*, intro. Esther Cloudman Dunn, 1932 (*The Modern Library*).
Brooke	*English Drama 1580–1642*, ed. C. F. Tucker Brooke and N. B. Paradise, 1933.
Clark	*World Drama*, ed. B. H. Clark, 1933, Vol. 1.
Rylands	*Elizabethan Tragedy*, ed. G. Rylands, 1933.
Spencer	*Elizabethan Plays*, ed. H. Spencer, 1933.
Baskervill	*Elizabethan and Stuart Plays*, ed. C. R. Baskervill, V. B. Heltzel, and A. H. Nethercot, 1934.
Parks	*The English Drama: An Anthology 900–1642*, ed. E. W. Parks and R. C. Beatty, 1935.
McIlwraith	*Five Elizabethan Tragedies*, ed. A. K. McIlwraith, 1938 (*The World's Classics*).
Ashton	*Types of English Drama*, ed. J. W. Ashton, 1940.
Morrell	*Four English Tragedies of the 16th and 17th Centuries*, ed. J. M. Morrell, 1953.

Act and Scene Divisions

Baskervill and the present edition	Verity, Clark, Rylands	Ward, Neilson, Tatlock, Bates, Matthews, Schelling, Smith, Walley, Dunn, Brooke, Parks	Oliphant	Spencer	McIlwraith, Ashton, Morrell
i	I. i	[identical with Verity as far as III. ii]	[identical with Ward except as indicated]	[identical with Ward except as indicated]	[identical with Verity as far as IV. iv]
ii	ii				
iii	iii				
iv	II. i				
v	ii				
vi	iii				
vii	III. i				
viii	ii				
ix	IV. i	III. iii			
x	ii	IV. i			
xi	iii	ii			
xii	iv	iii			
xiii	(1–33)v (34–185)vi	iv v	(1–67)iv (68–185)v	iv	v
xiv	v. i	v. i			v. i
xv	ii	ii			ii
xvi	iii	iii			iii
xvii	(1–22)iv (23–38)v (39–140)vi	iv v			iv

A WOMAN
KILLED WITH KINDNESS

[DRAMATIS PERSONAE

SIR FRANCIS ACTON.

SIR CHARLES MOUNTFORD.

JOHN FRANKFORD.

WENDOLL, \
CRANWELL, } *his friends.*

MALBY, *friend to Sir Francis.*

OLD MOUNTFORD, *uncle to Sir Charles.*

TYDY, *cousin to Sir Charles.*

SANDY, *former friend to Sir Charles.*

RODER, *former tenant to Sir Charles.*

SHAFTON, *false friend to Frankford.*

NICHOLAS, \
JENKIN, } *servants to Frankford.*

SPIGGOT, *butler to Frankford.*

ROGER BRICKBAT, \
JACK SLIME, } *country fellows.*

Sheriff.

Keeper of the Prison.

Sergeant.

Officers, Falconers, Huntsmen, Coachman, Carters, Musicians, Servants, Children.

ANNE, *wife to Frankford and sister to Sir Francis.*

SUSAN, *sister to Sir Charles.*

SISLY MILK-PAIL, *servingwoman to Frankford.*

JOAN MINIVER, \
JANE TRUBKIN, } *country wenches.*
ISBEL MOTLEY, /

Servingwomen.]

DRAMATIS PERSONAE] first given by Dodsley (1744) and expanded by later editors. The list above is adapted from that given by Bates.

The Prologue

I come but like a harbinger, being sent
To tell you what these preparations mean:
Look for no glorious state, our Muse is bent
Upon a barren subject, a bare scene.
We could afford this twig a timber-tree,   5
Whose strength might boldly on your favours build;
Our russet, tissue; drone, a honey-bee;
Our barren plot, a large and spacious field;
Our coarse fare, banquets; our thin water, wine;
Our brook, a sea; our bat's eyes, eagle's sight;   10
Our Poet's dull and earthy Muse, divine;
Our ravens, doves; our crow's black feathers, white.
    But gentle thoughts, when they may give the foil,
    Save them that yield, and spare where they may spoil.

Text in italics in Qq.   1. like] *Q1;* as *Q2.*   11. earthy] *Qq;* earthly *Dunn.*

3. *glorious*] ostentatious.
state] splendour; or, possibly, chair of state, throne.
   5. *afford . . . timber-tree*] wish this twig were a timber-tree. This usage
is without parallel in *O.E.D.*, but cf. the passage in a Heywood 'Epilogue'
(spoken at the court 'upon a New Yeares day at night'):
> We bring a mite that would present a mine,
> Our loves we pay, to whom our lives we owe,
> Water we bring, who could affoord it wine,
> Our art you see, our hearts we cannot show.
>
>   (Pearson, VI, 347.)

   7. *russet*] coarse woollen cloth.
tissue] fine cloth, often interwoven with silver or gold.
   13. *gentle thoughts*] i.e. those of the audience.
give the foil] overthrow. The phrase comes from wrestling, where the
foil is 'the fact of being almost thrown; a throw not resulting in a flat fall'
(*O.E.D.*).

A Woman
Killed with Kindness

[Scene i]

Enter MASTER JOHN FRANKFORD, MISTRESS ANNE,
SIR FRANCIS ACTON, SIR CHARLES MOUNTFORD, MASTER MALBY
MASTER WENDOLL, *and* MASTER CRANWELL.

Sir Fra. Some music there! None lead the bride a dance?
Sir Cha. Yes, would she dance 'The Shaking of the Sheets':
    But that's the dance her husband means to lead her.
Wen. That's not the dance that every man must dance,
    According to the ballad.
Sir Fra.   Music ho!   5
    By your leave, sister—by your husband's leave
    I should have said—the hand that but this day
    Was given you in the church I'll borrow. Sound!
    This marriage music hoists me from the ground.
Frank. Ay, you may caper, you are light and free;   10
    Marriage hath yok'd my heels, pray then pardon me.

0.1–2. *Mistress . . . Acton*] *Q2; Sir Francis Acton, Mistris Acton Q1.*
5. ballad] *Q1;* Ballet *Q2.*   11. pray then pardon] *Q1;* pray pardon *Q2;*
then pardon *conj. Daniel.*

---

    2. '*The Shaking . . . Sheets*'] Both a popular tune and the ballad sung to
it had this title; see the note to l. 5 below. Sir Charles is of course indulging
in the usual banter about the activity of the wedding night.
    5. *ballad*] Wendoll's allusion to death as common to every man is ap-
parent in the first stanza of eleven in the ballad printed in Chappell, 1, 228:
               Can you dance the shaking of the sheets,
                  a dance that every man must do?
               Can you trim it up with dainty sweets
                  and every thing that longs thereto?
             Make ready then your winding sheet
                 And see how you can bestir your feet,
                 For death is the man that all must meet.

Sir Fra. I'll have you dance too, brother.

Sir Cha.   Master Frankford,
You are a happy man, sir; and much joy
Succeed your marriage mirth, you have a wife
So qualify'd and with such ornaments   15
Both of the mind and body. First, her birth
Is noble, and her education such
As might become the daughter of a prince.
Her own tongue speaks all tongues, and her own hand
Can teach all strings to speak in their best grace,   20
From the shrill treble, to the hoarsest bass.
To end her many praises in one word,
She's beauty and perfection's eldest daughter,
Only found by yours, though many a heart hath sought her.

Frank. But that I know your virtues and chaste thoughts,   25
I should be jealous of your praise, Sir Charles.

Cran. He speaks no more than you approve.

Mal. Nor flatters he that gives to her her due.

Anne. I would your praise could find a fitter theme
Than my imperfect beauty to speak on.   30
Such as they be, if they my husband please,
They suffice me now I am married.
His sweet content is like a flattering glass,
To make my face seem fairer to mine eye:
But the least wrinkle from his stormy brow   35
Will blast the roses in my cheeks that grow.

Sir Fra. A perfect wife already, meek and patient.

---

13. You are] *Q1;* Y'are *Q2.*   14. mirth,] *Q1;* mirth: *Q2.*   21. shrill]
Q1; shril'st *Q2;* shrillest *Verity.*   23. beauty] *Q2;* beauty, *Q1.*   30.
beauty] *Qq;* beauties *Dodsley.*   33. flattering] *Q1;* flatt'ring *Q2.*

---

15. *qualify'd*] endowed with qualities.
25. *But*] were it not.
27. *approve*] make proof of.
30. *beauty*] Presumably Heywood was careless in the use of the plural
pronoun in l. 31; Dodsley's emendation resolves the inconsistency.
32. *suffice*] almost certainly accented on the first syllable; see the chapter
on 'Stress' in Kökeritz, pp. 332–9.

How strangely the word 'husband' fits your mouth,
Not marry'd three hours since, sister. 'Tis good;
You that begin betimes thus, must needs prove   40
Pliant and duteous in your husband's love.
Godamercies, brother, wrought her to it already?
'Sweet husband', and a curtsey the first day.
Mark this, mark this, you that are bachelors,
And never took the grace of honest man,   45
Mark this against you marry, this one phrase:
'In a good time that man both wins and woos
That takes his wife down in her wedding shoes.'
Frank. Your sister takes not after you, Sir Francis.
All his wild blood your father spent on you;   50
He got her in his age when he grew civil.
All his mad tricks were to his land entail'd,
And you are heir to all; your sister, she
Hath to her dower her mother's modesty.
Sir Cha. Lord, sir, in what a happy state live you;   55
This morning, which to many seems a burden

39. since, sister.] *This ed.;* since sister, *Qq;* since! Sister, *Dodsley.*   42.
Godamercies] *Q1;* Gramercies *Q2.*   to it] *Q1;* too't *Q2.*   already?]
Collier (1850); already, *Q1;* already: *Q2.*   43. curtsey] *Q2;* curtesie *Q1.*
56–7.] *Verity;* This ... too / Heauy ... pleasure. *Qq.*   56. morning] *Qq;*
marriage *or* marrying *conj. Daniel.*   burden] *Q1;* burthen *Q2 (and
throughout the play).*

---

38. *strangely*] unaccustomedly.
42. *Godamercies*] an exclamation of applause; a contraction of 'God have
mercies' (plural not recorded in *O.E.D.*).
45. *took ... man*] 'assumed the honorable estate of husband' (Bates).
46. *against*] in anticipation of the time when.
47–8.] Reed notes this remark as 'still a proverb in common use'; not in
Tilley or Oxford. Cf. Dekker's *The Honest Whore, Part II,* I. iii. 100–2:
'This wench (your new wife) will take you downe in your wedding shooes,
vnlesse you hang her vp in her wedding garters' (*Dramatic Works,* ed.
Bowers, 1953–, II, 152).
47. *In ... time*] at the right moment.
48.] that tames his wife at once.
50. *spent*] expended, exhausted.
51. *got*] begot.
civil] polite; 'quietly' civilized in contrast to 'wild'.
54. *to*] as, for; see Abbott, Sect. 189.

Too heavy to bear, is unto you a pleasure.
This lady is no clog, as many are;
She doth become you like a well-made suit
In which the tailor hath us'd all his art,   60
Not like a thick coat of unseason'd frieze,
Forc'd on your back in summer; she's no chain
To tie your neck and curb you to the yoke,
But she's a chain of gold to adorn your neck.
You both adorn each other, and your hands   65
Methinks are matches. There's equality
In this fair combination; you are both scholars,
Both young, both being descended nobly.
There's music in this sympathy, it carries
Consort and expectation of much joy,   70
Which God bestow on you, from this first day,
Until your dissolution—that's for aye.

Sir Fra. We keep you here too long, good brother Frankford.
Into the hall! Away, go, cheer your guests!
What, bride and bridegroom both withdrawn at once ?   75
If you be miss'd, the guests will doubt their welcome,
And charge you with unkindness.

Frank.   To prevent it,
I'll leave you here, to see the dance within.

Anne. And so will I.   [*Exeunt* FRANKFORD *and* ANNE.]

Sir Fra.   To part you it were sin.

---

63. curb you] *Pearson;* curbs you *Q1;* curbe ye *Q2.*   65. adorn] *Q2;*
adore *Q1.*   67. you are] *Q1;* y'are *Q2.*   74. go,] *Q1;* go *Q2.*   79.
Exeunt . . . Anne.] Verity; Exit Q2.

---

61. *unseason'd*] unseasonable.
frieze] a coarse woollen cloth (with a pun on the action of freezing).
65. *adorn*] It can be argued that the Q2 reading is a simple error of repetition from l. 64, characteristic of compositor B, but the Q1 reading
breaks the metaphor which in Q2 runs from l. 64 to l. 66.
65–6. *your . . . matches*] i.e. you are good matches for each other.
70. *Consort*] (a) harmony; (b) companionship.
74. *cheer*] entertain.
78. *within*] off-stage, understood as representing an inner part of the
house.

F

Now gallants, while the town musicians   80
Finger their frets within, and the mad lads
And country lasses, every mother's child
With nosegays and bride-laces in their hats,
Dance all their country measures, rounds, and jigs,
What shall we do? Hark, they are all on the hoigh,   85
They toil like mill-horses, and turn as round—
Marry, not on the toe. Ay, and they caper,
But without cutting. You shall see to-morrow
The hall floor peck'd and dinted like a millstone,
Made with their high shoes; though their skill be small, 90
Yet they tread heavy where their hobnails fall.

Sir Cha. Well, leave them to their sports. Sir Francis Acton,
I'll make a match with you: meet me to-morrow
At Chevy Chase, I'll fly my hawk with yours.

Sir Fra. For what? for what?

Sir Cha.   Why, for a hundred pound.   95

Sir Fra. Pawn me some gold of that.

Sir Cha.   Here are ten angels;
I'll make them good a hundred pound to-morrow
Upon my hawk's wing.

---

80. Now] *Q2; Frank* Now *Q1.*   85. they are] *Q1;* they're *Q2.*   88. But]
Qq; But not *Dodsley;* Not *Verity.*   93. me] *Q1; not in Q2.*

---

81. *frets*] divisions of the finger board on the lute.

83. *bride-laces*] lace ribbons given as favours to tie up the rosemary formerly worn at weddings.

84. *measures . . . jigs*] three sorts of dances, the first usually stately, the second danced in a circle, the third lively and sprightly.

85. *on the hoigh*] in a state of excitement; cf. Middleton, *The Family of Love*, III. ii: 'Young wenches now are all o' the hoigh' (*Works*, ed. Dyce, 1840, II, 151).

87. *not . . . toe*] i.e. flat-footed.

87–8. *caper . . . cutting*] The emendations lead into the idea of the next sentence, but the Qq reading makes satisfactory sense: to caper without cutting is to execute the leaps in dancing without twirling the feet properly. See *O.E.D.*, 'cut', *v.*, VII, 30.

96. *Pawn*] pledge.

angels] gold coins; minted from 1465 to the time of Charles I, varying in value from 6s. 8d. to 10s., they depicted the archangel Michael standing on the dragon.

Sir Fra.   'Tis a match, 'tis done.
    Another hundred pound upon your dogs,
    Dare you, Sir Charles ?

Sir Cha.   I dare. Were I sure to lose   100
    I durst do more than that. Here's my hand,
    The first course for a hundred pound.

Sir Fra.   A match.

Wen. Ten angels on Sir Francis Acton's hawk;
    As much upon his dogs.

Cran. I am for Sir Charles Mountford; I have seen   105
    His hawk and dog both try'd. What, clap you hands ?
    Or is't no bargain ?

Wen.   Yes, and stake them down.
    Were they five hundred they were all my own.

Sir Fra. Be stirring early with the lark to-morrow;
    I'll rise into my saddle ere the sun   110
    Rise from his bed.

Sir Cha.   If there you miss me, say
    I am no gentleman; I'll hold my day.

Sir Fra. It holds on all sides; come, to-night let's dance.
    Early to-morrow let's prepare to ride;   114
    We had need be three hours up before the bride.   [*Exeunt.*]

---

100. you] *Q1;* ye *Q2.*   106. you] *Q1;* ye *Q2.*   115. *Exeunt.*] *Reed;*
Exit Q2.

---

102. *course*] a matching of two hounds in which, when the game is afoot,
the dogs are released together; the winner is not necessarily the hound that
makes the kill, but the one judged best on a number of points in performance.

106. *clap you hands*] shake hands to confirm an agreement; cf. *H5*, v. ii.
133: 'And so clap hands and a bargain'.

107. *stake them down*] deposit money as a stake on the result of a contest;
cf. *Mer. V.*, III. ii. 215–16:
    Gra. We'll play with them the first boy for a thousand ducats.
    Ner. What! and stake down ?

112. *hold my day*] keep my appointed day; cf. Heywood's 'Apollo and
Daphne', in *Pleasant Dialogues and Dramma's*: 'Breake he, or not directly
keepe his day' (Pearson, VI, 294).

113. *holds*] remains valid.

[Scene ii]

Enter NICHOLAS *and* JENKIN, JACK SLIME, ROGER BRICKBAT, *with country Wenches, and two or three Musicians.*

Jenk. Come, Nick, take you Joan Miniver to trace withal; Jack
Slime, traverse you with Sisly Milk-pail, I will take Jane
Trubkin, and Roger Brickbat shall have Isbel Motley;
and now that they are busy in the parlour, come, strike up,
we'll have a crash here in the yard.   5

Nich. My humour is not compendious: dancing I possess not,
though I can foot it; yet since I am fall'n into the hands of
Sisly Milk-pail, I assent.

Jack. Truly, Nick, though we were never brought up like
serving courtiers, yet we have been brought up with serv-   10
ing creatures, ay and God's creatures too, for we have
been brought up to serve sheep, oxen, horses, and hogs,
and such like; and though we be but country fellows, it

---

ii. 8. assent] *Qᵢ;* consent *Q₂.*   12. and hogs] *Qᵢ;* Hogges *Q₂.*

---

ii. 1–3. *Joan Miniver, Jane Trubkin, Isbel Motley*] Their surnames signify
respectively a fur piece worn on ceremonial dress; a short, fat woman; a
coarse, mixed cloth.

1. *trace*] dance, 'apparently forward and back again at caprice'
(Bates).

2. *traverse*] dance, 'perhaps crossing or turning' (Bates).

5. *crash*] frolic; cf. Brome, *The New Academy*, III. i: 'Come Gentlemen,
shall we have a crash at cards?' (*Works*, Pearson, 1873, II, 48).

6. *humour*] disposition, as in Jonsonian comedy and in later Elizabethan
drama generally.

compendious] Nicholas erroneously uses the word in the sense of 'compre-
hensive', as in l. 23 below. Cf. Mistress Eyre's use of it in Dekker's *Shoe-
makers' Holiday* [III. ii. 6–8]:

Firke. Take it? well I goe, and he should not take it, *Firk* sweares to for-
sweare him, yes forsooth I goe to Guild Hall.
Wife. Nay when? thou art too compendious, and tedious.
                                        (*Dramatic Works*, ed. cit., I, 50.)

possess] am master of; not recorded in *O.E.D.* in this sense before the
19th century.

7–8. *yet . . . assent*] 'Since Jenkin had assigned her to Slime, we must
suppose that during Nick's speech she has indicated a preference for him'
(Spencer).

> may be in the way of dancing we can do the horse-trick as
> well as servingmen.   15

Roger. Ay, and the crosspoint, too.

Jenk. O Slime, O Brickbat, do not you know that comparisons
are odious ? Now we are odious ourselves, too; therefore
there are no comparisons to be made betwixt us.

Nich. I am sudden, and not superfluous;   20
> I am quarrelsome, and not seditious;
> I am peaceable, and not contentious;
> I am brief, and not compendious.
> Slime, foot it quickly. If the music overcome not my
> melancholy, I shall quarrel; and if they suddenly do not 25
> strike up, I shall presently strike thee down.

Jenk. No quarrelling, for God's sake! Truly, if you do, I shall
set a knave between you.

Jack. I come to dance, not to quarrel. Come, what shall it be ?
'Rogero'?   30

---

15. servingmen] *Q1;* the Seruing-men *Q2.*   24. Slime, foot] *Q1; Slime.*
Foote *Q2.*   26. thee] *Qq;* them *Dodsley.*   28. you] *Q1;* ye *Q2.*

---

14. *horse-trick*] ? a dance step; not in *O.E.D.*

16. *crosspoint*] a dance step. There is probably a play on words here;
horse and *cross* were slang terms meaning 'to have intercourse with',
and a *servingman* could be a lover as well as a courtier; see Farmer and
Henley.

17–18. *comparisons are odious*] proverbial (Tilley C576). With a play on
odorous; cf. *Ado.*, III. v. 18: 'comparisons are odorous'.

20. *sudden*] brief.

24. *Slime*] Q2 is clearly wrong in printing this proper name as a speech-
heading; ll. 24–6 fit the pompous attitude that Nick is assuming in this
scene, and Slime says in l. 29 'I come to dance, not to quarrel'.

music] It was a common notion that music was a cure for melancholy.

25. *suddenly*] immediately.

28. *knave*] male servant, i.e. himself.

30–3. '*Rogero*', '*The* . . . *World*', '*John* . . . *Now*'] three popular tunes; the
second is an alternative name for 'Sellenger's Round', mentioned in ll. 47–8
below. The tunes are reproduced in Chappell, I, 231, 256–7, and 268, respectively. Chappell points out that the comedy *Lingua* (1607) refers to the
music as that heard 'the first time the planets played; I remember Venus,
the treble, ran sweet division upon Saturn, the base. The first tune they
played was Sellenger's Round, in memory whereof, ever since, it hath been
called *The Beginning of the World*'.

Jenk. 'Rogero'? No. We will dance 'The Beginning of the
    World'.

Sisly. I love no dance so well as 'John, Come Kiss Me Now'.

Nich. I, that have ere now deserv'd a cushion, call for 'The
    Cushion Dance'.   35

Roger. For my part, I like nothing so well as 'Tom Tyler'.

Jenk. No, we'll have 'The Hunting of the Fox'.

Jack. 'The Hay', 'The Hay', there's nothing like 'The Hay'.

Nich. I have said, I do say, and I will say again—

Jenk. Every man agree to have it as Nick says.   40

All. Content.

Nich. It hath been, it now is, and it shall be—

Sisly. What, Master Nich'las, what?

Nich. 'Put on Your Smock a Monday'.

Jenk. So the dance will come cleanly off. Come, for God's sake   45
    agree of something. If you like not that, put it to the musi-
    cians, or let me speak for all, and we'll have 'Sellenger's
    Round'.

All. That, that, that!

Nich. No, I am resolv'd thus it shall be: 50
    First take hands, then take you to your heels.

34. I, ..., call] *Q1;* I ..., call *Q2.*   36. *Roger.]* *Q2; Rogero. Q1.*   39. I
do ... and I will] *Q1;* do ... and will *Q2.*   51. you] *Q1;* ye *Q2.*

---

34. *deserv'd a cushion*] i.e. earned the right to some luxury.
34–5. '*The Cushion Dance*'] an old round dance; a description of it (reprinted by Bates) appears in *The Dancing-Master*, 1703; a tune called
'Joan Sanderson, or The Cushion Dance' appears in Chappell, 1, 287.
36. '*Tom Tyler*'] another tune; one called 'Tom Tinker' is in Chappell,
1, 310.
37. '*The* ... *Fox*'] an unidentified tune.
38. '*The Hay*'] a rustic dance with a serpentine movement, rather noisy
and wild; a description appears in C. J. Sharp, *The Country Dance Book*,
Part II, 41–8.
44. '*Put* ... *Monday*'] another popular tune, otherwise known as 'Pretty
Nancy'; the tune is in Chappell, 1, 234.
Smock] a woman's undergarment, a chemise.
a] on; see Abbott, Sect. 140.
45. *cleanly*] adroitly; with a pun.
46. *of*] about; see Abbott, Sect. 174.
47–8. '*Sellenger's Round*'] See note on ll. 30–3 above.

Jenk. Why, would you have us run away?

Nich. No, but I would have you shake your heels.
    Music, strike up.

They dance; NICHOLAS, *dancing, speaks stately and scurvily,
    the rest after the country fashion.*

Jenk. Hey! lively, my lasses! Here's a turn for thee!   [*Exeunt.*] 55

[Scene iii]

Wind horns. Enter SIR CHARLES, SIR FRANCIS, MALBY, CRANWELL,
    WENDOLL, *Falconers, and Huntsmen.*

Sir Cha. So! well cast off. Aloft, aloft! Well flown!
    O now she takes her at the souse, and strikes her
    Down to the earth, like a swift thunder clap.
Wen. She hath stroke ten angels out of my way.

52. you] *Q1;* ye *Q2.*   54.1. *speaks*] *Qq; moves Oliphant.*   54.2. *rest
after*] *Qq; rest dance after Collier (1850).*   55. *Exeunt.*] *Reed; Exit. Q2.*
iii. 0.2. *Falconers*] *Verity; Faulkener Qq.*   2–3.] *Q1; as prose Q2.*   3. the
earth] *Q1;* th'earth *Q2.*

54.1–2.] The actors speak ad lib. during the dancing, Jenkin's final line
only being established to serve as a cue. The emendations by Collier and
Oliphant are unnecessary.

54.1. stately and scurvily] i.e. in a sorry attempt at dignity. Bates glosses
scurvily as 'haughtily', Ashton as 'sourly'; but cf. Jonson, *Cynthia's Revels*,
v. iv. 149: 'And his hat was carried skiruily' (*Works*, ed. Herford and
Simpson, 1925–52, IV, 143).

iii.] The situation is best described by Bates, whose extensive notes on
this scene are extremely valuable: 'Apparently the scene opens in the midst
of the trial, when the hawk of Sir Francis has been flown, and the falconer
of Sir Charles has just cast off the rival bird. Sir Francis' merlin had struck
the quarry, which escaped to the river. Thence it was twice driven out into
the fields by its pursuer, until finally the merlin, hiding in the stubble,
caught it on the ground and killed it there.'

0.1. Wind] blow.

1. *well cast off*] The prey in sight, Sir Charles praises the unhooding and
flinging of the hawk from the falconer's wrist.

2. *takes . . . souse*] swoops straight down from above, after the prey has
risen from the ground. See *The Boke of Saynt Albans* (1486): 'Iff yowre
hawke nym the fowle a lofte: ye shall say she toke it at the mounte or at
the souce' (Djb).

4. *stroke*] a common form of the past and perfect of *strike* during the 16th
and 17th centuries; see *O.E.D.*

Sir Fra. A hundred pound from me.

Sir Cha.   What, falconer?   5

Falc. At hand, sir.

Sir Cha. Now she hath seiz'd the fowl, and 'gins to plume her.

   Rebeck her not; rather stand still and cherk her.

   So! seize her gets, her jesses, and her bells.

   Away!   10

Sir Fra. My hawk kill'd, too.

Sir Cha.   Ay, but 'twas at the querre,

   Not at the mount like mine.

Sir Fra.   Judgement, my masters.

Cran. Yours miss'd her at the ferre.

Wen. Ay, but our merlin first had plum'd the fowl,

   And twice renew'd her from the river, too.   15

5. falconer] *Q1;* Faulc'ner *Q2.*   7–8.] *Q1; as prose Q2.*   8. Rebeck]
Qq; Rebuke *Bates.*   cherk] *Bates;* checke *Qq.*   14. had] *Q2;* hath *Q1.*
15. renew'd] *Q2;* renewed *Q1;* enew'd *conj. Deighton.*

---

7. *'gins to plume*] begins to pluck feathers from.

8. *Rebeck, cherk*] Bates explains her emendations: 'Don't startle her.
Stand still a minute if she seems likely to take flight and reassure her by
chirping to her.' Bates shows that the falconry terms in this scene derive
from the *Boke of Saynt Albans,* in one version of which, Gervase Mark-
ham's *The Gentleman's Academie,* 1595, 'the *r* has slipped into *c* and *cherke*
has become *checke,* although *rebuking* stands. For the slip from *rebuke* to
rebeck, Heywood himself or his printers may be responsible.' But though
checke does not fit here, *Rebeck* ('call back') may.

9. *gets*] some unidentified part of the hawk's harness; Verity suggests the
hawk's booty, *O.E.D.* equates the word with *jess,* citing this passage only.

   jesses] leg straps.

   bells] worn to frighten the prey and to aid the falconer in tracing a wan-
dering hawk.

11. *at the querre*] i.e. before the fowl rises from the ground. Bates cites a
passage from the *Boke of Saynt Albans* to show that the definition of *querre*
in *O.E.D.* ('The attack or swoop made by a hawk upon a bird; the act of
seizing or tearing the quarry') is incorrect.

12. *at the mount*] See note on l. 2 above.

13. *at the ferre*] on the opposite bank of a river. Bates glosses *ferre* as
'higher point', but the *Boke of Saynt Albans* reads, 'Iff yowre hawke
nym the fowle at the fer side of the Ryuer . . . from you Then she sleeth
the fowle at the fer Jutty. . . ' (Djb).

14. *merlin*] a variety of hawk.

15. *renew'd . . . river*] 'driven her from the river by a fresh attack' (Bates).
Deighton's conjecture is tempting, for the *Boke of Saynt Albans* has 'Yowre

Her bells, Sir Francis, had not both one weight,
Nor was one semitune above the other;
Methinks these Milan bells do sound too full,
And spoil the mounting of your hawk.

Sir Cha.   'Tis lost.

Sir Fra.   I grant it not. Mine likewise seiz'd a fowl   20
Within her talents, and you saw her paws
Full of the feathers; both her petty singles
And her long singles gripp'd her more than other.
The terrials of her legs were stain'd with blood;
Not of the fowl only she did discomfit   25
Some of her feathers, but she brake away.
Come, come, your hawk is but a rifler.

---

17. semitune] *Qq;* semi-tone *Collier (1850).*   24–5. blood; / Not of the fowl
only she did discomfit] *Q2;* blood; / Not of the Fowle onely, she did dis-
comfite, *Q1;* blood, / Not of the fowl only; she did discomfit *Neilson.*

---

hawke hath ennewed the fowle in to the ryuer' (Dija), but the sense of *enew*,
'to drive into the river', does not fit with the preposition *from.* Cf. *Troil.,*
v. v. 6–7:

>   Renew, renew! The fierce Polydamas
>   Hath beat down Menon.

16–17.] The *Boke of Saynt Albans* (D3) directs that the hawk's bells
must be of equal weight and a semitone apart in pitch.

17. *semitune*] variant of 'semitone'.

18. *Milan bells*] made of silver, they were regarded as the best bells.

21. *talents*] a common form of *talons*; see *O.E.D.*

22–3. *petty singles, long singles*] outer and middle claws. Bates again explains: 'Sir Francis is claiming that his hawk, in her swoop, really gripped
her bird better than Sir Charles' hawk gripped hers, but the first quarry,
though wounded, broke away.'

23. *other*] the other.

24–7.] Neilson suggests that Sir Francis is talking about Sir Charles's
hawk in these lines and repunctuates accordingly; the meaning implied by
the Qq punctuation is that Sir Francis's hawk managed to injure its prey
severely, not just tear away some feathers.

24. *terrials*] probably an error for the *terrets*—variously spelled *tyrrits,
territs, terriets*—leather loops used to attach the bells to the hawk's legs.

25–6. *Not . . . feathers*] i.e. the hawk drew blood, not merely tore out a
few of the fowl's feathers.

25. *discomfit*] destroy, tear out. Not in *O.E.D.* in this sense, but cf. late
pop. Latin *disconficere*, 'to finish up, destroy, consume'.

27. *rifler*] 'Oftentimes it happeneth with a Hawke, that for eagerness
when she shoulde nomme a fowle, she seaseth but the feathers, and ther-

Sir Cha.   How?

Sir Fra. Ay, and your dogs are trindle-tails and curs.

Sir Cha. You stir my blood.

    You keep not a good hound in all your kennel,   30
    Nor one good hawk upon your perch.

Sir Fra.   How, knight?

Sir Cha. So, knight? You will not swagger, sir?

Sir Fra. Why, say I did?

Sir Cha. Why, sir, I say you would gain as much by swagg'ring
    As you have got by wagers on your dogs;   35
    You will come short in all things.

Sir Fra.   Not in this!
    Now I'll strike home.

Sir Cha.   Thou shalt to thy long home,
    Or I will want my will.

Sir Fra. All they that love Sir Francis follow me.

Sir Cha. All that affect Sir Charles draw on my part.   40

Cran. On this side heaves my hand.

Wen.   Here goes my heart.

                They divide themselves.

SIR CHARLES, CRANWELL, *Falconer, and Huntsman fight against*
SIR FRANCIS, WENDOLL, *his Falconer, and Huntsman, and* SIR
CHARLES *hath the better, and beats them away, killing both of* SIR
    FRANCIS *his men.* [*Exeunt all except* SIR CHARLES.]

Sir Cha. My God! what have I done? what have I done?
    My rage hath plung'd into a sea of blood,

27–9.] *Q2; Q1, beginning a new page at l. 27, misassigns* How? *to Fran., l. 28*
to Char., and l. 29 to Fran.   30. a] *Q1;* one *Q2.*   34–6. Why, sir . . .
things] *Q1; as prose Q2.*   36–8.] *Pearson;* you . . . things. / Not . . . home. /
Thou . . . will. *Qq.*   41.4. *both] Q2;* one *Q1.*   41.5. *men] Q2;* huntsmen
Q1.   Exeunt . . . Charles.] *Verity.*

---

fore suche Hawkes be called Riflers if they do oft so' (*Boke of Saynt Albans*
[A8v]).

    28. *trindle-tails*] curly-tailed and hence low-bred dogs.

    32. *swagger*] bluster.

    37. *thy long home*] i.e. thy grave. Proverbial (Tilley H533); ultimately
from Ecclesiastes, xii. 5.

    41.4. *both*] For Q1's *one* see the Introduction, p. lxvi above.

In which my soul lies drown'd. Poor innocents,
For whom we are to answer. Well, 'tis done,   45
And I remain the victor. A great conquest,
When I would give this right hand, nay, this head,
To breathe in them new life whom I have slain.
Forgive me, God, 'twas in the heat of blood,
And anger quite removes me from myself: 50
It was not I, but rage, did this vile murder;
Yet I, and not my rage, must answer it.
Sir Francis Acton he is fled the field,
With him, all those that did partake his quarrel,
And I am left alone, with sorrow dumb,   55
And in my height of conquest, overcome.

Enter SUSAN.

Susan. O God, my brother wounded among the dead;
    Unhappy jest that in such earnest ends.
    The rumour of this fear stretch'd to my ears,
    And I am come to know if you be wounded.   60
Sir Cha. O sister, sister, wounded at the heart.
Susan. My God forbid!
Sir Cha. In doing that thing which he forbade,
    I am wounded, sister.
Susan.   I hope not at the heart.
Sir Cha. Yes, at the heart.
Susan.   O God! A surgeon there!   65
Sir Cha. Call me a surgeon, sister, for my soul;

---

44. drown'd.] *Dodsley;* drownd *Q1;* drown'd, *Q2.*   innocents] *Q2;*
Innocent *Q1.*   51. murder] *Q1;* murther *Q2 (and throughout the play).*
56.1. Susan] *Q2;* Iane *Q1 (and throughout this scene).*   57. *Susan.*]
Dodsley.   among] *Q1;* mong *Q2.*   58. jest] *Q1;* iests *Q2.*   62. My]
Qq; May *conj. Oliphant.*

---

53. *he*] In Elizabethan English 'the pronoun is frequently inserted after
a proper name as the subject' (Abbott, Sect. 243).
    54. *partake his quarrel*] fight on his side.
    56.1.] For Q1's *Iane* see the Introduction, p. lxvi above.
    58. *jest*] exploit (with a pun).
    59. *fear*] event to be feared.

The sin of murder it hath pierc'd my heart,
And made a wide wound there, but for these scratches,
They are nothing, nothing.

Susan.   Charles, what have you done?
Sir Francis hath great friends, and will pursue you   70
Unto the utmost danger of the law.

Sir Cha. My conscience is become my enemy,
And will pursue me more than Acton can.

Susan. O fly, sweet brother.

Sir Cha.   Shall I fly from thee?
What, Sue, art weary of my company?   75

Susan. Fly from your foe.

Sir Cha.   You, sister, are my friend,
And flying you, I shall pursue my end.

Susan. Your company is as my eyeball dear;
Being far from you, no comfort can be near.
Yet fly to save your life; what would I care   80
To spend my future age in black despair,
So you were safe? And yet to live one week
Without my brother Charles, through every cheek
My streaming tears would downwards run so rank
Till they could set on either side a bank,   85
And in the midst a channel; so my face
For two salt water brooks shall still find place.

Sir Cha. Thou shalt not weep so much, for I will stay
In spite of danger's teeth. I'll live with thee,

---

72. is] *Qq;* hath *Collier (1850).*   my] *Q1;* mine *Q2.*   75. What] *Q1;*
Why *Q2.*   Sue] *Q2; Iane Q1.*   83. every] *Qq;* either *Dodsley.*   85.
could] *Qq;* would *Dodsley.*   88. shalt] *Q1;* shall *Q2.*

---

71. *danger*] penalty.

77. *end*] i.e. death.

84. *rank*] profusely, abundantly; cf. *Troil.*, I. iii. 196: 'How rank soever
rounded in with danger'.

83. *every*] Dodsley's emendation is unnecessary. Francis Thynne defends 'every' meaning 'either' in his *Animadversions*, 1598: 'They did ride
euerye side of hym' (ed. Furnivall, 1875, p. 50).

87. *still*] always; the usual Elizabethan sense.

88. *shalt*] Q2's *shall* is probably a misprint, though very rarely the form
is found for the second person singular; see *O.E.D.*

Or I'll not live at all. I will not sell   90
My country and my father's patrimony,
No, thy sweet sight, for a vain hope of life.

Enter Sheriff with Officers.

Sher. Sir Charles, I am made the unwilling instrument
Of your attach and apprehension.
I am sorry that the blood of innocent men   95
Should be of you exacted. It was told me
That you were guarded with a troop of friends,
And therefore I come arm'd.
Sir Cha.   O master Sheriff,
I came into the field with many friends,
But, see, they all have left me; only one   100
Clings to my sad misfortune, my dear sister.
I know you for an honest gentleman;
I yield my weapons and submit to you.
Convey me where you please.
Sher.   To prison then,
To answer for the lives of these dead men.   105
Susan. O God! O God!
Sir Cha.   Sweet sister, every strain
Of sorrow from your heart augments my pain.
Your grief abounds and hits against my breast.
Sher. Sir, will you go?
Sir Cha.   Even where it likes you best.   [*Exeunt.*]

92. No,] *Qq;* Nor *Dodsley.*   92.1. Sheriff] *Q2; Shrieffe Q1.*   95. I am]
Q1; I'me *Q2.*   96. exacted] *Q1;* enacted *Q2.*   98. I come arm'd] *Q1;*
came thus arm'd *Q2;* I come thus armed *Pearson;* [I] came thus armed
Baskervill.   Sheriff] *Q2; Shriefe Q1.*   99. many] *Q2;* man *Q1.*
108. abounds] *Qq;* rebounds *conj. Brereton, Sykes.*   109. *Exeunt.*] *Dodsley.*

92. *No*] Dodsley's emendation is unnecessary.
94. *attach*] arrest.
96. *exacted*] The Q2 reading is almost certainly a misprint.
108. *abounds*] overflows. The conjecture by Brereton and Sykes reinforces the metaphor in the second half of the line, but no better than does
the reading of Qq: 'Your grief (or tears) overflows and, like a wave, pounds
against my breast'.
109. *likes*] pleases.

[Scene iv]

Enter MASTER FRANKFORD *in a study.*

Frank. How happy am I amongst other men
    That in my mean estate embrace content.
    I am a gentleman, and by my birth
    Companion with a king; a king's no more.
    I am possess'd of many fair revenues,   5
    Sufficient to maintain a gentleman.
    Touching my mind, I am study'd in all arts,
    The riches of my thoughts, and of my time
    Have been a good proficient. But the chief
    Of all the sweet felicities on earth,   10
    I have a fair, a chaste, and loving wife,
    Perfection all, all truth, all ornament.
    If man on earth may truly happy be,
    Of these at once possess'd, sure I am he.

Enter NICHOLAS.

Nich. Sir, there's a gentleman attends without to speak   15
    with you.

iv. 7–8. arts, . . . thoughts, . . . time] *Dodsley;* Arts; . . . thoughts . . . time,
Q1; Arts; . . . thoughts, . . . time, *Q2.*

---

    iv. 0.1. study] reverie; though Frankford may well enter the stage from
the 'study', or central opening in the rear wall of the stage, the word here
refers to his state of mind. See J. C. Adams, *The Globe Playhouse* (1942),
for a reconstruction of the stage that includes the 'study'; for an opposing
view see C. W. Hodges, *The Globe Restored* (1953).
    1–4.] Cf. *I Edward IV*:
                      and the meanest life
        Proportiond with content sufficiency,
        Is merrier then the mighty state of kinges. (Pearson, I, 47.)
    2. mean] moderate.
    5. *revenues*] commonly accented on the second syllable in 16th- and 17th-
century usage; see Kökeritz, p. 336.
    8–9. *and . . . proficient*] and have used my time profitably; *O.E.D.*, citing
this passage only, defines *proficient* as 'A thing that helps or conduces to
progress'. See, rather, proficient, B.2: 'One who has made good progress
in some art or branch of learning; an advanced pupil or scholar; an expert,
an adept' (earliest citation 1610).
    14. *at once*] at the same time.

Frank. On horseback?

Nich. Ay, on horseback.

Frank. Entreat him to alight; I will attend him.
    Knowest thou him, Nick?

Nich.   I know him; his name's Wendoll.
    It seems he comes in haste—his horse is booted   21
    Up to the flank in mire, himself all spotted
    And stain'd with plashing. Sure he rid in fear
    Or for a wager: horse and man both sweat;
    I ne'er saw two in such a smoking heat.   25

Frank. Entreat him in; about it instantly.   [*Exit* NICHOLAS.]
    This Wendoll I have noted, and his carriage
    Hath pleas'd me much; by observation
    I have noted many good deserts in him—
    He's affable and seen in many things,   30
    Discourses well, a good companion,
    And though of small means, yet a gentleman
    Of a good house, somewhat press'd by want.
    I have preferr'd him to a second place
    In my opinion and my best regard.   35

Enter WENDOLL, ANNE, *and* NICHOLAS.

Anne. O Master Frankford, Master Wendoll here
    Brings you the strangest news that e'er you heard.

Frank. What news, sweet wife? What news, good Master Wendoll?

18. Ay] *Q1* [I]; Yes *Q2*.   19. I will] *Q1;* and ile *Q2*.   20. Knowest]
Q1; Know'st *Q2*.   I know him] *Q1;* Know him, yes *Q2*.   26. *Exit*
Nicholas.] *Reed.*   28. much; by observation] *Q2;* much by obseruation:
Q1.   33. somewhat] *Qq;* though somewhat *Pearson.*   35.1. Anne] *Q2*
(*Mistris Frankford*); *Maister Franckeford Q1.*

---

    21. *booted*] covered, as if wearing boots.

    23. *plashing*] splashing.

    28. *observation*] See Abbott, Sect. 479, for the frequent pronunciation of
-*ion* as two syllables, especially at the end of a line of verse; in this play cf.
iv. 31; iv. 72; v. 31; vi. 3; vi. 42; vi. 144; vii. 60; vii. 84; viii. 62; viii. 215;
ix. 60; ix. 61; x. 37; xi. 33; xiv. 102; xv. 14; xvi. 83.

    30. *seen*] accomplished; cf. *Shr.*, I. ii. 133: 'a schoolmaster / Well seen in
music'.

    34. *second*] second only, presumably, to that held by Anne.

Wen. You knew the match made 'twixt Sir Francis Acton
　　And Sir Charles Mountford.

Frank. 　　　　　　　　True, with their hounds and hawks.

Wen. The matches were both play'd.

Frank. 　　　　　　　　Ha! and which won?　　41

Wen. Sir Francis, your wife's brother, had the worst
　　And lost the wager.

Frank. 　　　　　　　Why, the worse his chance;
　　Perhaps the fortune of some other day
　　Will change his luck.

Anne. 　　　　　　　O, but you hear not all.　　45
　　Sir Francis lost, and yet was loath to yield;
　　In brief the two knights grew to difference,
　　From words to blows, and so to banding sides,
　　Where valorous Sir Charles slew in his spleen
　　Two of your brother's men—his falconer　　50
　　And his good huntsman, whom he lov'd so well.
　　More men were wounded, no more slain outright.

Frank. Now trust me I am sorry for the knight;
　　But is my brother safe?

Wen. 　　　　　　　　All whole and sound,
　　His body not being blemish'd with one wound.　　55

39–40. You . . . Mountford] *Reed; as prose Qq.*　　41. which] *Qq;* who
Dodsley.　　45. *Anne.*] *Qq;* Wen. *Baskervill (conj. Daniel).*　　47. In brief]
Q1; At length *Q2.*　　50. falconer] *Q1;* Faulc'ner *Q2.*

---

41. *which*] used interchangeably with *who*; see Abbott, Sect. 265.

45–52. *O . . . outright*] The phrase 'your brother' in l. 50 (Sir Francis is,
after all, her sibling) makes Baskervill's reassignment of this speech tempting; but Anne has heard the whole story from Wendoll, and it is not surprising that she should get carried away in the excitement of the moment
and interrupt Wendoll's account.

47–52.] Cf. Painter, Fo. 287v:'There rose greate debate amongs them, and
proceeded so farre, as fondly they began to reuile one another with words,
and from tauting termes to earnest blowes, wherwith diuers in that skirmish
were hurt on both sides.' There is at least a similarity in sentence construction and rhythm.

47. *In brief*] in a few words; or, to parallel Q2's 'At length', 'shortly,
before long'—but the phrase is not in *O.E.D.* in this sense.

48. *banding sides*] forming hostile parties.

49. *Where*] whereupon.

But poor Sir Charles is to the prison led,
To answer at th' assize for them that's dead.
Frank. I thank your pains, sir; had the news been better,
Your will was to have brought it, Master Wendoll.
Sir Charles will find hard friends; his case is heinous,   60
And will be most severely censur'd on.
I am sorry for him. Sir, a word with you:
I know you, sir, to be a gentleman
In all things, your possibilities but mean;
Please you to use my table and my purse—   65
They are yours.
Wen.   O Lord, sir, I shall never deserve it.
Frank. O sir, disparage not your worth too much;
You are full of quality and fair desert.
Choose of my men which shall attend on you,
And he is yours. I will allow you, sir,   70
Your man, your gelding, and your table, all
At my own charge; be my companion.
Wen. Master Frankford, I have oft been bound to you
By many favours; this exceeds them all
That I shall never merit your least favour.   75
But when your last remembrance I forget,
Heaven at my soul exact that weighty debt.
Frank. There needs no protestation, for I know you
Virtuous, and therefore grateful. Prithee, Nan,
Use him with all thy loving'st courtesy.   80
Anne. As far as modesty may well extend,

62. I am] *Q1;* I'me *Q2.*   64. possibilities] *Q1;* possibility *Q2.*   66.
They are] *Qq;* They're *Ward.*   never] *Qq;* ne'er *Ward.*   69. on you]
Q1; you sir *Q2.*   71–2. table, all / At] *Pearson;* table, / Al at *Qq.*

---

60. *will . . . friends*] will find friends only with difficulty.
61. *censur'd on*] judged.
64. *possibilities*] resources.
68. *quality*] good natural gifts; cf. *Troil.*, IV. iv. 76: 'The Grecian youths
are full of quality'.
74–5. *this . . . That*] i.e. 'this favour exceeds the others so much that';
for the omission of *so* see Abbott, Sect. 406.
80. *Use*] treat.

G

It is my duty to receive your friend.

Frank. To dinner. Come, sir, from this present day
    Welcome to me for ever; come, away.

        [*Exeunt* MASTER FRANKFORD, WENDOLL, *and* ANNE.]

Nich. I do not like this fellow by no means;   85
    I never see him but my heart still earns.
    Zounds! I could fight with him, yet know not why;
    The Devil and he are all one in my eye.

Enter JENKIN.

Jenk. O Nick, what gentleman is that comes to lie at our
    house? My master allows him one to wait on him, and I   90
    believe it will fall to thy lot.

Nich. I love my master—by these hilts I do—
    But rather than I'll ever come to serve him,
    I'll turn away my master.

Enter SISLY.

Sisly. Nich'las, where are you, Nich'las? You must come in,   95
    Nich'las, and help the young gentleman off with his
    boots.

Nich. If I pluck off his boots, I'll eat the spurs,
    And they shall stick fast in my throat like burrs.   *Exit.*

Sisly. Then, Jenkin, come you.   100

Jenk. 'Tis no boot for me to deny it. My master hath given

---

83. dinner. Come, sir,] *This ed.;* dinner, come sir *Q1;* dinner: come sir, *Q2.*
84.1. *Exeunt . . . Anne.*] *Reed; Exit. Q2.*   85. not] *Q2;* nor *Q1.*   86.
earns] *Qq;* yearns *Dodsley.*   88.] *Q1;* The . . . eye. *Exit. Q2.*   my] *Q1;*
mine *Q2.*   89. that] *Q1;* that that *Q2.*   96. young] *Q1; not in Q2.*
99. *Exit.*] *Q1; not in Q2.*   101. 'Tis] *Q1;* Nay 'tis *Q2.*

85.] The double negative is common in early and Elizabethan English,
usually for emphasis; see Abbott, Sect. 406.

86. *earns*] grieves.

88.] Q2's *Exit* is clearly wrong.

89. *that*] The relative pronoun is often omitted (see Abbott, Sect. 244),
and the repetition of *that* would be characteristic of compositor B.
    lie] lodge.

92. *hilts*] Nick wears a dagger or daggers; cf. vi. 171.

101. *boot*] avail (with a pun).

me a coat here, but he takes pains himself to brush it
once or twice a day with a holly wand.

Sisly. Come, come, make haste, that you may wash your
hands again and help to serve in dinner.   [*Exit.*]   105

Jenk. [*to the audience.*] You may see, my masters, though it
be afternoon with you, 'tis but early days with us, for we
have not din'd yet. Stay but a little, I'll but go in and
help to bear up the first course and come to you again
presently.   *Exit.*   110

[Scene v]

Enter MALBY *and* CRANWELL.

Mal. This is the sessions day; pray, can you tell me
How young Sir Charles hath sped? Is he acquit,
Or must he try the law's strict penalty?

Cran. He's clear'd of all, 'spite of his enemies,
Whose earnest labours was to take his life;   5
But in this suit of pardon he hath spent

---

105. *Exit.*] *This ed.*   106. *to the audience*] *Spencer.*   107. 'tis but] *Qq;*
'tis yet but *Collier (1850).*   108. but a] *Q1;* a *Q2.*

v. 3. law's] *Dodsley;* Lawes *Qq;* laws' *Collier (1850).*   5. labours] *Q1;*
labour *Q2.*

---

104. *that*] so that; cf. Abbott, Sect. 283.

106–8. *though . . . yet*] Performances of plays began about two in the
afternoon; the usual dinner hour was eleven or twelve. See *Shakespeare's
England*, I, 15; II, 134; and cf. *The English Traveller*, I. i:

  Winc. This fellowes my best clocke,
    Hee still strikes trew to dinner.
  Clo. And to supper too sir, I know not how the day goes with you, but
    my stomacke hath strucke twelue, I can assure you that.
                              (Pearson, IV, 13.)

110. *presently*] probably, as in modern usage, 'after a short time'; but
O.E.D. notes that the growth of this sense from the earlier one, 'at once',
was so imperceptible that examples before 1650 are doubtful.

v. 2. *sped*] fared.

3. *try*] undergo.

5. *labours was*] The singular verb with a plural subject was common; see
Abbott, Sect. 333.

6. *of*] for; see Abbott, Sect. 174. Sir Charles has exhausted his resources
in securing influence and favour.

All the revenues that his father left him,
And he is now turn'd a plain countryman,
Reform'd in all things. See, sir, here he comes.

Enter SIR CHARLES *and his Keeper.*

Keep. Discharge your fees, and you are then at freedom.   10
Sir Cha. Here, master Keeper, take the poor remainder
  Of all the wealth I have. My heavy foes
  Have made my purse light, but, alas, to me,
  'Tis wealth enough that you have set me free.
Mal. God give you joy of your delivery;   15
  I am glad to see you abroad, Sir Charles.
Sir Cha. The poorest knight in England, Master Malby.
  My life hath cost me all the patrimony
  My father left his son. Well, God forgive them
  That are the authors of my penury.   20

Enter SHAFTON.

Shaf. Sir Charles, a hand, a hand—at liberty.
  Now by the faith I owe, I am glad to see it.
  What want you? Wherein may I pleasure you?
Sir Cha. O me! O most unhappy gentleman!
  I am not worthy to have friends stirr'd up   25
  Whose hands may help me in this plunge of want.
  I would I were in Heaven, to inherit there
  Th' immortal birthright which my Saviour keeps,
  And by no unthrift can be bought and sold;

9.1. *Charles*] *Q2; Francis Q1.*   18. the] *Q1;* my *Q2.*   21. *Shaf.*] *Q1;*
not in *Q2.*

---

7. *revenues*] See note on iv. 5 above.
9. *Reform'd*] transformed; not in *O.E.D.* in this sense.
12. *heavy*] oppressive, severe; and with an obvious play on words with
light in the next line.
16. *abroad*] out of confinement.
22. *owe*] own; the original meaning, very frequent in the 16th and 17th
centuries.
23. *want*] lack.
26. *plunge*] strait, difficulty.
29. *unthrift*] either (a) spendthrift, or (b) unthriftiness.

For here on earth, what pleasures should we trust ?   30
Shaf. To rid you from these contemplations,
 Three hundred pounds you shall receive of me—
 Nay, five for fail. Come, sir, the sight of gold
 Is the most sweet receipt for melancholy
 And will revive your spirits. You shall hold law   35
 With your proud adversaries. Tush, let Frank Acton
 Wage with knighthood-like expense with me,
 And he will sink, he will. Nay, good Sir Charles,
 Applaud your fortune, and your fair escape
 From all these perils.
Sir Cha.   O sir, they have undone me.   40
 Two thousand and five hundred pound a year
 My father at his death possess'd me of,
 All which the envious Acton made me spend,
 And notwithstanding all this large expense,
 I had much ado to gain my liberty;   45
 And I have now only a house of pleasure,
 With some five hundred pounds, reserv'd
 Both to maintain me and my loving sister.
Shaf. [*Aside*] That must I have; it lies convenient for me.
 If I can fasten but one finger on him,   50
 With my full hand I'll gripe him to the heart.
 'Tis not for love I proffer'd him this coin,
 But for my gain and pleasure. [*To Sir Charles.*] Come, Sir
  Charles,

37. Wage with knighthood-like] *This ed.;* Wage with Knighthood like *Q1;*
Wage his Knight-hood-like *Q2;* Wage with his Knight-hood like *Pearson;*
Wage, with his knighthood, like *Ward.*   38. And he] *Q1;* And a' *Q2.*
46. now only] *Q1;* onely now *Q2.*   49. Aside] *Collier (1850).*   53. *To
Sir Charles.*] *Verity (Aloud).*

31–40.] It is evident from 'Come, sir' (l. 33), 'Tush' (l. 36), and 'Nay'
(l. 38) that Sir Charles makes gestures of protest during this speech.
33. *for fail*] i.e. lest three be not enough.
35. *hold law*] engage in litigation.
37. *Wage*] contend, vie.
knighthood-like] appropriate to knighthood; the compound is not in *O.E.D.*
43. *envious*] malicious; cf. *Ham.*, IV. vii. 174: 'An envious sliver broke'.
46. *house of pleasure*] summerhouse.
48. *Both to maintain*] to maintain both.

I know you have need of money; take my offer.

Sir Cha. Sir, I accept it, and remain indebted   55
Even to the best of my unable power.
Come, gentlemen, and see it tend'red down.   *Exeunt.*

[Scene vi]

Enter WENDOLL *melancholy.*

Wen. I am a villain if I apprehend
But such a thought; then to attempt the deed—
Slave, thou art damn'd without redemption.
I'll drive away this passion with a song.
A song! Ha, ha! A song, as if, fond man,   5
Thy eyes could swim in laughter, when thy soul
Lies drench'd and drowned in red tears of blood.
I'll pray, and see if God within my heart
Plant better thoughts. Why, prayers are meditations,
And when I meditate—O God, forgive me—   10
It is on her divine perfections.
I will forget her; I will arm myself
Not to entertain a thought of love to her;
And when I come by chance into her presence,
I'll hale these balls until my eyestrings crack   15
From being pull'd and drawn to look that way.

Enter over the stage FRANKFORD, ANNE, *and* NICHOLAS.

57. *Exeunt.*] *Q1; not in Q2.*

vi. 1. *Wen.*] *Q1; not in Q2.*   7. drowned] *Q2;* drownd *Q1.*   13. to en-
tertain] *Q1;* t'entertaine *Q2.*

---

56. *unable*] weak, feeble; cf. *Shr.*, v. ii. 169: 'froward and unable worms'.
57. *tend'red down*] paid.

vi. 1. *apprehend*] conceive.
4. *song*] See note at ii. 24.
5. *fond*] foolish; the most common sense in the Elizabethan period.
15. *hale these balls*] pull these eyeballs away forcibly.
16.1. over the stage] This and similar stage-directions in other plays have
usually been taken to indicate that the persons involved come in at one of
the stage doors, cross the platform, and leave by the other door, but Allar-

O God! O God! with what a violence
I am hurry'd to my own destruction.
There goest thou the most perfect'st man
That ever England bred a gentleman;   20
And shall I wrong his bed? Thou God of thunder,
Stay in Thy thoughts of vengeance and of wrath
Thy great almighty and all-judging hand
From speedy execution on a villain,
A villain and a traitor to his friend.   25

Enter JENKIN [*behind*].

Jenk. Did your worship call?
Wen. [*not noticing Jenkin.*] He doth maintain me, he allows me
    largely
    Money to spend—
Jenk. [*Aside*] By my faith, so do not you me; I cannot get a
    cross of you.   30
Wen.   My gelding and my man.
Jenk. [*Aside*] That's Sorrel and I.
Wen. This kindness grows of no alliance 'twixt us—
Jenk. [*Aside*] Nor is my service of any great acquaintance.
Wen. I never bound him to me by desert—   35

18. I am] *Q1;* I'me *Q2.*   my] *Q1;* mine *Q2.*   19. perfect'st] *Q1;* perfect's *Q2;* perfect *Dodsley;* perfectest *Verity.*   25.1. *behind*] *Schelling.*
27. *not noticing Jenkin*] *Baskervill.*   29. *Aside*] *Oliphant.*   32. *Aside*]
Oliphant.   34. *Aside*] *Oliphant.*   35. me] *Q2;* be *Q1.*

---

dyce Nicoll in a recent article, 'Passing over the Stage', *Sh. S.*, XII (1959),
47–55, has provided a much more likely interpretation: that the characters
involved climb a flight of steps rising from the yard to one side of the stage,
cross over, and go down a flight at the opposite side. Wendoll, as Frankford, Anne, and Nick 'cross over', stands front-stage observing them.

    27. *largely*] generously.

    30. *cross*] coin; originally a coin with a cross stamped on one side.

    31.] The verse line begun at l. 28 continues here, after the interruption
of Jenkin's prose aside. The illusion of simultaneous speaking is thereby
increased.

    33. *alliance*] kinship.

    35-7.] Wendoll's astonishment at the enormity of his offence is reflected
in his incomplete constructions.

Of a mere stranger, a poor gentleman,
A man by whom in no kind he could gain!
He hath plac'd me in the height of all his thoughts,
Made me companion with the best and chiefest
In Yorkshire. He cannot eat without me,   40
Nor laugh without me. I am to his body
As necessary as his digestion,
And equally do make him whole or sick.
And shall I wrong this man? Base man! Ingrate!
Hast thou the power straight with thy gory hands   45
To rip thy image from his bleeding heart?
To scratch thy name from out the holy book
Of his remembrance, and to wound his name
That holds thy name so dear, or rend his heart
To whom thy heart was join'd and knit together?   50
And yet I must. Then, Wendoll, be content;
Thus villains, when they would, cannot repent.

Jenk. [*Aside*] What a strange humour is my new master in. Pray
       God he be not mad. If he should be so, I should never
       have any mind to serve him in Bedlam. It may be he is   55
       mad for missing of me.

Wen. [*seeing Jenkin.*] What, Jenkin? Where's your mistress?

Jenk. Is your worship marry'd?

Wen. Why dost thou ask?

Jenk. Because you are my master, and if I have a mistress,   60

38.] *Q1;* And he . . . in his highest thoughts *Q2.*   42. as his] *Qq;* as [is] his
Ward.   50. join'd and knit] *Q1;* knit and ioyn'd *Q2.*   53. *Aside*]
Oliphant.   55. he is] *Q1;* hee's *Q2.*   57. *seeing Jenkin.*] *Verity.*

---

36. *Of*] from.

37. *kind*] way.

38. *in . . . thoughts*] highest in his thoughts.

45. *straight*] without swerving; or, perhaps, in a common Elizabethan
sense, 'immediately'.

48. *name*] reputation, honour (with a play in the next line).

55. *Bedlam*] Bethlehem, the famous London hospital for the insane,
located in Heywood's time outside Bishopsgate, since then twice moved.

56. *missing of me*] missing me; in Elizabethan English *of* was often used
to separate gerund and object—see Abbott, Sect. 177.

I would be glad like a good servant to do my duty to
her.

Wen. I mean where's Mistress Frankford?

Jenk. Marry, sir, her husband is riding out of town, and she
went very lovingly to bring him on his way to horse. Do   65
you see, sir, here she comes, and here I go.

Wen. Vanish.   [*Exit* JENKIN.]

Enter ANNE.

Anne. You are well met, sir. Now in troth my husband
Before he took horse had a great desire
To speak with you. We sought about the house,   70
Hallow'd into the fields, sent every way,
But could not meet you; therefore he enjoin'd me
To do unto you his most kind commends.
Nay, more, he wills you as you prize his love,
Or hold in estimation his kind friendship,   75
To make bold in his absence and command
Even as himself were present in the house;
For you must keep his table, use his servants,
And be a present Frankford in his absence.

Wen. I thank him for his love.   80
[*Aside*] Give me a name, you whose infectious tongues
Are tipp'd with gall and poison; as you would
Think on a man that had your father slain,
Murd'red thy children, made your wives base strumpets,
So call me, call me so! Print in my face   85

---

63. where's Mistress] *Q1;* Mistris *Q2.*   67. *Exit Jenkin.] Reed.*
68. You are] *Q1;* Y'are *Q2.*   71. Hallow'd] *Pearson;* Hallowed *Q1;*
Hollow'd *Q2.*   72. enjoin'd] *Q2;* inioyned *Q1.*   73. kind] *Q2;* kinds
Q1.   81. *Aside] Collier (1850).*   82–4. poison; . . . strumpets,] *Reed;*
poison, . . . strumpets, *Q1;* poison, . . . strumpets *Q2.*   84. Murd'red]
Q2; Murdered *Q1.*   thy] *Q1;* your *Q2.*

---

65. *bring . . . horse*] accompany him to his horse.
73.] to deliver his kindest remembrances to you.
kind] Q1's 'kinds' is probably a misprint for 'kinde' (as in Q2), but the
compositor may have tried to set 'kindst'.
78. *keep*] maintain.

The most stigmatic title of a villain
For hatching treason to so true a friend.

Anne. Sir, you are much beholding to my husband;
You are a man most dear in his regard.

Wen. I am bound unto your husband and you too.   90
[*Aside*] I will not speak to wrong a gentleman
Of that good estimation, my kind friend.
I will not! Zounds, I will not! I may choose,
And I will choose. Shall I be so misled?
Or shall I purchase to my father's crest   95
The motto of a villain? If I say
I will not do it, what thing can enforce me?
Who can compel me? What sad destiny
Hath such command upon my yielding thoughts?
I will not. Ha! some fury pricks me on;   100
The swift Fates drag me at their chariot wheel
And hurry me to mischief. Speak I must—
Injure myself, wrong her, deceive his trust.

Anne. Are you not well, sir, that you seem thus troubled?
There is sedition in your countenance.   105

Wen. And in my heart, fair angel, chaste and wise:
I love you. Start not, speak not, answer not.
I love you—nay, let me speak the rest.
Bid me to swear, and I will call to record
The host of Heaven.

91. *Aside*] Collier (*1850*).   98. Who] *Q1;* What *Q2.*   104. you seem]
Q1; ye seeme *Q2.*   108. me] *Q2;* we *Q1.*

---

86. *stigmatic*] ignominious, infamous.
88. *beholding*] indebted, beholden.
92. *estimation*] reputation.
95. *purchase*] acquire otherwise than by inheritance or descent; cf. *Ant.*,
I. iv. 12–14:
> His faults in him seem as the spots of Heaven,
> More fiery by night's blackness, hereditary
> Rather than purchased.

98. *sad*] steadfast.
105. *sedition*] discord, the passions rebelling against the reason and the
will. Not in *O.E.D.* in this figurative use.

Anne.   The host of Heaven forbid   110
    Wendoll should hatch such a disloyal thought.
Wen. Such is my fate; to this suit I was born,
    To wear rich Pleasure's crown, or Fortune's scorn.
Anne. My husband loves you.
Wen.   I know it.
Anne.   He esteems you
    Even as his brain, his eyeball, or his heart.   115
Wen. I have try'd it.
Anne. His purse is your exchequer, and his table
    Doth freely serve you.
Wen.   So I have found it.
Anne. O with what face of brass, what brow of steel,
    Can you unblushing speak this to the face   120
    Of the espous'd wife of so dear a friend?
    It is my husband that maintains your state;
    Will you dishonour him? I am his wife
    That in your power hath left his whole affairs;
    It is to me you speak?
Wen.   O speak no more,   125
    For more than this I know and have recorded
    Within the red-leav'd table of my heart.
    Fair, and of all belov'd, I was not fearful
    Bluntly to give my life into your hand,

---

112. suit] *Qq;* fate *conj. Deighton.*   117. your] *Q2;* you *Q1.*   121. espous'd] *Q2;* espoused *Q1.*   123–4.] *Qq;* Will you dishonor him that in your power / Hath left his whole affaires? I am his wife, *Pearson;* Will you dishonor him—I am his wife— / That . . . affairs? *Baskervill.*

---

116. *try'd it*] put it to the test.
123–4.] The emendations of Pearson and Baskervill are unnecessary, for in Elizabethan English *his* can serve as the antecedent of a relative pronoun; thus, 'I am the wife of him who left his whole affairs in your power'. See Abbott, Sect. 218, and cf. *Tw. N.,* I. v. 305: 'Love make his heart of flint that you shall love'.
127. *table*] notebook.
128–30. *I . . . means*] I was not afraid to give my life abruptly into your hand and, at the same venture, all my earthly means. Baskervill's repunctuation yields the reading 'At one throw, risk'.

And at one hazard all my earthly means.   130
Go, tell your husband; he will turn me off,
And I am then undone. I care not, I—
'Twas for your sake. Perchance in rage he'll kill me.
I care not—'twas for you. Say I incur
The general name of villain through the world,   135
Of traitor to my friend—I care not, I.
Beggary, shame, death, scandal, and reproach—
For you I'll hazard all. What care I ?
For you I'll live, and in your love I'll die.

Anne. You move me, sir, to passion and to pity;   140
The love I bear my husband is as precious
As my soul's health.

Wen.   I love your husband too,
And for his love I will engage my life.
Mistake me not, the augmentation
Of my sincere affection borne to you   145
Doth no whit lessen my regard of him.
I will be secret, lady, close as night,
And not the light of one small glorious star
Shall shine here in my forehead to bewray
That act of night.

Anne. [*Aside*]   What shall I say ?   150
My soul is wand'ring and hath lost her way.
[*To him.*] O Master Wendoll, O.

Wen.   Sigh not, sweet saint,

---

130. one hazard] *Qq;* one, hazard *Baskervill.*   138. What] *Q1;* why what
Q2.   139. live] *Q1;* loue *Q2.*   150. *Aside*] *Spencer.*

---

135. *The general name*] the name among people in general.
138.] The Q2 reading makes a more regular line, but a long caesura can
easily substitute for an extra syllable.
139.] The antithesis between *live* and *die* makes the Q1 reading clearly
preferable.
140. *passion*] anger (not amorousness).
147. *close*] secret; cf. note on l. 176 below.
148. *glorious*] boastful.
149. *bewray*] reveal.

For every sigh you breathe draws from my heart
A drop of blood.

Anne. [*Aside*]   I ne'er offended yet;
My fault, I fear, will in my brow be writ: 155
Women that fall not quite bereft of grace
Have their offences noted in their face.
I blush and am asham'd. [*To him.*] O Master Wendoll,
Pray God I be not born to curse your tongue,
That hath enchanted me. This maze I am in   160
I fear will prove the labyrinth of sin.

Enter NICHOLAS [*behind*].

Wen. The path of pleasure and the gate to bliss,
Which on your lips I knock at with a kiss. [*Kisses her.*]
Nich. [*Aside*] I'll kill the rogue.
Wen. Your husband is from home, your bed's no blab—   165
     Nay, look not down and blush. [*Exeunt* WENDOLL *and* ANNE.]
Nich.   Zounds, I'll stab.
     Ay, Nick, was it thy chance to come just in the nick?

---

154. *Aside*] *This ed.*   155. my] *Q2; not in Q1.*   161.1. *behind*] *Collier*
(*1850*).   163. *Kisses her.*] *This ed.*   164. *Aside*] *Verity.*   166. *Exeunt*
. . . *Anne.*] *Dodsley; Exit. Q2.*   166–7.] *Q2;* Zounds . . . stab: / I . . .
come / Iust . . . slaue, *Q1.*

153–4.] It was a popular belief that every time one sighed his heart lost
a drop of blood; Wendoll rather charmingly implies that his heart is hers.
Donne employs the same conceit in his 'Song', 'Sweetest love I do not go',
ll. 25–6:

> When thou sigh'st, thou sigh'st not winde,
>   But sigh'st my soule away. (ed. Grierson, 1912, I, 19.)

155.] a favourite idea of Heywood's; cf. xvii. 56 below and, among others,
2 Edward IV:

> If all thy faults were in thy forehead writ,
> Perhaps thou wouldst thyself appeare no lesse,
> But much more horrible then she doth now.
>   (Pearson, I, 168.)

165. *blab*] tattle-tale; cf. *2 Edward IV*: 'This tongue was never knowne
to be a blab' (Pearson, I, 148).

167. *in the nick*] at the right moment (with an obvious pun); cf. *Oth.*,
v. ii. 314–17 (the Q1 reading):

I love my master, and I hate that slave;
I love my mistress, but these tricks I like not.
My master shall not pocket up this wrong;   170
I'll eat my fingers first. [*Drawing his dagger.*] What say'st thou,
    metal?
Does not the rascal Wendoll go on legs
That thou must cut off? Hath he not hamstrings
That thou must hock? Nay, metal, thou shalt stand
To all I say. I'll henceforth turn a spy,   175
And watch them in their close conveyances.
I never look'd for better of that rascal
Since he came miching first into our house.
It is that Satan hath corrupted her,
For she was fair and chaste. I'll have an eye   180
In all their gestures. Thus I think of them—
If they proceed as they have done before,
Wendoll's a knave, my mistress is a &c.   *Exit.*

171. *Drawing his dagger.*] Oliphant.   172. the] *Q1;* that *Q2.*   174.
shalt] *Q1;* shall *Q2.*   183. &c.] *Q1;* —— *Q2.*

---

and this, it seems,
Roderigo meant to have sent this damned villain,
But that, belike, Iago in the nick
Came in and satisfied him.

170. *pocket up*] submit to; cf. *John*, III. i. 200: 'Well, ruffian, I must
pocket up these wrongs'.

171. *metal*] (a) dagger; (b) courage. In l. 174 below, Q1 spells the word
as 'mettal', Q2 as 'mettle'; here, both have 'mettle'.

172. *go*] walk.

174. *hock*] cut, so as to disable.

176. *close conveyances*] secret underhand dealings.

178. *miching*] sneaking; or, possibly, 'pretending poverty', for which cf.
Randle Cotgrave, *A dictionarie of the French and English tongues*, 1611: 'to
miche it, or a rich man to make shew of pouertie' (from *O.E.D.*). The most
famous appearance of the word is of course in *Ham.*, III. ii. 148–9: 'Marry,
this is miching mallecho; it means mischief'.

180. *fair*] unspotted.

181. *gestures*] movements. Cf. George Turbervile, *Tragical Tales*, 1587,
ed. Maidment, 1837, p. 127: 'Hee usde his gestures so unto this gallant
dame . . . that she at length his friend in love became'.

183. *&c.*] Is this to be regarded as a rhetorical device or a piece of over-
nice reticence? The only other even remotely similar example that I know

[Scene vii]

Enter SIR CHARLES *and* SUSAN.

Sir Cha. Sister, you see we are driven to hard shift
          To keep this poor house we have left unsold;
          I am now enforc'd to follow husbandry,
          And you to milk; and do we not live well?
          Well, I thank God.
Susan.   O brother, here's a change,   5
          Since old Sir Charles died, in our father's house.
Sir Cha. All things on earth thus change, some up, some down;
          Content's a kingdom, and I wear that crown.

                    Enter SHAFTON *with a Sergeant.*

Shaf. Good morrow, good morrow, Sir Charles; what, with your
              sister
          Plying your husbandry?—Sergeant, stand off—   10
          You have a pretty house here, and a garden,
          And goodly ground about it. Since it lies
          So near a lordship that I lately bought,
          I would fain buy it of you. I will give you—

vii. 6. died,] *Verity;* died *Qq.*   9. *Shaf.*] *Q1; not in Q2.*   morrow, good
morrow] *Q1;* morrow, morrow *Q2.*

---

of in contemporary dramatic printing is also from Heywood, in the first
part of *The Iron Age,* v:
      Ther. Then haue at thee *Menelaus,* thou art a king and a ——
      Aia. No more, but if on any, rayle on mee.
          Desert should still be snarl'd at, vice passe free.
      Ther. . . . what thankes hast thou for spending thy meanes, . . . and all
          for a ——
      Aiax. Peace. (Pearson, III, 342.)
Here, however, the dashes may well indicate no more than an interruption by Ajax.

   vii. 3. *husbandry*] agriculture; with a suggestion of the meaning 'eco-
nomy, thrift'.
     8. *Content's a kingdom*] proverbial (Tilley C623); cf. *3H6,* III. i. 64–5:
                         my crown is call'd content;
                 A crown it is that seldom kings enjoy.
     8.1. *Sergeant*] an officer charged with the arrest of offenders.
     13. *lordship*] estate, manor.

Sir Cha. O pardon me; this house successively   15
    Hath 'long'd to me and my progenitors
    Three hundred year. My great-great-grandfather,
    He in whom first our gentle style began,
    Dwelt here, and in this ground increas'd this molehill
    Unto that mountain which my father left me.   20
    Where he the first of all our house begun,
    I now the last will end and keep this house,
    This virgin title never yet deflower'd
    By any unthrift of the Mountfords' line.
    In brief, I will not sell it for more gold   25
    Than you could hide or pave the ground withal.
Shaf. Ha, ha! A proud mind and a beggar's purse.
    Where's my three hundred pounds—beside the use?
    I have brought it to an execution
    By course of law; what, is my money ready?   30
Sir Cha. An execution, sir, and never tell me
    You put my bond in suit? You deal extremely.
Shaf. Sell me the land and I'll acquit you straight.
Sir Cha. Alas, alas! 'Tis all trouble hath left me
    To cherish me and my poor sister's life.   35
    If this were sold, our names should then be quite

---

17. year] *Q1;* yeeres *Q2.*   28. beside] *Q1;* besides *Q2.*   29. an]
Q1; not in Q2.   30. money] *Q1;* monies *Q2.*   36. names] *Dodsley;*
meanes *Qq.*

---

17. *year*] a common form for the plural, from the O.E. plural *géar*. J. B.
Leishman, ed., *The Three Parnassus Plays*, 1949, has a note on this form,
p. 95.
18. *gentle style*] title to gentility.
19–20. *molehill . . . mountain*] alluding to the proverb 'To make a mountain of a molehill' (Tilley M1035).
28. *use*] interest.
29. *brought . . . execution*] had prepared a warrant of seizure.
32. *put . . . suit*] put my bond in force in a court of law. The earliest citation in *O.E.D.* for 'put in suit' in this sense is 1618. See also *O.E.D. bond*,
III, 9.
extremely] with great severity.
36. *names*] A strained sense might be obtained by taking the Qq *means* as
'resources, possessions', but Dodsley's emendation seems justified.

THE
UNIVERSITY OF WINNIPEG
PORTAGE & BALMORAL
WINNIPEG 2, MAN.
CANADA

SC. VII]   A WOMAN KILLED WITH KINDNESS   39

Raz'd from the bead-roll of gentility.
You see what hard shift we have made to keep it
Ally'd still to our own name. This palm you see
Labour hath glow'd within; her silver brow,   40
That never tasted a rough winter's blast
Without a mask or fan, doth with a grace
Defy cold winter and his storms outface.

Susan. Sir, we feed sparing, and we labour hard,
We lie uneasy, to reserve to us   45
And our succession this small plot of ground.

Sir Cha. I have so bent my thoughts to husbandry
That I protest I scarcely can remember
What a new fashion is, how silk or satin
Feels in my hand; why, pride is grown to us   50
A mere, mere stranger. I have quite forgot
The names of all that ever waited on me;
I cannot name ye any of my hounds,
Once from whose echoing mouths I heard all the music
That e'er my heart desired. What should I say?   55
To keep this place I have chang'd myself away.

---

37. Raz'd] *Dodsley;* Raced *Q1;* Rac'd *Q2.*   bead-roll] *Collier (1850);* bed-roll *Qq.*   40. within;] *Dodsley;* within *Qq.*   54. the] *Q1; not in Q2.*

---

37. *bead-roll*] list.

40. *Labour . . . within*] i.e. has been made red by labour.

40-1. *brow . . . tasted*] Similarly, Jonson attributes taste to eyes in *Every Man in His Humour,* IV. vii. 1 (ed. cit., III, 375) and *The Case Is Altered,* IV. iv. 18–20 (ed. cit., III, 155).

42. *mask*] 'sometimes made of velvet, and sometimes of silk lined with fine leather, worn out of doors by city-wives and women of humbler rank as well as by ladies' (Bates). Cf. *Gent.,* IV. iv. 159–62:

> since she did neglect her looking-glass
> And threw her sun-expelling mask away,
> The air hath starv'd the roses in her cheeks
> And pinch'd the lily-tincture of her face.

43. *his*] its; the common form of the neuter possessive singular into the 17th century. The first occurrence of *its* recorded by *O.E.D.* is in 1598.

44. *sparing*] first recorded as an adverb in *O.E.D.* 1623.

46. *succession*] descendants, heirs.

51. *mere*] absolute.

56. *I . . . away*] i.e. I have altered my mode of life completely.

H

Shaf. [to the Sergeant.] Arrest him at my suit. [*To Sir Charles.*]
　　Actions and actions
　　Shall keep thee in perpetual bondage fast.
　　Nay, more, I'll sue thee by a late appeal
　　And call thy former life in question.　　　　　　　60
　　The Keeper is my friend; thou shalt have irons,
　　And usage such as I'll deny to dogs.
　　Away with him!
Sir Cha. You are too timorous; but trouble is my master,
　　And I will serve him truly. My kind sister,　　　65
　　Thy tears are of no force to mollify
　　This flinty man. Go to my father's brother,
　　My kinsmen and allies; entreat them from me
　　To ransom me from this injurious man
　　That seeks my ruin.
Shaf.　　　　　　　　Come, irons, irons, away!　　　70
　　I'll see thee lodg'd far from the sight of day.

　　　　　　　　　　　　　　Exeunt. [Manet SUSAN.]

　　　　Enter SIR FRANCIS *and* MALBY [*behind*].

Susan. My heart's so hard'ned with the frost of grief
　　Death cannot pierce it through. Tyrant too fell!

---

57. *to the Sergeant.*] *Verity.*　　58. perpetual] *Q1;* continuall *Q2.*　　62–
3.] *Pearson; Qq set as one line.*　　63–4.] *Pearson;* Away . . . timorous; / But
. . . master, *Verity.*　　64. You] *Q1;* Ye *Q2.*　　timorous] *Qq;* tyrannous
Oliphant (conj. Neilson).　　68. from] *Q1;* for *Q2.*　　70. irons, irons] *Q1;*
irons, irons; come *Q2;* irons! Come *Ward.*　　71.1. *Exeunt.*] *Q1; not in Q2.*
Manet Susan.] *Verity (subs.).*　　71.2. *Enter . . . Malby.*] *Q1; Q2 places
after l. 74.*　　behind] *Ashton (subs.).*

---

　　59. *sue . . . appeal*] prosecute thee on a criminal accusation undertaken
after the usual time. For *appeal* cf. *Ant.*, III. i. 10–12: 'not resting here,
accuses him of letters he had formerly wrote to Pompey; upon his own
appeal, seizes him'.
　　60.] 'And put in jeopardy the life which you formerly saved' (Spencer).
　　64. *timorous*] dreadful, terrible. Cf. Richard Johnson, *The Most Famous
History of the seuen Champions of Christendome* (1608): 'Yet for the honour
thou hast done in *Iuda*, I grant thee this loue, by the law of Armes to choose
thy death, els hadst thou suffered a timorous torment' (p. 45).
　　68. *allies*] relatives.

So lead the fiends condemned souls to Hell.

Sir Fra. Again to prison! Malby, hast thou seen   75
A poor slave better tortur'd? Shall we hear
The music of his voice cry from the grate
'Meat for the Lord's sake'? No, no, yet I am not
Throughly reveng'd. They say he hath a pretty wench
Unto his sister; shall I, in mercy sake   80
To him and to his kindred, bribe the fool
To shame herself by lewd, dishonest lust?
I'll proffer largely, but, the deed being done,
I'll smile to see her base confusion.

Mal. Methinks, Sir Francis, you are full reveng'd   85
For greater wrongs than he can proffer you.
See where the poor sad gentlewoman stands.

Sir Fra. Ha, ha! now I will flout her poverty,
Deride her fortunes, scoff her base estate;
My very soul the name of Mountford hates.   90
But stay, my heart, O what a look did fly

78. Lord's] *Q2;* Lord *Q1.*   80. Unto] *Q1;* To *Q2.*   mercy] *Q1;* my
mercy *Q2.*   88. I will] *Q1;* will I *Q2.*   90. hates] *Q1;* hate *Q2.*
91. O] *Dodsley* (oh); or *Qq.*

---

77. *grate*] grating of the prison.
78. *Meat*] food.
Meat . . . sake] Since little was provided for prisoners to eat, those who
were too poor to bribe the guards had no recourse but to beg; cf. *Shakespeare's England,* II, 507.
79. *Throughly*] thoroughly.
wench] young woman, but with some of the pejorative connotations fully
developed in modern usage.
80. *Unto*] as, for; cf. Abbott, Sect. 189.
in mercy sake] in the name of mercy.
82. *dishonest*] unchaste.
83. *largely*] generously.
84. *base confusion*] degrading ruin.
91–4.] Lawrence Babb, *The Elizabethan Malady,* 1951, suggests
that these lines are 'a conventional aside representing the speaker's
thoughts. Under the circumstances Sir Francis could not actually speak'
(p. 144).
91. O] *O.E.D.* records *or* as an introductory particle meaning 'now', but
the only two citations are dated *c.* 1413 and *c.* 1450; Dodsley's emendation
is less strained.

To strike my soul through with thy piercing eye.
I am enchanted, all my spirits are fled,
And with one glance my envious spleen stroke dead.

Susan. [*seeing them.*] Acton, that seeks our blood!   *Runs away.*
Sir Fra.   O chaste and fair!
Mal. Sir Francis, why Sir Francis, zounds, in a trance?   96
Sir Francis, what cheer, man? Come, come, how is't?
Sir Fra. Was she not fair? Or else this judging eye
Cannot distinguish beauty.
Mal.   She was fair.
Sir Fra. She was an angel in a mortal's shape,   100
And ne'er descended from old Mountford's line.
But soft, soft, let me call my wits together.
A poor, poor wench, to my great adversary
Sister, whose very souls denounce stern war
One against other. How now, Frank, turn'd fool   105
Or madman, whether? But no! master of
My perfect senses and directest wits.
Then why should I be in this violent humour
Of passion and of love? and with a person
So different every way, and so oppos'd   110
In all contractions and still-warring actions?
Fie, fie, how I dispute against my soul.
Come, come, I'll gain her, or in her fair quest
Purchase my soul free and immortal rest.   *Exeunt.*

---

95. *seeing them.*] *This ed.*   *Runs*] *Q2; Run Q1.*   96. zounds, in] *Q1;* in
Q2.   105. One] *Q1;* Each *Q2.*   106. no!] *Collier (1850);* no *Qq;* no;
Dodsley.   114. *Exeunt.*] *Q1;* not in *Q2.*

---

94. *envious spleen*] malicious anger.
102. *soft, soft*] wait a moment.
104. *whose very souls*] i.e. Mountford's and mine.
denounce] proclaim.
106. *whether*] which one.
111. *contractions*] dealings.
113. *her fair quest*] quest of fair her.

[Scene viii]

Enter 3 or 4 Servingmen [including SPIGGOT *the Butler and* NICHO-
LAS], *one with a voider and a wooden knife to take away all, another
the salt and bread, another the tablecloth and napkins, another the
carpet.* JENKIN *with two lights after them.*

Jenk. So, march in order and retire in battle 'ray. My master
and the guests have supp'd already; all's taken away. Here,
now spread for the servingmen in the hall. Butler, it be-
longs to your office.

Spig. I know it, Jenkin. What do you call the gentleman that   5
supp'd there to-night?

Jenk. Who, my master?

Spig. No, no, Master Wendoll, he is a daily guest; I mean the
gentleman that came but this afternoon.

Jenk. His name is Master Cranwell. God's light! Hark, within   10
there, my master calls to lay more billets on the fire. Come,
come! Lord how we that are in office here in the house are
troubled. One spread the carpet in the parlour and stand
ready to snuff the lights; the rest be ready to prepare their
stomachs. More lights in the hall there. Come, Nich'las.   15
                              [*Exeunt. Manet* NICHOLAS.]

Nich. I cannot eat, but had I Wendoll's heart
I would eat that; the rogue grows impudent.

viii. 0.1–2. *including . . . Nicholas*] Spencer.   0.2. *away all*] *Q1; away Q2.*
1. '*ray*] *Q1;* array *Q2.*   5. I know . . . What] *Q1;* I know . . . Ienkin /
VVhat *Q2.*   do you] *Q1;* de'ye *Q2.*   6. there] *Qq;* here *Dodsley.*
8. *Spig.*] *Q1 (But.);* wen. *Q2.*   he is] *Q1;* hee's *Q2.*   10. name is] *Q1;*
name's *Q2.*   11. on] *Q1;* vppon *Q2.*   15.1. *Exeunt . . . Nicholas.*] Reed;
Exit *Q2.*

---

viii. 0.2. *voider*] tray or basket used for clearing the table.
0.4. *carpet*] table-cover of tapestry work. 'Carpets were not at this period
laid on the floor; except occasionally to kneel on, or for purposes of state'
(Ben Jonson, *Works*, ed. Gifford and Cunningham, 1904, I, 447 n.).
lights] candles.
1. '*ray*] order, array, especially of soldiers.
8. *he*] Cf. note on iii. 53 above.
10. *God's light*] a common oath, frequently abbreviated to ''slight'.
12. *office*] service.
15. *stomachs*] appetites.

O I have seen such vild, notorious tricks,
Ready to make my eyes dart from my head.
I'll tell my master, by this air I will;   20
Fall what may fall, I'll tell him. Here he comes.

Enter FRANKFORD, *as it were brushing the crumbs from his
clothes with a napkin, and newly risen from supper.*

Frank. Nich'las, what make you here ? Why are not you
         At supper in the hall there with your fellows ?
Nich. Master, I stay'd your rising from the board
         To speak with you.
Frank.   Be brief, then, gentle Nich'las,   25
         My wife and guests attend me in the parlour.
         Why dost thou pause ? Now, Nich'las, you want money,
         And unthrift-like would eat into your wages
         Ere you have earn'd it. Here's, sir, half a crown;
         Play the good husband, and away to supper.   30
Nich. [*Aside*] By this hand, an honourable gentleman. I will
         not see him wrong'd. [*To him.*] Sir, I have serv'd you
         long; you entertain'd me seven years before your beard.
         You knew me, sir, before you knew my mistress.
Frank. What of this, good Nich'las ?   35
Nich. I never was a make-bate or a knave;

21.2. *and*] *Q1; as Q2.*   23. there with] *Q1;* among *Q2.*   29. Here's,
sir] *Q1;* heere sirs *Q2.*   31. *Aside*] *Oliphant.*

---

   18. *vild*] vile.
   22. *make*] do.
   24. *stay'd*] waited for.
   26. *attend*] wait for.
   28. *unthrift-like*] like a spendthrift; this passage is the only one cited in
O.E.D.
   29. *it*] 'Wages' was often construed as singular, 14th to 18th centuries.
   30. *Play . . . husband*] be thrifty.
   33. *entertain'd me*] took me into service.
   seven . . . beard] i.e. seven years before you were old enough to grow
a beard.
   36. *make-bate*] trouble-maker. Cf. Sidney's *Arcadia* II (1590): 'The
farmer . . . disdaining this fellow should play the preacher, who had bin one
of the chiefest make-bates, strake him a great wound vpon the face with
his sword' (p. 221).

    I have no fault but one—I am given to quarrel,
    But not with women. I will tell you, master,
    That which will make your heart leap from your breast,
    Your hair to startle from your head, your ears to tingle.   40
Frank. What preparation's this to dismal news?
Nich. 'Sblood, sir, I love you better than your wife—
    [*Frankford threatens him.*] I'll make it good.
Frank. Thou art a knave, and I have much ado
    With wonted patience to contain my rage   45
    And not to break thy pate. Thou art a knave;
    I'll turn you with your base comparisons
    Out of my doors.
Nich. Do, do. There's not room for Wendoll and me too both
    in one house. O master, master, that Wendoll is a villain. 50
Frank. [*striking him.*] Ay, saucy!
Nich. Strike, strike, do strike; yet hear me: I am no fool;
    I know a villain when I see him act
    Deeds of a villain. Master, master, that base slave
    Enjoys my mistress and dishonours you.   55
Frank. Thou hast kill'd me with a weapon whose sharp'ned point
    Hath prick'd quite through and through my shivering heart.
    Drops of cold sweat sit dangling on my hairs
    Like morning's dew upon the golden flowers,

---

37. I am] *Q1;* I'me *Q2.*   40. to startle] *Qq;* start *Ward.*   43. *Frankford
. . . him.] This ed.*   44. Thou art] *Q1;* Y'are *Q2.*   46. Thou art]
Q1; Th'art *Q2.*   48–50.] *This ed.;* Out . . . dores. / Do, do, / Theres . . .
to, / Both . . . maister, / That . . . villen. *Qq;* Out . . . room / For . . . house. /
Oh . . . villain. *Verity.*   49. There's] *Q1;* There is *Q2.*   51. *striking
him.] Baskervill.*   56. sharp'ned] *Q1;* sharp *Q2.*   57. shivering] *Q1;*
shiu'ring *Q2.*

38–40.] Cf. *Ham.,* I. v. 15–20:
    I could a tale unfold whose lightest word
    Would harrow up thy soul, freeze thy young blood,
    Make thy two eyes, like stars, start from their spheres,
    Thy knotted and combined locks to part,
    And each particular hair to stand an end,
    Like quills upon the fretful porpentine.
40. *startle*] start, make a sudden involuntary movement.
55. *Enjoys*] i.e. carnally.

And I am plung'd into a strange agony.   60
What didst thou say? If any word that touch'd
His credit or her reputation,
It is as hard to enter my belief
As Dives into Heaven.

Nich.   I can gain nothing;
They are two that never wrong'd me. I knew before   65
'Twas but a thankless office, and perhaps
As much as is my service or my life
Is worth. All this I know, but this and more,
More by a thousand dangers could not hire me
To smother such a heinous wrong from you.   70
I saw, and I have said.

Frank. [*Aside*] 'Tis probable; though blunt, yet he is honest.
Though I durst pawn my life, and on their faith
Hazard the dear salvation of my soul,
Yet in my trust I may be too secure.   75
May this be true? O may it? Can it be?
Is it by any wonder possible?
Man, woman, what thing mortal may we trust
When friends and bosom wives prove so unjust?
[*To him.*] What instance hast thou of this strange report? 80

Nich. Eyes, eyes.

Frank. Thy eyes may be deceiv'd I tell thee,
For should an angel from the heavens drop down

60. a strange agony] *Q1;* strange agonies *Q2.*   64–8.] *Pearson;* As . . .
Heauen. / I . . . two / That . . . before / Twas . . . perhaps / As . . . woorth, /
Al . . . more, *Qq.*   67. is] *Q2; not in Q1.*   72. *Aside*] *Verity.*   78.
may] *Q1;* can *Q2.*   81. Eyes, eyes] *Q1;* Eyes master, eyes *Q2.*

64. *Dives*] the rich man sent to Hell in Jesus' parable of Dives and
Lazarus (see Luke, xvi. 19–31).
74. *dear . . . soul*] salvation of my dear soul; cf. xiii. 138.
dear] precious.
75. *secure*] over-confident; cf. *Wiv.,* II. i. 240: 'Though Page be a secure
fool'.
80. *instance*] evidence; cf. *A Challenge for Beauty,* II:
          Perhaps shee's fayre, what Instance can you give,
          That shee's of such prov'd vertue. (Pearson, v, 31.)
83–5.] Cf. *A Challenge for Beauty,* IV:

And preach this to me that thyself hast told,
He should have much ado to win belief,   85
In both their loves I am so confident.
Nich. Shall I discourse the same by circumstance?
Frank. No more; to supper, and command your fellows
To attend us and the strangers. Not a word;
I charge thee on thy life, be secret then,   90
For I know nothing.
Nich. I am dumb, and now that I have eas'd my stomach, I
will go fill my stomach.   *Exit.*
Frank. Away, begone.
She is well born, descended nobly;   95
Virtuous her education; her repute
Is in the general voice of all the country
Honest and fair; her carriage, her demeanour
In all her actions that concern the love
To me her husband, modest, chaste, and godly.   100
Is all this seeming gold plain copper?
But he, that Judas that hath borne my purse,

89–90.] *This ed.; word, / I ... life Q1;* word / I ... life, *Q2;* word, / I ...
life; *Dodsley.*

Vnlesse an Angell should descend and speak't,
And for an instance streight produce that Ring,
It wins with me no credence. (Pearson, v, 53.)
87. *discourse*] relate.
by circumstance] in detail.
89. *strangers*] visitors.
92. *eas'd my stomach*] Cf. the modern slang expression 'Got it off my
chest'.
95–101.] Cf. the similar speech by Mr Generous about his wife in *The
Late Lancashire Witches*:
I know her a good woman and well bred,
Of an unquestion'd carriage, well reputed
Amongst her neighbours, reckon'd with the best
And ore me most indulgent; though in many
Such things might breed a doubt and jealousie,
Yet I hatch no such phrensie. (Pearson, IV, 192.)
102. *Judas*] See John, xiii. 29: 'Judas had the [money-]bagge' and cf.
'An Order for Prayer and Thanksgiving', 1598, in *Liturgies and Occasional
Forms of Prayer Set Forth in the Reign of Queen Elizabeth*, Parker Society,
1847, p. 681: 'D. Bagshaw, the Pope's Judas, or purse-bearer'.

And sold me for a sin—O God, O God,
Shall I put up these wrongs ? No, shall I trust
The bare report of this suspicious groom   105
Before the double gilt, the well-hatch'd ore
Of their two hearts ? No, I will loose these thoughts;
Distraction I will banish from my brow
And from my looks exile sad discontent.
Their wonted favours in my tongue shall flow;   110
Till I know all, I'll nothing seem to know.
Lights and a table there. Wife, Master Wendoll, and
gentle Master Cranwell—

Enter ANNE, MASTER WENDOLL, MASTER CRANWELL,
NICHOLAS, *and* JENKIN, *with cards, carpet, stools, and
other necessaries.*

Frank. O you are a stranger, Master Cranwell, you,
And often balk my house; faith, you are a churl.   115
Now we have supp'd, a table and to cards.

Jenk. A pair of cards, Nich'las, and a carpet to cover the table.

106. well-hatch'd] *Verity* (-hatched); wel hatch *Qq.*   107. loose] *Qq;*
lose *Dodsley.*   112. there.] *Q2;* there *Q1.*   113.2. carpet] *Q1; Carpets
Q2.*   114.] *Q1;* O master *Cranwel*, you are are [*sic*] a stranger heere, *Q2.*
115. you are] *Q1;* y'are *Q2.*

---

103. *sold . . . sin*] See Matthew, xxvii. 3–4: 'Then when Judas which betrayed him, sawe that he was condemned, hee repented himselfe, and
brought againe the thirtie pieces of siluer to the chiefe Priestes, and Elders,
Saying, I haue sinned betraying the innocent blood'.
104. *put up*] put up with.
No] i.e. rather.
106. *double gilt*] the refined gold (with a pun on 'guilt' and possibly on
the meaning 'thief' for *gilt*, the first example recorded by *O.E.D.* being
dated 1620).
well-hatch'd] richly inlaid; *O.E.D.* does not record the compound.
ore] *O.E.D.* records no figurative use of the term before *a.* 1628.
107. *loose*] let loose, rid myself of.
110. *Their wonted favours*] my usual kindnesses to them. For *favour* see
the quotation in *O.E.D.*, sb., 2b, from Bishop Hall's *Meditations and Vows*,
II, Sect. 23: 'So shal I . . . accept of small favours with great thankfulnes'
(1608–11).
115. *balk*] pass by, avoid.
117. *pair*] pack.

Where's Sisly with her counters and her box? Candles
and candlesticks there! [*Enter* SISLY *and a Servingman
with counters and candles.*] Fie, we have such a household   120
of serving creatures! Unless it be Nick and I, there's not
one amongst them all can say 'bo' to a goose; [*to Nicholas*] well said, Nick.

They spread a carpet, set down lights and cards. [*Exeunt all the
Servants except* NICHOLAS.]

Anne. Come, Master Frankford, who shall take my part?
Frank. Marry, that will I, sweet wife.   125
Wen. No, by my faith, sir, when you are together I sit out;
  it must be Mistress Frankford and I, or else it is no
  match.
Frank. I do not like that match.
Nich. [*Aside*] You have no reason, marry, knowing all.   130
Frank. 'Tis no great matter, neither. Come, Master Cran-
  well, shall you and I take them up?
Cran. At your pleasure, sir.
Frank. I must look to you, Master Wendoll, for you will be
  playing false—nay, so will my wife, too.   135
Nich. [*Aside*] Ay, I will be sworn she will.
Anne. Let them that are taken playing false forfeit the set.
Frank. Content; [*Aside*] it shall go hard but I'll take you.
Cran. Gentlemen, what shall our game be?

119–20. *Enter . . . candles.] This ed.*   122–3. *to Nicholas] This ed.*
123.1–2. *Exeunt . . . Nicholas.] This ed.*   126. faith, sir] *Q1;* Faith, *Q2.*
130. *Aside] Dodsley.*   134. you will] *Q1;* you'l *Q2.*   136. *Aside]*
Dodsley.   Ay, I] *Q1* (I, I); I *Q2.*   137. playing false] *Q1;* false *Q2.*
138. *Aside] This ed.*

---

122. *say . . . goose*] proverbial (Tilley B481).

123. *well said*] well done; cf. *Ant.*, IV. iv. 28: 'So, so; come, give me
that; this way; well said'.

124. *take my part*] be my partner.

129.] There is *double entendre* in practically every exchange in this part
of the scene, especially in the names of the card games.

132. *take them up*] play against them.

137. *taken . . . false*] caught cheating.

set] game.

Wen. Master Frankford, you play best at noddy.   140

Frank. You shall not find it so; [*Aside*] indeed you shall not!

Anne. I can play at nothing so well as double ruff.

Frank. If Master Wendoll and my wife be together, there's
    no playing against them at double hand.

Nich. I can tell you, sir, the game that Master Wendoll is   145
    best at.

Wen. What game is that, Nick?

Nich. Marry, sir, knave out of doors.

Wen. She and I will take you at lodam.

Anne. Husband, shall we play at saint?   150

Frank. [*Aside*] My saint's turn'd devil; [*to her*] no, we'll
    none of saint. You're best at new-cut, wife; [*Aside*]
    you'll play at that!

Wen. If you play at new-cut, I am soonest hitter of any here,
    for a wager.   155

141. *Aside*] *This ed.*   151. *Aside*] *Neilson.*   152. You're] *Q1;* You are
Q2.   *Aside*] *This ed.*   154. I am] *Q1;* I'me *Q2.*

---

140. *noddy*] (a) a card game resembling cribbage; (b) fool, booby. The
pun was a common one; cf. *The Second Part of the Return from Parnassus*,
The Prologue, ll. 16–17: 'Gentlemen, you that can play at noddy, or rather
play vpon Noddies' (ed. Leishman, 1949, p. 219).

142. *double ruff*] one of the variants of ruff, a card game similar to whist;
with a glance at the meaning 'excitement', 'passion' for *ruff*.

144. *double hand*] unidentified, but probably another card game; not in
O.E.D.

148. *knave . . . doors*] apparently another familiar game. Bates cites the
subtitle of 'A Proper new Ballad on the Old Parliament: Or, the second
part of Knave out of Doores'.

149. *lodam*] Florio identifies this game with one called in Italian *carica
l'asino*, 'load the ass' (*O.E.D.*). In view of the double meanings of the names
of the card games in this passage, this line would support that derivation.

150. *saint*] variant form for a game usually known as 'cent', similar to
piquet, one hundred being the number of points required to win.

151. *My . . . devil*] Daniel compares Shakespeare's sonnet [CXLIV, 7]:
'And would corrupt my saint to be a devil'.

152. *new-cut*] 'An old card game' (*O.E.D.*); Bates records a number of
allusions. The sexual application is obvious.

154. *hitter*] ? point-maker; cf. the use of the verb 'hit' meaning to 'take
up' (a man) in backgammon. The noun *hitter* is not recorded in *O.E.D.* in
any sense before 1813. Farmer and Henley record the phrase 'hit on the
tail', meaning 'copulate', and I suspect a similar second meaning here.

Frank. [*Aside*] 'Tis me they play on. Well, you may draw out,
    For all your cunning; 'twill be to your shame.
    I'll teach you at your new-cut a new game.
    [*To them.*] Come, come.
Cran. If you cannot agree upon the game, to post and pair.   160
Wen. We shall be soonest pairs, and my good host,
    When he comes late home, he must kiss the post.
Frank. Whoever wins, it shall be to thy cost.
Cran. Faith, let it be vide-ruff, and let's make honours.
Frank. If you make honours, one thing let me crave: 165
    Honour the king and queen; except the knave.
Wen. Well, as you please for that. Lift who shall deal.
Anne. The least in sight. What are you, Master Wendoll?
Wen. [*cutting the cards.*] I am a knave.
Nich. [*Aside*]   I'll swear it.
Anne. [*Cutting.*]   I a queen.
Frank. [*Aside*] A quean thou should'st say; [*to them*] well, the
    cards are mine.   170
    They are the grossest pair that e'er I felt.

---

156. *Aside*] Neilson.   159. *To them.*] *This ed.; Neilson ends the aside after* on (*l. 156*).   169. *cutting the cards.*] *This ed.*   *Aside*] *Verity.*   *Cutting.*] *This ed.*   a queen] *Q1;* am Queene *Q2.*   170. *Aside*] *Verity.*

---

156. *draw out*] i.e. so pick your cards as to lose the game.

160. *post and pair*] 'A game on the cards, played with three cards each, wherein much depended on *vying*, or betting on the goodness of your own hand' (Robert Nares, *A Glossary*, 1882, II, 676). Farmer and Henley record as one meaning for *post*, 'an act of coition'; not in *O.E.D.* in this sense.

162. *kiss the post*] be shut out; cf. *1 Edward IV*: 'Make haste thou art best, for fear thou kiss the post' (Pearson, I, 47).

164. *vide-ruff*] another variant of ruff, with the same suggestion as in l. 142 above.

make honours] ?name the highest cards; the phrase is not recorded in *O.E.D.*, nor does *honours* as a cardplaying term appear there earlier than 1674.

167. *Lift . . . deal*] cut for the deal.

168. *least*] lowest.

170. *quean*] harlot.

171. *grossest pair*] (a) thickest pack; (b) most immoral couple.

felt] (a) handled; (b) tested, sounded out.

Anne. Shuffle, I'll cut; [*Aside*] would I had never dealt!

Frank. [*deals.*] I have lost my dealing.

Wen.   Sir, the fault's in me.

    This queen I have more than my own, you see.

    Give me the stock. [*Deals.*]

Frank   My mind's not on my game;   175

    [*Aside*] Many a deal I have lost, the more's your shame.

    [*To them.*] You have serv'd me a bad trick, Master Wendoll.

Wen. Sir, you must take your lot. To end this strife,

    I know I have dealt better with your wife.

Frank. [*Aside*] Thou hast dealt falsely, then.   180

Anne. What's trumps?

Wen. Hearts. Partner, I rub.

Frank. [*Aside*] Thou robb'st me of my soul, of her chaste love;

    In thy false dealing thou hast robb'd my heart.

    Booty you play; I like a loser stand,   185

    Having no heart, or here or in my hand.

---

172. *Aside*] *This ed.*   173. *deals.*] *This ed.*   174. *my*] *Q1; mine Q2.*
175. *Deals.*] *This ed.*   176. *Aside*] *This ed.*   180. *Aside*] *This ed.*
183. *Aside*] *Verity.*

---

172. *dealt*] (a) dealt the cards; (b) had sexual intercourse. For the sexual meaning, cf. the song in *The Rape of Lucrece*:

    Some love the rough, and some th' smooth,
    Some great, and others small things,
    But Oh your lecherous Englishman:
    He loves to deale in all things.

(Pearson, v, 216.) The same song, with slight variants, appears in the fifth act of *A Challenge for Beauty* (Pearson, v, 65).

173. *lost my dealing*] made a mistake in dealing.

175. *stock*] that portion of the cards not dealt out; Brooke glosses as 'kitty'.

177. *trick*] (a) hand of cards; (b) piece of roguery.

182. *rub*] take all the cards of one suit; Frankford plays on the homonym *rob* in the next line.

185. *Booty you play*] you join with a confederate to victimize another player. Cf. James Mabbe, tr., Matheo Aleman, *The Rogue: or the life of Guzman de Alfarache* 1 (1623): 'We are three of vs, let vs all play booty, and joyne together to coozen the Cardinall' (p. 222).

186. *or here or*] either here or; a common correlative—see Abbott, Sect. 136.

here] i.e. in his breast.

[*To them.*] I will give o'er the set; I am not well.
Come, who will hold my cards?
Anne. Not well, sweet Master Frankford?
       Alas, what ail you? 'Tis some sudden qualm.   190
Wen. How long have you been so, Master Frankford?
Frank. Sir, I was lusty and I had my health,
       But I grew ill when you began to deal.
       Take hence this table.

[*The Servants enter and remove the table, cards, &c.*]

                         Gentle Master Cranwell,
You are welcome; see your chamber at your pleasure.   195
I am sorry that this megrim takes me so
I cannot sit and bear you company.
Jenkin, some lights, and show him to his chamber.
                    [*Exeunt* CRANWELL *and* JENKIN.]
Anne. A night gown for my husband, quickly there.

[*Enter a Servant with a gown, and exit.*]

       It is some rheum or cold.
Wen.   Now, in good faith,   200
       This illness you have got by sitting late
       Without your gown.

187. *To them.*] *This ed.; Ve rity ends the aside after* heart (*l. 184*).   194. The
. . . *&c.*] *This ed.*   195. You are] *Q1;* Y'are *Q2.*   196. so] *Q1;* so, *Q2;*
so; *Reed.*   198. Jenkin] *Qq; Anne.* Jenkin *conj. Neilson.*   198.1.
Exeunt . . . Jenkin.] *Verity.*   199.1. *Enter . . . exit.*] *This ed.*   200–2.]
Ward; It . . . cold? / Now . . . got / By . . . gowne. / I . . . *Wendol, Qq.*

187. *give . . . set*] give up the game.
190. *qualm*] feeling of sickness; Frankford understands it in its other
meaning, 'sickening fear, sinking of the heart'.
192. *lusty*] vigorous, healthy.
196. *megrim*] migraine, severe headache.
198.] There is no real justification for Neilson's suggested reassignment
of this line.
199. *night gown*] dressing gown.
200. *rheum*] inflammation, cold.
202. *gown*] I suspect some sort of *double entendre,* but I can find no analogous use. The General Editor suggests that there may be a relationship
with 'bona-roba'.

Frank.   I know it, Master Wendoll.
         Go, go to bed, lest you complain like me.
         Wife, prithee wife, into my bedchamber.
         The night is raw and cold and rheumatic.   205
         Leave me my gown and light; I'll walk away my fit.
Wen. Sweet sir, good night.
Frank. Myself, good night.   [*Exit* WENDOLL.]
Anne.   Shall I attend you, husband?
Frank. No, gentle wife, thou'lt catch cold in thy head;
         Prithee, begone, sweet, I'll make haste to bed.   210
Anne. No sleep will fasten on mine eyes, you know,
         Until you come.
Frank.   Sweet Nan, I prithee, go.   [*Exit* ANNE.]
         [*To Nicholas.*] I have bethought me; get me by degrees
         The keys of all my doors, which I will mould
         In wax, and take their fair impression,   215
         To have by them new keys. This being compass'd,
         At a set hour a letter shall be brought me,
         And when they think they may securely play,
         They are nearest to danger. Nick, I must rely
         Upon thy trust and faithful secrecy.   220
Nich. Build on my faith.
Frank.   To bed then, not to rest;
         Care lodges in my brain, grief in my breast.   *Exeunt.*

---

208. *Exit Wendoll.*] *Reed.*   209. catch] *Q2;* catcht *Q1.*   212. *Exit
Anne.*] *Verity; Exit. Qq* [*following* come (*l. 212*)].   213. *To Nicholas.*]
Walley.   219. are nearest] *Q1;* neerest are *Q2.*   222. *Exeunt.*] *Q1;*
not in *Q2.*

---

205. *rheumatic*] producing rheum; accented on the first syllable, for
which see Kökeritz, p. 336.
208. *Myself*] my own, my alter ego.
211.] Cf. *The English Traveller*, IV. iii: 'I finde no sleepe can fasten on
mine eyes' (Pearson, IV, 69).
215. *fair*] clean, unblemished.

[Scene ix]

Enter SUSAN, OLD MOUNTFORD, SANDY, RODER, *and* TYDY.

Old Mount. You say my nephew is in great distress—
Who brought it to him but his own lewd life?
I cannot spare a cross. I must confess
He was my brother's son; why, niece, what then?
This is no world in which to pity men.   5

Susan. I was not born a beggar, though his extremes
Enforce this language from me; I protest
No fortune of mine own could lead my tongue
To this base key. I do beseech you, uncle,
For the name's sake, for Christianity,   10
Nay, for God's sake, to pity his distress.
He is deny'd the freedom of the prison,
And in the hole is laid with men condemn'd;
Plenty he hath of nothing but of irons,
And it remains in you to free him thence.   15

Old Mount. Money I cannot spare; men should take heed.
He lost my kindred when he fell to need.   *Exit.*

Susan. Gold is but earth; thou earth enough shalt have
When thou hast once took measure of thy grave.
You know me, Master Sandy, and my suit.   20

Sandy. I knew you, lady, when the old man liv'd;

ix. 0.1. *Susan*] *This ed.; Sir Charles, his sister Q1; Sir Charles his Sister Q2.*
4. my] *Q2;* me *Q1.*   8. own] *Q2; not in Q1.*   17. *Exit.*] *Q1; not in Q2.*

---

ix. 2. *lewd*] wicked, unprincipled.
6. *extremes*] extremities.
10. *the name's sake*] i.e. the family name, reputation.
12. *freedom . . . prison*] Those with money to spend usually had considerable liberty; see *Shakespeare's England*, II, 508; and cf. *Meas.*, IV. ii. 154–5:
'He hath evermore had the liberty of the prison'.
13. *the hole*] the worst sort of cell; from the name of one of the worst cells
in the Counter, a London prison.
with men condemn'd] It was standard practice to mingle trivial offenders
with the most hardened criminals. See Griffiths, I, 3.
18. *earth*] *O.E.D.* records only one citation, 1612, for *earth* as 'a dis-
paraging term for precious metal'.
19. *took*] a standard form for the past participle of *take*, 16th to 18th
centuries; see *O.E.D.*

I

I knew you ere your brother sold his land.
Then you were Mistress Sue, trick'd up in jewels;
Then you sung well, play'd sweetly on the flute;
But now I neither know you nor your suit.   [*Exit.*]   25

Susan. You, Master Roder, was my brother's tenant:
Rent-free he plac'd you in that wealthy farm
Of which you are possess'd.

Roder.   True, he did;
And have I not there dwelt still for his sake?
I have some business now, but without doubt   30
They that have hurl'd him in will help him out.   *Exit.*

Susan. Cold comfort still. What say you, cousin Tydy?

Tydy. I say this comes of roisting, swagg'ring.
Call me not cousin; each man for himself!
Some men are born to mirth and some to sorrow;   35
I am no cousin unto them that borrow.   *Exit.*

Susan. O Charity, why art thou fled to Heaven,
And left all things on this earth uneven?
Their scoffing answers I will ne'er return,
But to myself his grief in silence mourn.   40

Enter SIR FRANCIS *and* MALBY.

Sir Fra. She is poor; I'll therefore tempt her with this gold.
Go, Malby, in my name deliver it,

24. flute] *Q1;* Lute *Q2.*   25. *Exit.*] *Reed.*   28. True] *Qq;* True, [true]
Ward.   33. swagg'ring] *Qq;* swaggering *Collier (1825).*

---

24. *sung*] a standard form for the past tense of *sing,* 16th to 19th centuries;
see *O.E.D.*

26. *was*] a common form with 'you', 16th to 18th centuries; see *O.E.D.*

32. *Cold comfort*] proverbial (Tilley C542).

33. *roisting*] rudely revelling.

37–8.] Cf. *Fortune by Land and Sea,* III. iv:
        Who said that charity was fled to heaven,
        And had no known abiding here on earth. (Pearson, VI, 407.)

38. *uneven*] unjust; presumably a perfect rhyme with 'Heaven' in Heywood's time—see Kökeritz, p. 204.

39. *return*] i.e. to Sir Charles.

40. *mourn*] probably not a perfect rhyme with 'return', but closer than
in modern English; see Kökeritz, p. 249.

And I will stay thy answer.

Mal. Fair Mistress, as I understand your grief
  Doth grow from want, so I have here in store   45
  A means to furnish you, a bag of gold
  Which to your hands I freely tender you.

Susan. I thank you, Heavens; I thank you, gentle sir!
  God make me able to requite this favour.

Mal. This gold Sir Francis Acton sends by me,   50
  And prays you &c.

Susan. Acton! O God, that name I am born to curse.
  Hence, bawd; hence, broker! See, I spurn his gold;
  My honour never shall for gain be sold.

Sir Fra. Stay, lady, stay!

Susan.   From you I'll posting hie, 55
  Even as the doves from feather'd eagles fly. [*Exit.*]

Sir Fra. She hates my name, my face—how should I woo?
  I am disgrac'd in everything I do.
  The more she hates me and disdains my love,
  The more I am rapt in admiration   60
  Of her divine and chaste perfections.
  Woo her with gifts I cannot, for all gifts
  Sent in my name she spurns. With looks I cannot,
  For she abhors my sight. Nor yet with letters,
  For none she will receive. How then? how then? 65
  Well, I will fasten such a kindness on her
  As shall o'ercome her hate and conquer it.
  Sir Charles, her brother, lies in execution
  For a great sum of money; and, besides,

44. *Mal.*] *Q1; Fran. Q2.* understand] *Q2;* vnderstand, *Q1.* 51. you
&c.] *Q1;* you *Q2.* 52. I am] *Q1;* I'me *Q2.* 56. feather'd] *Q2;*
feathered *Q1.* *Exit.*] *Q2; not in Q1.*

---

43. *stay*] wait for.
45. *in store*] in abundance.
51. *&c.*] indicating whispering.
53. *broker*] procurer, pander.
55. *posting*] hurriedly; not in *O.E.D.* as adv.
68. *lies in execution*] is imprisoned.

The appeal is su'd still for my huntsmen's death,   70
Which only I have power to reverse.
In her I'll bury all my hate of him.
Go seek the Keeper, Malby; bring me to him.
To save his body, I his debts will pay;
To save his life, I his appeal will stay.   *Exeunt.*   75

[Scene x]

Enter SIR CHARLES *in prison, with irons; his feet bare, his*
garments all ragged and torn.

Sir Cha. Of all on the earth's face most miserable,
Breathe in the hellish dungeon thy laments.
Thus like a slave ragg'd, like a felon gyv'd—
That hurls thee headlong to this base estate.
O unkind uncle! O my friends ingrate!   5
Unthankful kinsmen! Mountfords all too base,
To let thy name lie fetter'd in disgrace.
A thousand deaths here in this grave I die:

70. huntsmen's] *Q2;* Huntsmans *Q1.*   73. me to him] *Q1;* him to me *Q2.*
75. Exeunt.] *Q1; not in Q2.*

x. 0.1. *feet*] *Q2; face Q1.*   2. the] *Q1;* this *Q2.*   3. slave ragg'd,] *Q2;*
slaue, ragd *Q1.*   4–5.] *Qq; Spencer transposes these lines.*   4. That] *Qq;*
What *Verity.*   6. Mountfords] *Qq;* Mountford's *Collier (1825);* Mountford *Morrell.*   7. thy] *Qq;* the *Collier (1825).*   lie] *Q1;* be *Q2.*   fetter'd] *Q2;* fettered *Q1.*

---

70. *appeal is su'd*] prosecution is in hand.
73. *me to him*] Though the Q2 reading perhaps seems more natural, Q1
fits well in the theatrical context of the two men leaving the stage.

x. 0.1. *feet*] Q1's *face* seems improbable.
2. *the*] The Q2 *this* is perhaps preferable.
3. *gyv'd*] shackled; Fenton speaks of the prisoner as 'clogged with heavye
shackels and clinkinge yrons' (ed. cit., I, 44); Painter says that he was 'fettered with great and weyghty Gives' (Fo. 294v).
4–5.] The reading of the Qq must be interpreted as reflecting the inco-
herence of Sir Charles's anguish; the emendations of Verity and Spencer,
especially the latter, are attractive.
5. *ingrate*] ungrateful.

Fear, hunger, sorrow, cold—all threat my death
And join together to deprive my breath.   10
But that which most torments me, my dear sister
Hath left to visit me, and from my friends
Hath brought no hopeful answer; therefore I
Divine they will not help my misery.
If it be so, shame, scandal, and contempt   15
Attend their covetous thoughts, need make their graves.
Usurers they live, and may they die like slaves.

Enter Keeper.

Keep. Knight, be of comfort, for I bring thee freedom
    From all thy troubles.
Sir Cha.   Then I am doom'd to die;
    Death is th'end of all calamity.   20
Keep. Live! your appeal is stay'd, the execution
    Of all your debts discharg'd, your creditors
    Even to the utmost penny satisfy'd,
    In sign whereof your shackles I knock off.
    You are not left so much indebted to us   25
    As for your fees; all is discharg'd, all paid.
    Go freely to your house or where you please;
    After long miseries embrace your ease.
Sir Cha. Thou grumblest out the sweetest music to me
    That ever organ play'd. Is this a dream?   30
    Or do my waking senses apprehend
    The pleasing taste of these applausive news?

20. th'end] *Q1;* the end *Q2.*   21. stay'd] *Q2;* stayed *Q1.*

---

9. *threat*] threaten.
10. *deprive*] deprive me of.
12. *left*] ceased.
17. *Usurers*] It was believed unchristian to take any interest whatever for money lent, and a usurer was one who did so.
20.] ? proverbial; not in Oxford or Tilley, but cf. Tilley D148: 'Death pays all debts'.
21. *your . . . stay'd*] The charge against you has been withdrawn.
21–2. *execution . . . debts*] all judgments for debt.
32. *applausive*] worthy of applause, agreeable.

Slave that I was to wrong such honest friends,
My loving kinsmen and my near allies.
Tongue, I will bite thee for the scandal breath   35
Against such faithful kinsmen; they are all
Compos'd of pity and compassion,
Of melting charity, and of moving ruth.
That which I spake before was in my rage;
They are my friends, the mirrors of this age,   40
Bounteous and free. The noble Mountfords' race
Ne'er bred a covetous thought or humour base.

Enter SUSAN.

Susan. I can no longer stay from visiting
My woeful brother; while I could I kept
My hapless tidings from his hopeful ear.   45
Sir Cha. Sister, how much am I indebted to thee
And to thy travail!
Susan.   What, at liberty?
Sir Cha. Thou seest I am, thanks to thy industry.
O unto which of all my courteous friends
Am I thus bound? My uncle Mountford, he   50
Even of an infant lov'd me; was it he?
So did my cousin Tydy; was it he?
So Master Roder, Master Sandy too.
Which of all these did this high kindness do?
Susan. Charles, can you mock me in your poverty,   55
Knowing your friends deride your misery?

---

34. kinsmen] *Qq;* kinsman *Collier (1850).*   35. breath] *Qq;* breath'd
Pearson.   40. age,] *Verity;* age: *Qq.*   41. free.] *Q2;* free, *Q1.*   Mount-
fords'] *Reed;* Mountfords *Qq;* Mountford's *Collier (1825).*   47. travail]
Collier (1850); trauel *Qq.*   55. your] *Qq;* my *Ward.*

---

35. *scandal breath*] scandalous talk; *scandal* as adj. not recorded in *O.E.D.*
Here one must take it as adjectival or accept Pearson's emendation.
  40. *mirrors*] paragons, exemplars.
  41. *free*] generous.
  42. *humour*] See note at ii. 6.
  47. *travail*] exertion, trouble.

Now I protest I stand so much amaz'd
To see your bonds free and your irons knock'd off
That I am rapt into a maze of wonder,
The rather for I know not by what means   60
This happiness hath chanc'd.
Sir Cha.   Why, by my uncle,
My cousins, and my friends; who else, I pray,
Would take upon them all my debts to pay?
Susan. O brother, they are men all of flint,
Pictures of marble, and as void of pity   65
As chased bears. I begg'd, I su'd, I kneel'd,
Laid open all your griefs and miseries,
Which they derided—more than that, deny'd us
A part in their alliance, but in pride
Said that our kindred with our plenty died.   70
Sir Cha. Drudges too much! What, did they? O known evil:
Rich fly the poor as good men shun the Devil.
Whence should my freedom come? Of whom alive,
Saving of those, have I deserv'd so well?
Guess, sister, call to mind, remember me.   75
These I have rais'd, these follow the world's guise,

64. men all] *Qq;* men [made] all *Ward.*   71. Drudges] *Qq;* Drudges!
Dodsley.   76. these] *Q1;* they *Q2.*

---

57. *Now*] hardly more than an exclamation, the temporal sense obscured.
65. *Pictures*] statues; cf. the second part of *If You Know Not Me, You
Know No Body*:
                    new marble pictures we'le haue wrought,
          And in a new ship from beyond sea brought. (Pearson, I, 300.)
Similarly, *statue* was used for 'picture'; cf. *Gent.*, IV. iv. 207–8, where
Julia speaks to Silvia's picture:
                    were there sense in his idolatry
          My substance should be statue in thy stead.
66. *chased*] tormented, harassed; in the sport of bear-baiting. See
Shakespeare's England, II, 429–30.
71. *Drudges too much*] slaves too base.
72.] ? proverbial; not in Oxford or Tilley, but cf. Tilley P468: 'The poor
have few friends'.
75. *remember*] remind.
76. *rais'd*] named (not in *O.E.D.* in this sense); less probably, 'elevated
to their present position'.

Whom, rich in honour, they in woe despise.

Susan. My wits have lost themselves; let's ask the Keeper.

Sir Cha. Gaoler!

Keep. At hand, sir.   80

Sir Cha. Of courtesy resolve me one demand—
    What was he took the burden of my debts
    From off my back, stay'd my appeal to death,
    Discharg'd my fees, and brought me liberty?

Keep. A courteous knight, one call'd Sir Francis Acton.   85

Susan. Acton!

Sir Cha. Ha! Acton! O me, more distress'd in this
    Than all my troubles. Hale me back,
    Double my irons, and my sparing meals
    Put into halves, and lodge me in a dungeon   90
    More deep, more dark, more cold, more comfortless.
    By Acton freed! Not all thy manacles
    Could fetter so my heels as this one word
    Hath thrall'd my heart, and it must now lie bound
    In more strict prison than thy stony gaol.   95
    I am not free, I go but under bail.

Keep. My charge is done, sir, now I have my fees;
    As we get little, we will nothing leese.   *Exit.*

Sir Cha. By Acton freed, my dangerous opposite.
    Why, to what end? or what occasion? ha!   100
    Let me forget the name of enemy

---

77. in honour] *Qq;* [they] honour *Neilson.*   85. one] *Q1;* and *Q2.*
86.] *Q1; not in Q2.*   88. Than all] *Qq;* Than [in] all *Oliphant.*   92.
Acton] *Q2;* action *Q1.*   98. *Exit.*] *Q1; not in Q2.*   100. or] *Qq;*
on *Pearson.*

77.] i.e. 'Those who are honorable but unfortunate they despise' (Baskervill); Neilson's emendation yields a different reading.

81. *resolve . . . demand*] answer me one question.

82. *What*] who; see Abbott, Sect. 254.

86.] This almost certainly genuine line could easily have been dropped
by the Q2 compositor.

97.] For the practice of feeing the gaoler, see Griffiths, I, 2–3.

98. *leese*] lose.

99. *opposite*] adversary.

And with indifference balance this high favour. Ha!
Susan. [*Aside*] His love to me, upon my soul 'tis so;
　　That is the root from whence these strange things grow.
Sir Cha. [*Aside*] Had this proceeded from my father, he　　105
　　That by the law of nature is most bound
　　In offices of love, it had deserved
　　My best employment to requite that grace.
　　Had it proceeded from my friends, or him,
　　From them this action had deserv'd my life—　　　110
　　And from a stranger more, because from such
　　There is less execution of good deeds.
　　But he, nor father, nor ally, nor friend,
　　More than a stranger, both remote in blood
　　And in his heart oppos'd my enemy,　　　　　115
　　That this high bounty should proceed from him—
　　O there I lose myself. What should I say,
　　What think, what do, his bounty to repay?
Susan. You wonder, I am sure, whence this strange kindness
　　Proceeds in Acton. I will tell you, brother:　　　120
　　He dotes on me and oft hath sent me gifts,
　　Letters, and tokens; I refus'd them all.
Sir Cha. I have enough; though poor, my heart is set
　　In one rich gift to pay back all my debt.　　　*Exeunt.*

---

103. *Aside*] *Dodsley.*　　me,] *Qq;* me? *Collier (1825).*　　105. *Aside*]
This ed.　　107. deserved] *Q1;* deseru'd *Q2.*　　109. him] *Qq;* allies
Dodsley; his *Ward.*　　112. execution] *Qq;* expectation *Dodsley.*　　119–
20.] *Reed; as prose Qq.*　　123. enough; though poor,] *Q2;* inough,
though poor, *Q1;* enough, though poor; *Dodsley.*

---

102. *indifference*] impartiality.
　balance] weigh.
　105–18.] Cf. Painter, Fo. 297v: 'I attended my delyueraunce by sute of
those whome I counted for Kin and fryends. . . But thys surmounteth all,
a mortall Ennimy, not reconcyled or requyred, without demaund of assur-
aunce for the pleasure which he doth, payeth the debts of his aduersarie'.
As at iv. 47–52, the parallel is hardly verbal, but the passages are very close
to each other.
　105. Aside] In view of Susan's 'You wonder, I am sure' (l. 119), it must
be assumed that she does not hear this speech by her brother.
　109. *him*] i.e. his father.
　112. *execution*] Dodsley's emendation is attractive.

[Scene xi]

Enter FRANKFORD *with a letter in his hand,*
and NICHOLAS *with keys.*

Frank. This is the night, and I must play the touch,
    To try two seeming angels. Where's my keys?
Nich. They are made according to your mould in wax.
    I bade the smith be secret, gave him money,
    And there they are. The letter, sir.   5
Frank. True, take it; there it is.
    And when thou seest me in my pleasant'st vein
    Ready to sit to supper, bring it me.
Nich. I'll do't; make no more question but I'll do't.   *Exit.*

Enter ANNE, CRANWELL, WENDOLL, *and* JENKIN.

Anne. Sirra, 'tis six o'clock already stroke;   10
    Go bid them spread the cloth and serve in supper.
Jenk. It shall be done forsooth, mistress. Where is Spiggot
    the butler to give us out salt and trenchers?   *[Exit.]*
Wen. We that have been a-hunting all the day
    Come with prepar'd stomachs, Master Frankford;   15
    We wish'd you at our sport.
Frank. My heart was with you, and my mind was on you;
    Fie, Master Cranwell, you are still thus sad.

---

xi. 0.1–2. *with . . . keys*] *This ed.; Enter Franckeford and Nick with keyes, and
a letter in his hand. Qq.*   1. and] *Q1;* that *Q2.*   the touch] *Q1;* my part
Q2.   5.] *Q2;* And there they are. / *Nich.* The Letter sir. *Q1.*   there]
Q1; heere *Q2.*   7. pleasant'st] *Q1;* pleasants *Q2.*   12. forsooth, mistress.] *Verity;* forsooth: mistris *Q1;* forsooth. Mistris *Q2.*   Where is] *Q1;*
wheres *Q2.*   13. out] *Q1;* our *Q2.*   *Exit.*] *Verity.*   15. prepar'd] *Q1;*
prepared *Q2.*   stomachs, Master Frankford;] *Dodsley;* stomacks maister
Frankeford, *Q1;* stomackes master Frankford; *Q2;* stomachs: Master
Frankford, *Reed.*

---

xi. 1. *play the touch*] The metaphor here in the Q1 reading is from the
use of a touchstone to test gold or silver. Cf. *R3*, IV. ii. 8–9:
      Ah Buckingham, now do I play the touch
      To try if thou be current gold indeed.
    10. *six o'clock*] Five-thirty was the customary hour for supper; see *Shake-*
speare's England, II, 134.
    13. *trenchers*] plates.

A stool, a stool! Where's Jenkin, and where's Nick?
'Tis supper time at least an hour ago.   20
What's the best news abroad?
Wen.   I know none good.
Frank. [*Aside*] But I know too much bad.

> *Enter* [SPIGGOT *the*] *Butler and* JENKIN *with a tablecloth,*
> *bread, trenchers, and salt* [*, then exeunt*].

Cran. Methinks, sir, you might have that interest
In your wife's brother to be more remiss
In this hard dealing against poor Sir Charles,   25
Who, as I hear, lies in York Castle, needy,
And in great want.
Frank. Did not more weighty business of my own
Hold me away, I would have labour'd peace
Betwixt them, with all care; indeed I would, sir.   30
Anne. I'll write unto my brother earnestly
In that behalf.
Wen.   A charitable deed,
And will beget the good opinion
Of all your friends that love you, Mistress Frankford.
Frank. That's you for one; I know you love Sir Charles.   35
[*Aside*] And my wife too well.
Wen.   He deserves the love
Of all true gentlemen; be yourselves judge.
Frank. But supper, ho! Now as thou lovest me, Wendoll,
Which I am sure thou dost, be merry, pleasant,

22. *Aside*] *Verity.*   22.2. *, then exeunt*] *Collier* (*1850*).   23. interest]
Q2; intrest *Q1.*   25. this] *Q1;* his *Q2.*   26–7.] *Q1;* Who . . . Castle /
Needy . . . want. *Q2.*   28. my] *Q1;* mine *Q2.*   34. Mistress] *Q2;*
maister *Q1.*   36. *Aside*] *Neilson.*   too well] *Qq;* too, well *Collier*
(*1825*).   38. lovest] *Q1;* lou'st *Q2.*

21. *abroad*] in the outside world.
23–4. *interest In*] influence with.
24. *remiss*] lenient. Cf. 'Jupiter and Io' in *Pleasant Dialogues and
Dramma's*:
> For thy remisnesse
> In *Io's* late affliction, speake, 'tis granted. (Pearson, VI, 278.)

And frolic it to-night. Sweet Master Cranwell,   40
Do you the like. Wife, I protest, my heart
Was ne'er more bent on sweet alacrity.
Where be those lazy knaves to serve in supper?

Enter NICHOLAS.

Nich. Sir, here's a letter.
Frank. Whence comes it? and who brought it?   45
Nich. A stripling that below attends your answer,
   And as he tells me it is sent from York.
Frank. Have him into the cellar; let him taste
   A cup of our March beer. Go, make him drink.

                                        [*Reads the letter.*]

Nich. I'll make him drunk, if he be a Trojan.   [*Exit.*] 50
Frank. My boots and spurs! Where's Jenkin? God forgive me,
   How I neglect my business. Wife, look here;
   I have a matter to be try'd to-morrow
   By eight o'clock, and my attorney writes me
   I must be there betimes with evidence,   55
   Or it will go against me. Where's my boots?

Enter JENKIN *with boots and spurs.*

Anne. I hope your business craves no such dispatch
   That you must ride to-night.
Wen. [*Aside*]   I hope it doth.

44.] *Q1;* Here's a Letter sir. *Q2.*   48–9.] *Reed;* Haue . . . cup / Of . . .
drinke. *Q1; as prose Q2.*   49.1. *Reads the letter.*] *Verity.*   50. if] *Qq;*
[an] if *Oliphant.*   *Exit.*] *Walley.*   51–2.] *Q1; as prose Q2.*   58. *Aside*]
Dodsley.

---

42. *alacrity*] enjoyment; not in *O.E.D.* in this sense.
49. *March beer*] a strong beer brewed in March.
50. *Trojan*] The usual meaning for this slang term seems to be 'a good
fellow' (see *O.E.D.*), but in his *Philocothonista*, 1635, Heywood includes it
as one of many slang terms for 'drunkard'. The passage is reprinted by
Bates. William Kemp affords an example of the more usual meaning shad-
ing into Heywood's in his *Kemps nine daies wonder*, 1600: 'he was a kinde
good fellow, a true Troyan; and if euer be my lucke to meete him at more
leasure, Ile make him full amendes with a Cup of Canarie' (ed. Dyce, 1840,
p. 13).

Frank. God's me! No such dispatch?

    Jenkin, my boots. Where's Nick? Saddle my roan,   60

    And the gray dapple for himself. Content ye,

    It much concerns me. [*Exit* JENKIN.] Gentle Master Cranwell

    And Master Wendoll, in my absence use

    The very ripest pleasure of my house.

Wen. Lord, Master Frankford, will you ride to-night?   65

    The ways are dangerous.

Frank.   Therefore will I ride

    Appointed well, and so shall Nick, my man.

Anne. I'll call you up by five o'clock to-morrow.

Frank. No, by my faith, wife, I'll not trust to that;

    'Tis not such easy rising in a morning   70

    From one I love so dearly. No, by my faith,

    I shall not leave so sweet a bedfellow

    But with much pain. You have made me a sluggard

    Since I first knew you.

Anne.   Then if you needs will go

    This dangerous evening, Master Wendoll,   75

    Let me entreat you bear him company.

Wen. With all my heart, sweet mistress. My boots there!

Frank. Fie, fie, that for my private business

    I should disease my friend and be a trouble

    To the whole house. Nick!   80

Nich. [*offstage.*] Anon, sir.

Frank. Bring forth my gelding—[*to Wendoll*] as you love me, sir,

    Use no more words; a hand, good Master Cranwell.

Cran. Sir, God be your good speed.

---

62. me.] *Q2;* me *Q1.*   Exit Jenkin.] *This ed.*   64. pleasure] *Q1;*
pleasures *Q2.*   81. offstage.] *Walley.*   82. gelding—] *Dodsley;*
gelding *Q1;* Gelding, *Q2.*   to Wendoll] *Oliphant.*

---

    59. *God's me*] a corruption of 'God save me'.

    61. *Content ye*] you may be sure.

    66. *ways are dangerous*] Travellers were subject to the constant threat of
ambush by highwaymen; see *Shakespeare's England,* I, 207–8.

    67. *Appointed*] equipped, armed.

    79. *disease*] dis-ease, inconvenience.

Frank. Good night, sweet Nan; nay, nay, a kiss and part.   85
  [*Aside*] Dissembling lips, you suit not with my heart.   [*Exit.*]
Wen. [*Aside*] How business, time, and hours all gracious proves
  And are the furtherers to my newborn love.
  I am husband now in Master Frankford's place
  And must command the house. [*To Anne.*] My pleasure is   90
  We will not sup abroad so publicly,
  But in your private chamber, Mistress Frankford.
Anne. [*to Wendoll.*] O sir, you are too public in your love,
  And Master Frankford's wife—
Cran.   Might I crave favour,
  I would entreat you I might see my chamber;   95
  I am on the sudden grown exceeding ill
  And would be spar'd from supper.
Wen.   Light there, ho!
  See you want nothing, sir, for if you do,
  You injury that good man, and wrong me too.
Cran. I will make bold. Good night.   [*Exit.*]
Wen.   How all conspire   100
  To make our bosom sweet and full entire.
  Come, Nan, I prithee let us sup within.
Anne. O what a clog unto the soul is sin.
  We pale offenders are still full of fear;
  Every suspicious eye brings danger near,   105
  When they whose clear heart from offence are free,
  Despise report, base scandals to outface,

---

86. *Aside*] Dodsley.   *Exit.*] *Q2; not in Q1*.   87. *Aside*] Neilson.
proves] *Q1;* proue *Q2*.   88. furtherers] *Qq;* furthers *McIlwraith*.
90. *To Anne.*] Neilson.   93. *to Wendoll.*] *Bates*.   99. injury] *Q1;*
iniure *Q2*.   100. *Exit.*] *Q2; not in Q1*.   106. heart] *Qq;* hearts *Dodsley*.
107. to] *Q1;* do *Q2*.

---

  87. *proves*] again the singular verb with plural subject; see Abbott, Sect.
333.
  99. *injury*] There is no need to adopt Q2, for *O.E.D.* records *injury*
meaning 'injure' from *c.* 1484 to 1651.
  101. *bosom*] intimacy.
  104. *pale*] weak.
  106. *When*] whereas.
  107. *report*] rumour, common talk.

And stand at mere defiance with disgrace.
Wen. Fie, fie, you talk too like a Puritant.
Anne. You have tempted me to mischief, Master Wendoll;   110
   I have done I know not what. Well, you plead custom;
   That which for want of wit I granted erst
   I now must yield through fear. Come, come, let's in.
   Once o'er shoes, we are straight o'er head in sin.
Wen. My jocund soul is joyful above measure;   115
   I'll be profuse in Frankford's richest treasure.   *Exeunt.*

[Scene xii]

   Enter SISLY, JENKIN, [SPIGGOT *the*] *Butler, and other*
            Servingmen.

Jenk. My mistress and Master Wendoll, my master, sup in her
   chamber to-night; Sisly, you are preferr'd from being the
   cook to be chambermaid. Of all the loves betwixt thee and
   me, tell me what thou thinkest of this.

109. Puritant] *Q1;* Puritan *Q2.*

xii. 0.1–2. Butler . . . Servingmen] *Q1; and* Butler *Q2.*   4. thinkest] *Q1;*
thinkst *Q2.*

---

108. *mere*] absolute.
109. *Puritant*] Puritan, i.e. prude. The word is not uncommonly thus
used by villains and is obliquely complimentary to the reformers. *O.E.D.,*
which records only two instances, not including this one, calls the word
'Alteration of Puritan, after Protestant'.
110. *mischief*] wickedness.
112. *erst*] at first.
113–14. *Come . . . sin*] a common idea; cf., for example, Heywood and
Rowley, *Fortune by Land and Sea,* I. iii. 88–9:
   He seekes his fate, and murderers once being in
   Wade further till they drown: sin pulls on sin. (Pearson, VI, 378.)
Cf. also *Gent.,* I. i. 23–4:
   That's a deep story of a deeper love;
   For he was more than over shoes in love.

xii. 2. *preferr'd*] promoted.
3–4. *Of . . . me*] Cf. *Gammer Gurton's Needle,* v. ii: 'For all the loves on
earth, Hodge, let me see it' (W. C. Hazlitt, ed., Dodsley's *A Select Collection of Old English Plays,* 1874, III, 254).

Sisly. Mum; there's an old proverb, 'When the cat's away the   5
    mouse may play'.

Jenk. Now you talk of a cat, Sisly, I smell a rat.

Sisly. Good words, Jenkin, lest you be call'd to answer them.

Jenk. Why, 'God make my mistress an honest woman'. Are
    not these good words ? 'Pray God my new master play not   10
    the knave with my old master'. Is there any hurt in this ?
    'God send no villainy intended, and if they do sup to-
    gether, pray God they do not lie together. God keep my
    mistress chaste and make us all His servants'. What harm
    is there in all this ? Nay, more, here is my hand; thou shalt   15
    never have my heart unless thou say 'Amen'.

Sisly. 'Amen, I pray God', I say.

Enter Servingmen.

Ser. My mistress sends that you should make less noise, to
    lock up the doors, and see the household all got to bed;
    you, Jenkin, for this night are made the porter, to see the   20
    gates shut in.

Jenk. Thus by little and little I creep into office. Come to ken-
    nel, my masters, to kennel; 'tis eleven o'clock already.

Ser. When you have lock'd the gates in, you must send up the
    keys to my mistress.   25

---

13. keep] *Q1;* make *Q2.*   20. this] *Q2;* his *Q1* (*catchword on preceding
page* this).

5–6. *When . . . play*] proverbial (Tilley C175).

7. *I . . . rat*] proverbial (Tilley R31).

8. *answer*] suffer the consequences for.

9. *God . . . woman*] Cf. *1 Edward IV*: 'God make him an honest man!'
(Pearson, I, 41).

21. *shut in*] closed.

22. *office*] i.e. office of a bawd or pander; not in *O.E.D.* in this sense.
Cf. *Oth.,* iv. ii. 88–92:

> I took you for that cunning whore of Venice
> That married with Othello. You, mistress,
> That have the office opposite to St. Peter,
> And keep the gate of hell!
>   *Re-enter* EMILIA.
>   You, you, ay, you!
> We have done our course; there's money for your pains.

Sisly. Quickly, for God's sake, Jenkin; for I must carry them.
  I am neither pillow nor bolster, but I know more than
  both.

Jenk. To bed, good Spiggot; to bed, good honest serving crea- 29
  tures, and let us sleep as snug as pigs in pease-straw. *Exeunt.*

[Scene xiii]

     Enter FRANKFORD *and* NICHOLAS.

Frank. Soft, soft. We have tied our geldings to a tree
  Two flight-shoot off, lest by their thund'ring hooves
  They blab our coming back. Hear'st thou no noise?
Nich. Hear? I hear nothing but the owl and you.
Frank. So; now my watch's hand points upon twelve,   5
  And it is dead midnight. Where are my keys?

xiii. 1–3.] *Verity; as prose Qq.* 1. our] *Q1;* your *Q2.* 2. thund'ring]
Q1; thundering *Q2.* 3. back] *Q1; not in Q2.* 4. Hear] *Q1; not in Q2.*
6. dead] *Q1;* iust *Q2.*

---

30. *as . . . pease-straw*] proverbial (Tilley, P296).
pease-straw] stalks and leaves of the pea plant, used as fodder.

 xiii.] G. F. Reynolds, *The Staging of Elizabethan Plays at the Red Bull
Theater: 1605–1625,* 1940, p. 125, suggests a staging for this scene. He has
Frankford and Nicholas enter at one side door, exeunt at the other (l. 21),
enter again from the same side as before (l. 22), and cross to the opposite
side again ('the last door', l. 23), where Frankford enters alone. He returns
(l. 40) 'for a passionate speech on what he has found, goes into the room
again [l. 65], drives Wendoll out on the main stage [l. 67.1], is followed by
Mistress Frankford [l. 77.1], and finally exits to his study [l. 131] . . . presumably Center'. The hypothesis (discussed by Reynolds, pp. 131–63) that
there was a movable structure on the stage, with entrances through the
sides as well as in front, would afford another solution to the problem of the
series of doors needed here.
 1. *We . . . tree*] This sort of evasion is common in the Elizabethan drama
in order to avoid bringing horses on the stage; cf. the coach in xvi. 1, and,
for the most famous example, *1H4,* II. ii.
 2. *Two flight-shoot*] more than two ordinary bow-shots, for flight-shoot-
ing employed a special 'flight-arrow', lightly feathered for long range;
'Langland, in his Itinerary, states this distance [flight-shoot] to be about
the breadth of the Thames above London Bridge' (Rylands).
 3. *blab*] betray.
 6. *dead*] The Q1 reading is more effective than Q2's *just.*

K

Nich. Here, sir.

Frank. This is the key that opes my outward gate,
      This is the hall door, this my withdrawing chamber.
      But this, that door that's bawd unto my shame,   10
      Fountain and spring of all my bleeding thoughts,
      Where the most hallowed order and true knot
      Of nuptial sanctity hath been profan'd.
      It leads to my polluted bedchamber,
      Once my terrestrial heaven, now my earth's hell,   15
      The place where sins in all their ripeness dwell—
      But I forget myself; now to my gate.

Nich. It must ope with far less noise than Cripple-gate, or
      your plot's dash'd.

Frank. So, reach me my dark-lantern to the rest.   20
      Tread softly, softly.

Nich.   I will walk on eggs this pace.

Frank. A general silence hath surpris'd the house,
      And this is the last door. Astonishment,
      Fear, and amazement play against my heart,
      Even as a madman beats upon a drum.   25

9. is] *Q1; not in Q2.*   my] *Q1;* the *Q2.*   24. play against] *Q1;* beate
vpon *Q2.*

---

8. *outward*] outer.

9. *withdrawing chamber*] a private room, attached to a more public one,
to withdraw to.

18. *Cripple-gate*] one of the northern gates of London; presumably it
had a reputation for creaking when opened. 'This allusion to Cripplegate,
by which playgoers might leave the city on their way to the Red Bull
theatre, passing through Red Cross Street to Long Lane, and then to St.
John Street, would have less point when spoken at the Rose, or Curtain,
or the Cockpit in Drury Lane' (Bates).

20. *dark-lantern*] a lantern with a slide by which the light can be concealed.

rest] i.e. of the gates. Baskervill and Ashton take 'to the rest' as 'in addition to the other equipment'.

21. *I . . . pace*] i.e. I wouldn't break eggs walking with steps like these;
proverbial (Tilley E91).

22. *surpris'd*] overcome.

24. *play against*] This seems more effective than the Q2 reading, which
uses the same verb phrase in ll. 24 and 25; compositor B is known to pick
up words from one line and repeat them in another.

O keep my eyes, you Heavens, before I enter,
From any sight that may transfix my soul;
Or if there be so black a spectacle,
O strike mine eyes stark blind; or if not so,
Lend me such patience to digest my grief   30
That I may keep this white and virgin hand
From any violent outrage or red murder.
And with that prayer I enter.   [*Exit.*]
Nich. Here's a circumstance!
A man may be made cuckold in the time   35
That he's about it. And the case were mine
As 'tis my master's—'sblood, that he makes me swear—
I would have plac'd his action, ent'red there;
I would, I would.

[*Enter* FRANKFORD.]

Frank. O, O!   40
Nich. Master, 'sblood, master, master!
Frank. O me unhappy, I have found them lying
Close in each other's arms, and fast asleep.
But that I would not damn two precious souls
Bought with my Saviour's blood and send them laden   45

33. *Exit.*] *Reed.*   34–7. Here's . . . swear] *Q1; as prose Q2*.   34. cir-
cumstance] *Q1;* circumstance indeed *Q2*.   35. cuckold] *Q1;* a Cuckold
Q2.   36. That] *Q1; not in Q2*.   38. ent'red] *Q1;* enter'd *Q2*.   39.1.
Enter Frankford.] *Reed.*   43. other's] *Q1;* other *Q2*.

───────────────────────────────

26–32.] Cf. *A Challenge for Beauty*, v. i:
　　　Wearied with pleasure, shee lies fast asleepe,
　　　Laid in a strangers armes, sh'as stay'd my speech,
　　　'Tas dim'd mine eyes from sight, and patience,
　　　Restrain'd my head from fury. (Pearson, v, 59.)
34. *circumstance*] roundabout behaviour, 'beating about the bush'; cf.
Tourneur, *The Atheist's Tragedy*, I. iv. 32: 'Time cuts off circumstance;
I must be briefe' (*Works*, ed. Nicoll, [1930], p. 188).
36. *And*] if.
37. *he*] Frankford.
38. *plac'd his action*] 'Established his case' (Ward).
44–8.] This would have been their fate if they died without a chance to
repent; contrast Hamlet's refusal to kill Claudius at his prayers lest he go
straight to Heaven (*Ham.*, III. iii. 73–96).

    With all their scarlet sins upon their backs
    Unto a fearful Judgement, their two lives
    Had met upon my rapier.
Nich. 'Sblood, master, have you left them sleeping still? Let
    me go wake them.   50
Frank. Stay, let me pause awhile.
    O God, O God, that it were possible
    To undo things done, to call back yesterday;
    That Time could turn up his swift sandy glass,
    To untell the days, and to redeem these hours;   55
    Or that the Sun
    Could, rising from the west, draw his coach backward,
    Take from the account of time so many minutes,
    Till he had all these seasons call'd again,
    Those minutes and those actions done in them,   60
    Even from her first offence; that I might take her
    As spotless as an angel in my arms.
    But O! I talk of things impossible,
    And cast beyond the moon. God give me patience,
    For I will in to wake them.   *Exit.* 65
Nich. Here's patience perforce;
    He needs must trot afoot that tires his horse.

Enter WENDOLL, *running over the stage in a night gown, he* [FRANK-
FORD] *after him with his sword drawn; the Maid in her smock stays
      his hand and clasps hold on him. He pauses awhile.*

49. 'Sblood, master] *Q1;* Master what *Q2.*   49–50.] *Q1;* Master . . .
still? / Let . . . em. *Q2.*   50. them] *Q1;* em *Q2.*   55. these] *Qq;* the
conj. Daniel.   58. the account] *Q1;* th'account *Q2.*   65. to] *Q1;* and
Q2.   67.3. *pauses*] *Q1; pauses for Q2.*

---

    53. *call back yesterday*] Cf. *R2,* III. ii. 69: 'O! call back yesterday, bid
time return'.
    55. *untell*] un-reckon.
    64. *cast . . . moon*] conjecture wildly, or perhaps *cast* is a past participle
going with *things* (l. 63) and *cast beyond the moon* means 'translunary'.
    66. *patience perforce*] i.e. patience of necessity; proverbial (Tilley P111).
    67.] presumably proverbial; not in Oxford or Tilley.
    67.1. over the stage] Cf. note on vi. 16.1.
night gown] dressing gown.

Frank. I thank thee, maid; thou like the angel's hand
  Hast stay'd me from a bloody sacrifice.
  Go, villain, and my wrongs sit on thy soul   70
  As heavy as this grief doth upon mine.
  When thou record'st my many courtesies
  And shalt compare them with thy treacherous heart,
  Lay them together, weigh them equally,
  'Twill be revenge enough. Go, to thy friend   75
  A Judas; pray, pray, lest I live to see
  Thee Judas-like, hang'd on an elder tree.

Enter ANNE *in her smock, night gown, and night attire.*

Anne. O by what word, what title, or what name
  Shall I entreat your pardon? Pardon! O
  I am as far from hoping such sweet grace   80
  As Lucifer from Heaven. To call you husband—
  O me most wretched, I have lost that name;
  I am no more your wife.
Nich.   'Sblood, sir, she swoons.
Frank. Spare thou thy tears, for I will weep for thee;
  And keep thy countenance, for I'll blush for thee. 85
  Now I protest I think 'tis I am tainted,
  For I am most asham'd, and 'tis more hard
  For me to look upon thy guilty face
  Than on the sun's clear brow. What wouldst thou speak?
Anne. I would I had no tongue, no ears, no eyes, 90
  No apprehension, no capacity.

---

68. the] *Q1;* an *Q2.* 69. sacrifice.] *Qq;* sacrifice. *Exit Maid. Verity.*
73. shalt] *Q1;* shall *Q2.* 83. swoons] *Dodsley;* sounds *Qq.* 85. coun-
tenance] *Q1;* count'nance *Q2.* 89.] *Q1;* Then . . . brow: / What . . .
speak? *Q2.* What . . . speak?] *Qq;* What! . . . speak? *Ward;* What
wouldst thou? Speak. *conj. this ed.*

68–9. *thou . . . sacrifice*] an allusion to the sacrifice of Isaac, Genesis, xxii.
11–12.
  77. *Judas-like . . . elder tree*] See Matthew, xxvii. 5; it was traditionally
believed that the tree on which Judas hanged himself was an elder.
  91. *apprehension, capacity*] i.e. the active and passive powers of the
mind.

When do you spurn me like a dog? When tread me
Under your feet? When drag me by the hair?
Though I deserve a thousand thousand fold
More than you can inflict, yet, once my husband,   95
For womanhood—to which I am a shame,
Though once an ornament—even for His sake
That hath redeem'd our souls, mark not my face
Nor hack me with your sword, but let me go
Perfect and undeformed to my tomb.   100
I am not worthy that I should prevail
In the least suit, no, not to speak to you,
Nor look on you, nor to be in your presence;
Yet as an abject this one suit I crave,
This granted I am ready for my grave.   105

Frank. My God with patience arm me. Rise, nay, rise,
And I'll debate with thee. Was it for want
Thou play'dst the strumpet? Wast thou not supply'd
With every pleasure, fashion, and new toy—
Nay, even beyond my calling?

Anne.   I was.   110

Frank. Was it then disability in me,
Or in thine eye seem'd he a properer man?

Anne. O no.

Frank.   Did I not lodge thee in my bosom?
Wear thee here in my heart?

Anne.   You did.

Frank. I did indeed; witness my tears I did.   115

---

93. your feet] *Q1;* feete *Q2.*   96. a shame] *Dodsley;* ashamd *Qq.*
113–14. Did ... bosom? / Wear ... heart?] *Q2;* Did ... weare thee / Here
... hart. *Q1.*   113. I not] *Q1;* not I *Q2.*   my] *Q2;* thy *Q1.*   114.
here in] *Q1;* in *Q2.*

---

96. *a shame*] Miniscule *e* and *d* look very much alike in Elizabethan handwriting; Dodsley's emendation is almost certainly correct.
104. *abject*] castaway.
109. *toy*] trinket, gew-gaw.
110. *calling*] rank, station in life.
112. *properer*] worthier.

Go bring my infants hither.

> [*Exit Maid and return with two Children.*]

     O Nan, O Nan,
If either fear of shame, regard of honour,
The blemish of my house, nor my dear love
Could have withheld thee from so lewd a fact,
Yet for these infants, these young harmless souls,   120
On whose white brows thy shame is character'd,
And grows in greatness as they wax in years—
Look but on them, and melt away in tears.
Away with them, lest as her spotted body
Hath stain'd their names with stripe of bastardy,   125
So her adult'rous breath may blast their spirits
With her infectious thoughts. Away with them!

> [*Exeunt Maid and Children.*]

Anne. In this one life I die ten thousand deaths.
Frank. Stand up, stand up: I will do nothing rashly.
I will retire awhile into my study,   130
And thou shalt hear thy sentence presently.   *Exit.*
Anne. 'Tis welcome, be it death. O me, base strumpet,
That having such a husband, such sweet children,
Must enjoy neither. O to redeem my honour
I would have this hand cut off, these my breasts sear'd,   135
Be rack'd, strappado'd, put to any torment;

---

116. *Exit . . . Children*] Collier (*1850*). 117. either] *Q1;* neither *Q2.*
126. adult'rous] *Q1;* adulterous *Q2.* 127.1. *Exeunt . . . Children.*]
Collier (*1850*). 134. my] *Q1;* mine *Q2.*

116.1. two Children] The time scheme of the play is indefinite. Except
for the two children here, the events of both plots seem to take place within
a relatively short period.
 119. *fact*] deed.
 125. *stripe of bastardy*] O.E.D., citing this passage only, defines *stripe* as
'a mark of disgrace'. Possibly there is an allusion to the bend sinister, a
mark of bastardy in heraldry.
 131. *presently*] immediately.
 136. *strappado'd*] The strappado is a form of torture in which the victim's
hands are secured to a rope and pulley behind his back and he is then
hoisted from the ground and allowed to fall part way back.

Nay, to whip but this scandal out, I would hazard
The rich and dear redemption of my soul.
He cannot be so base as to forgive me,
Nor I so shameless to accept his pardon.   140
[*To the audience.*] O women, women, you that have yet kept
Your holy matrimonial vow unstain'd,
Make me your instance: when you tread awry,
Your sins like mine will on your conscience lie.

> *Enter* SISLY, SPIGGOT, *all the Servingmen, and*
> JENKIN, *as newly come out of bed.*

All. O mistress, mistress, what have you done, mistress ?   145
Nich. 'Sblood, what a caterwauling keep you here!
Jenk. O Lord, mistress, how comes this to pass ? My master
    is run away in his shirt, and never so much as call'd me
    to bring his clothes after him.
Anne. See what guilt is: here stand I in this place,   150
    Asham'd to look my servants in the face.

> *Enter* MASTER FRANKFORD *and* CRANWELL,
> *whom seeing she falls on her knees.*

Frank. My words are regist'red in Heaven already;
    With patience hear me: I'll not martyr thee
    Nor mark thee for a strumpet, but with usage
    Of more humility torment thy soul   155
    And kill thee even with kindness.
Cran.   Master Frankford—
Frank. Good Master Cranwell—woman, hear thy judgement:
    Go make thee ready in thy best attire,
    Take with thee all thy gowns, all thy apparel;

137. whip] *Qq;* wipe *Dodsley.*   139. me,] *This ed.;* me ? *Q1;* me; *Q2.*   141.
To the audience.] *This ed.*   have yet] *Q1;* yet haue *Q2.*   143. instance:]
Collier (*1825*)*;* instance, *Qq.*   146. 'Sblood, what] *Q1;* VVhat *Q2.*

---

   137. *whip*] The Qq reading continues the idea of purging sin by torture;
Dodsley's emendation is tame in comparison.
   143. *instance*] example.
   148. *in his shirt*] in his night attire.

Leave nothing that did ever call thee mistress,   160
Or by whose sight being left here in the house
I may remember such a woman by.
Choose thee a bed and hangings for a chamber,
Take with thee everything that hath thy mark,
And get thee to my manor seven mile off,   165
Where live. 'Tis thine; I freely give it thee.
My tenants by shall furnish thee with wains
To carry all thy stuff within two hours;
No longer will I limit thee my sight.
Choose which of all my servants thou likest best,   170
And they are thine to attend thee.

Anne.   A mild sentence.

Frank. But as thou hop'st for Heaven, as thou believ'st
Thy name's recorded in the Book of Life,
I charge thee never after this sad day
To see me, or to meet me, or to send   175
By word, or writing, gift, or otherwise
To move me, by thyself or by thy friends,
Nor challenge any part in my two children.
So farewell, Nan, for we will henceforth be
As we had never seen, ne'er more shall see.   180

Anne. How full my heart is in my eyes appears;
What wants in words, I will supply in tears.

Frank. Come, take your coach, your stuff; all must along.
Servants and all make ready, all be gone.
It was thy hand cut two hearts out of one.   [*Exeunt.*]   185

---

163. a chamber] *Q1;* thy chamber *Q2.*   164. that] *Q1;* which *Q2.*
170. likest] *Q1;* lik'st *Q2.*   181. my eyes] *Q1;* mine eies *Q2.*   185.
Exeunt.] *Dodsley.*

---

167. *by*] nearby, in the neighbourhood.
169. *limit*] allow; not in *O.E.D.* in this sense. Cf. *The Wise-woman of
Hogsdon,* IV. i: 'Since I see you haue left his dangerous company, I limit
you to bee a welcome guest vnto my Table' (Pearson, V, 319).
   my sight] i.e. sight of me.
173. *Book of Life*] record of the names of those who shall inherit eternal
life. See Philippians, iv. 3, and Revelation, xx. 12.
180. *seen*] i.e. each other.

[Scene xiv]

       Enter SIR CHARLES, *gentlemanlike, and* [SUSAN]
          his Sister, gentlewomanlike.

Susan. Brother, why have you trick'd me like a bride?
    Bought me this gay attire, these ornaments?
    Forget you our estate, our poverty?
Sir Cha. Call me not brother, but imagine me
    Some barbarous outlaw or uncivil kern,   5
    For if thou shut'st thy eye and only hear'st
    The words that I shall utter, thou shalt judge me
    Some staring ruffin, not thy brother Charles.
    O Susan!
Susan. O brother, what doth this strange language mean?   10
Sir Cha. Dost love me, sister? Wouldst thou see me live
    A bankrupt beggar in the world's disgrace
    And die indebted to my enemies?
    Wouldst thou behold me stand like a huge beam
    In the world's eye, a byword and a scorn?   15
    It lies in thee of these to acquit me free,
    And all my debt I may outstrip by thee.
Susan. By me? why I have nothing, nothing left;
    I owe even for the clothes upon my back;
    I am not worth, &c.
Sir Cha.   O sister, say not so.   20
    It lies in you my downcast state to raise,

---

xiv. 8. ruffin] *Q1;* Ruffian *Q2.*   9. Susan] *Q1;* Sister *Q2.*   12. bank-
rupt] *Q1;* Bankrout *Q2.*   13. my] *Q1;* mine *Q2.*   20. &c.] *Q1; not in*
Q2.

---

    xiv. 1. *trick'd*] decked.
    5. *uncivil*] uncivilized, barbarous.
    kern] peasant; or, perhaps, in its common Elizabethan sense of 'Irish
foot-soldier', certainly thought of by the English as 'barbarous'.
    8. *staring*] frantic, wild.
    ruffin] ruffian, with overtones of the Elizabethan meaning, 'pander'.
    14–15. *huge . . . eye*] alluding to a passage in the Sermon on the Mount,
Matthew, vii. 3: 'And why seest thou the mote that is in thy brother's eye,
and perceiuest not the beame that is in thine owne eye.'
    20. *&c.*] indicating that Sir Charles interrupts.

To make me stand on even points with the world.
Come, sister, you are rich! Indeed you are,
And in your power you have without delay
Acton's five hundred pound back to repay.   25

Susan. Till now I had thought you lov'd me. By mine honour—
Which I had kept as spotless as the moon—
I ne'er was mistress of that single doit
Which I reserv'd not to supply your wants.
And do you think that I would hoard from you?   30
Now by my hopes in Heaven, knew I the means
To buy you from the slavery of your debts,
Especially from Acton, whom I hate,
I would redeem it with my life or blood.

Sir Cha. I challenge it, and kindred set apart   35
Thus ruffian-like I lay siege to your heart.
What do I owe to Acton?

Susan. Why, some five hundred pounds, toward which I swear
In all the world I have not one denier.

Sir Cha. It will not prove so. Sister, now resolve me: 40
What do you think—and speak your conscience—
Would Acton give might he enjoy your bed?

Susan. He would not shrink to spend a thousand pound
To give the Mountfords' name so deep a wound.

Sir Cha. A thousand pound! I but five hundred owe;   45
Grant him your bed, he's paid with interest so.

26. you] *Q1;* y'had *Q2.*   mine] *Q1;* my *Q2.*   27. had] *Q1;* haue *Q2.*
30. do you] *Q1;* de'ye *Q2.*   35. and . . . apart] *Q1;* and . . . apart; *Q2;*
and, . . . apart, *Reed.*   36. your] *Q1;* thy *Q2.*   38.] *Q1;* Why . . .
pounds, / Towards . . . sweare, *Q2.*   39. denier] *Dodsley;* deneare *Qq.*
46. interest] *Q1;* intrest *Q2.*

22. *on . . . points*] Cf. the modern 'on even terms'.
27. *had*] Possibly the Q2 *have* should be adopted, but the Q1 reading
fits the tense sequence of the other verbs in ll. 26–9.
28. *doit*] the type of a small sum; from the name of a small Dutch coin
worth half a farthing.
39. *denier*] another type of a small sum; from the name of a French coin
worth one-twelfth of a sou. The Qq spelling indicates the rhyme with
'swear' in l. 38.
40. *resolve*] tell, explain to.

Susan. O brother!
Sir Cha.   O sister! only this one way,
    With that rich jewel you my debts may pay.
    In speaking this my cold heart shakes with shame,
    Nor do I woo you in a brother's name,   50
    But in a stranger's. Shall I die in debt
    To Acton, my grand foe, and you still wear
    The precious jewel that he holds so dear?
Susan. My honour I esteem as dear and precious
    As my redemption.
Sir Cha.   I esteem you, sister,   55
    As dear for so dear prizing it.
Susan.   Will Charles
    Have me cut off my hands and send them Acton?
    Rip up my breast, and with my bleeding heart
    Present him as a token?
Sir Cha.   Neither, sister,
    But hear me in my strange assertion: 60
    Thy honour and my soul are equal in my regard,
    Nor will thy brother Charles survive thy shame.
    His kindness like a burden hath surcharged me,
    And under his good deeds I stooping go,
    Not with an upright soul. Had I remain'd   65
    In prison still, there doubtless I had died;
    Then unto him that freed me from that prison
    Still do I owe that life. What mov'd my foe
    To enfranchise me? 'Twas, sister, for your love!
    With full five hundred pounds he bought your love,   70
    And shall he not enjoy it? Shall the weight
    Of all this heavy burden lean on me,
    And will not you bear part? You did partake
    The joy of my release; will you not stand

55–6.] *Q1;* I . . . deare, / For . . . it. *Q2.*   59. sister] *Q2;* Iane *Q1.*
68. that] *Q1;* this *Q2.*

---

52. *grand*] chief, arch.
69. *enfranchise*] release from confinement.

    In joint-bond bound to satisfy the debt?   75
    Shall I be only charged?
Susan.   But that I know
    These arguments come from an honour'd mind,
    As in your most extremity of need,
    Scorning to stand in debt to one you hate—
    Nay, rather would engage your unstain'd honour   80
    Than to be held ingrate—I should condemn you.
    I see your resolution and assent;
    So Charles will have me, and I am content.
Sir Cha. For this I trick'd you up.
Susan.   But here's a knife,
    To save mine honour, shall slice out my life.   85
Sir Cha. I know thou pleasest me a thousand times
    More in that resolution than thy grant.
    [*Aside*] Observe her love: to soothe it to my suit
    Her honour she will hazard though not lose;
    To bring me out of debt, her rigorous hand   90
    Will pierce her heart. O wonder, that will choose,
    Rather than stain her blood, her life to lose.
    [*To her.*] Come, you sad sister to a woeful brother,
    This is the gate; I'll bear him such a present,
    Such an acquittance for the knight to seal,   95
    As will amaze his senses and surprise
    With admiration all his phantasies.

76. charged] *Q1;* charg'd *Q2.*   85. slice] *Qq;* sluice *conj. Daniel.*
86. I know] *Qq;* Aye, now *Dodsley;* Ay! know *Verity.*   87. that] *Q1;* thy
Q2.   88. *Aside*] *Verity.*   love:] *Dodsley;* loue *Q1;* loue; *Q2.*   it to]
Q2; them in *Q1.*

---

75. *In . . . bound*] bound with me jointly. *Joint-bond* is not recorded in
O.E.D.
    80. *engage*] compromise.
    88. *to . . . suit*] to make her honour comply with my suit. The sense of
the Q1 reading is obscure.
    95. *acquittance*] document of release. There is probably a double mean-
ing in the phrase 'seal an acquittance'; cf. Donne, Elegie XIX, 'Going to
Bed', l. 32: 'Then where my hand is set, my seal shall be' (ed. Grierson,
1912, I, 121).
    97. *admiration*] wonder.   *phantasies*] powers of imagination.

Enter SIR FRANCIS *and* MALBY.

Susan. Before his unchaste thoughts shall seize on me,
 'Tis here shall my imprison'd soul set free.
Sir Fra. How! Mountford with his sister hand in hand!   100
 What miracle's afoot?
Mal.   It is a sight
 Begets in me much admiration.
Sir Cha. Stand not amaz'd to see me thus attended.
 Acton, I owe thee money, and being unable
 To bring thee the full sum in ready coin,   105
 Lo! for thy more assurance here's a pawn,
 My sister, my dear sister, whose chaste honour
 I prize above a million. Here—nay, take her;
 She's worth your money, man; do not forsake her.
Sir Fra. [*Aside*] I would he were in earnest.   110
Susan. Impute it not to my immodesty.
 My brother being rich in nothing else
 But in his interest that he hath in me,
 According to his poverty hath brought you
 Me, all his store, whom howsoe'er you prize   115
 As forfeit to your hand, he values highly,
 And would not sell but to acquit your debt
 For any emperor's ransom.
Sir Fra. [*Aside*]   Stern heart, relent;
 Thy former cruelty at length repent.
 Was ever known in any former age   120
 Such honourable wrested courtesy?
 Lands, honours, lives, and all the world forgo
 Rather than stand engag'd to such a foe.
Sir Cha. Acton, she is too poor to be thy bride,

99. imprison'd] *Q2;* imprisoned *Q1.* 110. *Aside*] *This ed.* 118. *Aside*]
Verity. 122. lives] *Q1;* life *Q2.*

98–9.] Possibly this speech is an aside.
99.] i.e. the knife is here that shall free my imprisoned soul.
106. *pawn*] pledge; cf. i. 96.
110.] Perhaps the line is spoken to Malby rather than as an aside.
121. *wrested*] distorted.

And I too much oppos'd to be thy brother.   125
There, take her to thee; if thou hast the heart
To seize her as a rape or lustful prey,
To blur our house that never yet was stain'd,
To murder her that never meant thee harm,
To kill me now whom once thou savedst from death,   130
Do them at once on her; all these rely
And perish with her spotted chastity.

Sir Fra. You overcome me in your love, Sir Charles.
I cannot be so cruel to a lady
I love so dearly. Since you have not spar'd   135
To engage your reputation to the world,
Your sister's honour which you prize so dear,
Nay, all the comforts which you hold on earth,
To grow out of my debt, being your foe,
Your honour'd thoughts, lo, thus I recompense: 140
Your metamorphos'd foe receives your gift
In satisfaction of all former wrongs.
This jewel I will wear here in my heart,
And where before I thought her for her wants
Too base to be my bride, to end all strife,   145
I seal you my dear brother, her my wife.

Susan. You still exceed us. I will yield to fate
And learn to love where I till now did hate.

Sir Cha. With that enchantment you have charm'd my soul
And made me rich even in those very words.   150
I pay no debt but am indebted more;
Rich in your love I never can be poor.

Sir Fra. All's mine is yours; we are alike in state.

---

130. savedst] *Q1;* sau'dst *Q2.*   131. them] *Qq;* then, *Dodsley.*   once on
her; all these rely] *Q2;* once on her, all these relie *Q1;* once: on her all these
rely, *Verity.*   138. comforts] *Q1;* comfort *Q2.*   140. honour'd] *Q2;*
honored *Q1.*   153. All's] *Q2* [Al's]; Alas *Q1.*

---

127. *lustful prey*] prey to your lust.
131. *at once*] at one stroke.
    rely] i.e. rely on.
144. *where*] whereas.
    wants] circumstances of want.

Let's knit in love what was oppos'd in hate.
Come, for our nuptials we will straight provide,   155
Bless'd only in our brother and fair bride.   [*Exeunt.*]

[Scene xv]

Enter CRANWELL, FRANKFORD, *and* NICHOLAS.

Cran. Why do you search each room about your house,
    Now that you have dispatch'd your wife away?
Frank. O sir, to see that nothing may be left
    That ever was my wife's. I lov'd her dearly,
    And when I do but think of her unkindness,   5
    My thoughts are all in Hell, to avoid which torment,
    I would not have a bodkin or a cuff,
    A bracelet, necklace, or rebato wire,
    Nor anything that ever was call'd hers
    Left me, by which I might remember her.   10
    Seek round about.
Nich. 'Sblood, master, here's her lute flung in a corner.
Frank. Her lute! O God, upon this instrument
    Her fingers have run quick division,
    Sweeter than that which now divides our hearts.   15
    These frets have made me pleasant, that have now
    Frets of my heartstrings made. O Master Cranwell,

156. *Exeunt.*] *Q1; not in Q2.*

xv. 4. lov'd] *Q2;* loued *Q1.*   9. call'd] *Q2; not in Q1.*   14. run] *Q1;*
ran *Q2;* rung *Ward.*   15. Sweeter] *Qq;* Swifter *Dodsley.*

---

155. *straight*] immediately.

xv. 7. *bodkin*] an ornamental pin for fastening the hair.
    8. *rebato wire*] wire used to support the elaborate ruffs, or collars, worn
by well-to-do women.
    14. *run quick division*] executed a rapid melodic passage. Cf. *Rom.*, III. v.
29–30, where there is the same pun with the verb *divide*:
            Some say the lark makes sweet division;
            This doth not so, for she divideth us.
    16. *frets*] See the note on i. 81; here, as frequently in Heywood's time,
there is also a pun.
    pleasant] merry.

Oft hath she made this melancholy wood,
Now mute and dumb for her disastrous chance,
Speak sweetly many a note, sound many a strain   20
To her own ravishing voice, which being well strung,
What pleasant, strange airs have they jointly sung.—
Post with it after her.—Now nothing's left;
Of her and hers I am at once bereft.

Nich. I'll ride and overtake her, do my message,   25
And come back again.   [*Exit.*]

Cran.   Meantime, sir, if you please,
I'll to Sir Francis Acton and inform him
Of what hath pass'd betwixt you and his sister.

Frank. Do as you please. How ill am I bestead
To be a widower ere my wife be dead.   [*Exeunt.*] 30

[Scene xvi]

> *Enter* ANNE, *with* JENKIN, *her maid* SISLY, *her
> Coachman, and three Carters.*

Anne. Bid my coach stay. Why should I ride in state,
Being hurl'd so low down by the hand of fate?
A seat like to my fortunes let me have,
Earth for my chair, and for my bed a grave.

Jenk. Comfort, good mistress; you have watered your coach   5
with tears already. You have but two mile now to go to
your manor. A man cannot say by my old Master Frankford as he may say by me, that he wants manors, for he
hath three or four, of which this is one that we are going
to.   10

22. sung] *Q1;* rung *Q2.*   26. *Exit.*] *Reed.*   30. *Exeunt.*] *Reed.*
xvi. 10. to] *Q1;* to now *Q2.*

---

19. *for . . . chance*] because of her misfortune.

xvi. 1. *coach*] Cf. the note on xiii. 1 above.
7. *by*] with respect to.
8. *manors*] (a) estates; (b) manners.

L

Sisly. Good mistress, be of good cheer. Sorrow you see hurts
    you, but helps you not; we all mourn to see you so sad.
Carter. Mistress, I spy one of my landlord's men
    Come riding post; 'tis like he brings some news.
Anne. Comes he from Master Frankford, he is welcome;   15
    So are his news, because they come from him.

Enter NICHOLAS.

Nich. [*handing her the lute.*] There.
Anne. I know the lute. Oft have I sung to thee;
    We both are out of tune, both out of time.
Nich. Would that had been the worst instrument that e'er you   20
    played on. My master commends him to ye; there's all he
    can find that was ever yours. He hath nothing left that
    ever you could lay claim to but his own heart—and he
    could afford you that. All that I have to deliver you is this:
    he prays you to forget him, and so he bids you farewell.   25
Anne. I thank him; he is kind and ever was.
    All you that have true feeling of my grief,
    That know my loss, and have relenting hearts,
    Gird me about, and help me with your tears
    To wash my spotted sins. My lute shall groan;   30
    It cannot weep, but shall lament my moan.   [*She plays.*]

Enter WENDOLL [*behind*].

Wen. Pursued with horror of a guilty soul
    And with the sharp scourge of repentance lash'd,
    I fly from my own shadow. O my stars!

---

13. spy one] *Q1;* see some *Q2.*   16. are] *Q1;* is *Q2.*   17. *handing . . .
lute.*] *Verity.*   18. the lute] *Qq;* thee, Lute *conj.* G. B. *Johnston,
N. & Q.,* CCIII (1958), 525–6.   21. to] *Q1;* vnto *Q2.*   23. lay claim
to] *Q2;* claim to lay *Q1.*   31. *She plays.*] *Collier (1850).*   31.1. *behind*]
Collier (1850).   32. *Wen.*] *Q1; not in Q2.*   Pursued] *Q1;* Pursu'd *Q2.*
34. my] *Q1;* mine *Q2.*

---

14. *post*] with speed.
18. *the lute*] Johnston's conjecture is interesting, but not really necessary.
20. *instrument*] There is a punning reference to *instrument* as the female
sex organ. See Farmer and Henley.

What have my parents in their lives deserv'd   35
That you should lay this penance on their son?
When I but think of Master Frankford's love
And lay it to my treason, or compare
My murd'ring him for his relieving me,
It strikes a terror like a lightning's flash   40
To scorch my blood up. Thus I like the owl
Asham'd of day, live in these shadowy woods
Afraid of every leaf or murmuring blast,
Yet longing to receive some perfect knowledge
How he hath dealt with her. [*Sees Anne.*] O my sad fate!   45
Here, and so far from home, and thus attended!
O God, I have divorc'd the truest turtles
That ever liv'd together, and being divided
In several places, make their several moan;
She in the fields laments and he at home.   50
So poets write that Orpheus made the trees

36. their] *Q1;* your *Q2.*   39. murd'ring] *Q1;* murthering *Q2.*   45. *Sees
Anne.*] *Collier (1825).*

---

38. *lay*] compare.
41–2. *like ... day*] Cf. *3H6*, v. iv. 55–7:
> And he, that will not fight for such a hope,
> Go home to bed, and, like the owl by day,
> If he arise, be mock'd and wonder'd at.
44. *perfect*] correct.
47. *turtles*] turtle-doves.
49. *several*] separate.
51–4.] A similar rationalization of the Orpheus myth appears in Horace,
The Art of Poetry, ll. 391–6: 'While men still roamed the woods, Orpheus,
the holy prophet of the gods, made them shrink from bloodshed and brutal
living; hence the fable that he tamed tigers and ravening lions; hence too
the fable than Amphion, builder of Thebes's citadel, moved stones by the
sound of his lyre, and led them whither he would by his supplicating spell'
(trans. Fairclough, 1926, p. 483). The idea appears often in Renaissance
mythographers and critics; the most famous in English is probably that in
Sidney's *Defence of Poesie*, 1595, B2. A version closer to Heywood's is in
Alexander Ross, *Mystagogus Poeticus*, 2nd ed., 1648, p. 336: 'By *Orpheus*
charming of stones ... with his musick, is meant, how Governours ... did
bring rude and ignorant people ... to civilitie, and religion'. Orpheus appears as a presenter in Heywood's *Londini Status Pacatus*, where he says:
> The very Trees I did so much intrance,

And stones to dance to his melodious harp,
Meaning the rustic and the barbarous hinds,
That had no understanding part in them;
So she from these rude carters tears extracts,   55
Making their flinty hearts with grief to rise
And draw down rivers from their rocky eyes.

Anne. [*to Nicholas.*] If you return unto your master, say—
Though not from me, for I am all unworthy
To blast his name so with a strumpet's tongue—   60
That you have seen me weep, wish myself dead.
Nay, you may say too—for my vow is pass'd—
Last night you saw me eat and drink my last.
This to your master you may say and swear,
For it is writ in Heaven and decreed here.   65

Nich. I'll say you wept; I'll swear you made me sad.
Why how now, eyes? what now? what's here to do?
I am gone, or I shall straight turn baby too.

Wen. [*Aside*] I cannot weep; my heart is all on fire.
Curs'd be the fruits of my unchaste desire.   70

---

57. down] *Q2; not in Q1.*   58. *to Nicholas.*] *Verity.*   your] *Q1;* my *Q2.*
60. so] *Q2; not in Q1.*   68. I am] *Q1;* I'me *Q2.*   69. *Aside*] *Neilson.*

They shooke their bowes because they could not dance:
But, Stones not rooted, but above the ground
Mov'd in rare postures to my Harps sweet sound.
                                        (Pearson, v, 367.)
  53. *hinds*] rustics.
  57.] Cf. *The Rape of Lucrece*: 'To heare him sing drawes rivers from mine
eyes' (Pearson, v, 181); and *Fortune by Land and Sea*, II. i:
                    Your substance I despise,
          But to lose that [love] draws rivers from my eyes.
                                        (Pearson, VI, 380–1.)
  60.] Cf. *Loves Maistresse*, III:
              'Tis some infectious strumpet, and her breath
              Will blast our cheekes. (Pearson, v, 128.)
  62. *pass'd*] made.
  65. *here*] a rhyme with 'swear'; see Kökeritz, p. 207.
  69–70.] Cf. *The Rape of Lucrece*:
          I'me bent on both my thoughts are all on fire,
          Choose thee, thou must imbrace death, or desire.
                                        (Pearson, v, 223.)

Anne. Go break this lute upon my coach's wheel,
        As the last music that I e'er shall make—
        Not as my husband's gift, but my farewell
        To all earth's joy; and so your master tell.
Nich. If I can for crying.
Wen. [*Aside*]   Grief, have done,   75
        Or like a madman I shall frantic run.
Anne. You have beheld the woefullest wretch on earth,
        A woman made of tears. Would you had words
        To express but what you see; my inward grief
        No tongue can utter, yet unto your power   80
        You may describe my sorrow and disclose
        To thy sad master my abundant woes.
Nich. I'll do your commendations.
Anne.   O no.
        I dare not so presume; nor to my children.
        I am disclaim'd in both; alas, I am.   85
        O never teach them when they come to speak
        To name the name of mother; chide their tongue
        If they by chance light on that hated word;
        Tell them 'tis nought, for when that word they name,
        Poor pretty souls, they harp on their own shame. 90
Wen. [*Aside*] To recompense her wrongs, what canst thou do?
        Thou hast made her husbandless and childless too.
Anne. I have no more to say. Speak not for me,
        Yet you may tell your master what you see.
Nich. I'll do't.   *Exit.* 95
Wen. [*Aside*] I'll speak to her and comfort her in grief.
        O, but her wound cannot be cur'd with words.
        No matter though, I'll do my best good will
        To work a cure on her whom I did kill.
Anne. So, now unto my coach, then to my home,   100

71. upon] *Q2; not in Q1.*   75. Aside] *Neilson.*   77. woefullest] *Q1;*
wofull'st *Q2.*   91. Aside] *Neilson.*   96. Aside] *Neilson.*

---

80. *unto your power*] so far as you are able.
83. *do your commendations*] present your remembrances.

So to my deathbed, for from this sad hour
I never will nor eat, nor drink, nor taste
Of any cates that may preserve my life;
I never will nor smile, nor sleep, nor rest,
But when my tears have wash'd my black soul white,   105
Sweet Saviour, to Thy hands I yield my sprite.

Wen. [*coming forward.*] O Mistress Frankford—
Anne.   O for God's sake fly!
The Devil doth come to tempt me ere I die.
My coach! This sin that with an angel's face
Courted mine honour till he sought my wrack,   110
In my repentant eyes seems ugly black.

Exeunt all [*except* WENDOLL *and* JENKIN],
the Carters whistling.

Jenk. What, my young master that fled in his shirt! How
come you by your clothes again? You have made our
house in a sweet pickle, have you not, think you? What,
shall I serve you still or cleave to the old house?   115
Wen. Hence, slave! Away with thy unseasoned mirth;
Unless thou canst shed tears, and sigh, and howl,
Curse thy sad fortunes, and exclaim on fate,
Thou art not for my turn.

---

107. *coming forward.*] *Collier* (*1850*).   109. sin] *Qq;* fiend *Dodsley*.   110.
Courted] *Q1;* Coniur'd *Q2*.   111. eyes] *Q1;* eye *Q2*.   ugly black] *Qq;*
ugly, black *Collier* (*1850*).   111.1. *except Wendoll and Jenkin*] *Reed*.
114. have you] *Q1;* ha'ye *Q2*.   116. unseasoned] *Q1;* vnseason'd *Q2*.

---

103. *cates*] food.

109. *sin*] Dodsley's emendation is especially attractive since in Elizabethan handwriting 'sinne' (which is the spelling of both quartos) and
'fiend' might look very much alike.

110. *Courted*] The readings of both quartos are acceptable, Q2's somewhat more vivid. But there is no particular reason to desert Q1.
wrack] ruin.

111.2. the Carters whistling] Carters were famous for their whistling;
cf. *2H4*, III. ii. 343–6: 'a' came ever in the rearward of the fashion and sung
those tunes to the over-scutched huswives that he heard the carmen whistle,
and sware they were his fancies or his good-nights'.

116. *unseasoned*] unseasonable.

119. *for my turn*] suitable for my requirements.

Jenk. Marry, and you will not, another will; farewell and be   120
    hang'd. Would you had never come to have kept this
    coil within our doors. We shall ha' you run away like a
    sprite again.   [*Exit.*]

Wen. She's gone to death, I live to want and woe,
    Her life, her sins, and all upon my head,   125
    And I must now go wander like a Cain
    In foreign countries and remoted climes,
    Where the report of my ingratitude
    Cannot be heard. I'll over, first to France,
    And so to Germany, and Italy,   130
    Where when I have recovered, and by travel
    Gotten those perfect tongues, and that these rumours
    May in their height abate, I will return;
    And I divine, however now dejected,
    My worth and parts being by some great man prais'd,   135
    At my return I may in court be rais'd.   *Exit.*

123. *Exit.*] *Reed.*   129. over,] *Q1;* ouer *Q2.*

---

120. *and*] if.

121–2. *kept this coil*] stirred up this trouble.

126. *wander . . . Cain*] an allusion to the Lord's punishment of Cain; see
Genesis, iv. 12.

127. *remoted*] remote, distant.

132. *Gotten . . . tongues*] learned perfectly the languages of those coun-
tries.

    that] when.

134–6.] Daniel suggests an allusion to 'Carr', presumably Robert Carr,
Earl of Somerset, who had accompanied James I from Scotland as a page,
was soon discharged, went to France, returned, was taken into favour by
James, and was knighted on 23 December 1607. If so, the passage must
have been added between the time of the original production and the 1607
quarto.

134. *divine*] predict.

[Scene xvii]

> *Enter* SIR FRANCIS, SIR CHARLES, CRANWELL, [MALBY,]
> *and* SUSAN.

Sir Fra. Brother, and now my wife, I think these troubles
        Fall on my head by justice of the Heavens,
        For being so strict to you in your extremities,
        But we are now aton'd. I would my sister
        Could with like happiness o'ercome her griefs   5
        As we have ours.

Susan. You tell us, Master Cranwell, wondrous things
        Touching the patience of that gentleman,
        With what strange virtue he demeans his grief.

Cran. I told you what I was witness of;   10
        It was my fortune to lodge there that night.

Sir Fra. O that same villain Wendoll! 'Twas his tongue
        That did corrupt her; she was of herself
        Chaste and devoted well. Is this the house?

Cran. Yes sir, I take it here your sister lies.   15

Sir Fra. My brother Frankford show'd too mild a spirit
        In the revenge of such a loathed crime;
        Less than he did, no man of spirit could do.
        I am so far from blaming his revenge

---

xvii. o.1. *Malby,*] *Reed.*   7. wondrous] *Q2;* wonderous *Q1.*   10. wit-
ness] *Qq;* a witness *Reed.*

---

xvii.] Baskervill's was the first text to print the remainder of the play as
one scene; earlier editors divided it either into three scenes (dividing after
ll. 22 and 38 of the present edition) or into two (dividing after l. 38).
Reynolds, *op. cit.*, describes the conventions by which the episodes were
staged in Heywood's time: 'The scene begins on the way to the country
house, then as a "journeying" scene shifts to before the house, and finally
is changed to within the house apparently by the drawing of a curtain when
Mistress Anne is discovered in bed. Or it may be the last change was shown
by shoving the bed out upon the stage' (p. 117).
    4. *aton'd*] put at one, reconciled.
    9. *demeans*] expresses.
    12. *same*] in 16th- and 17th-century usage expressive of contempt.
    14. *devoted well*] faithful, true to her marriage vows; Spencer glosses
'pious'.
    15. *lies*] lives.

That I commend it; had it been my case,   20
Their souls at once had from their breasts been freed;
Death to such deeds of shame is the due meed.

Enter JENKIN *and* SISLY.

Jenk. O my mistress, my mistress, my poor mistress!
Sisly. Alas that ever I was born! What shall I do for my poor
   mistress?   25
Sir Cha. Why, what of her?
Jenk. O Lord, sir, she no sooner heard that her brother and
   his friends were come to see how she did, but she for very
   shame of her guilty conscience fell into a swoon, and we
   had much ado to get life into her.   30
Susan. Alas that she should bear so hard a fate;
   Pity it is repentance comes too late.
Sir Fra. Is she so weak in body?
Jenk. O sir, I can assure you there's no help of life in her, for
   she will take no sustenance. She hath plainly starved her-   35
   self, and now she is as lean as a lath. She ever looks for the
   good hour. Many gentlemen and gentlewomen of the
   country are come to comfort her.

Enter ANNE *in her bed.*

22.1. *and Sisly*] *Q1; not in Q2.*   23. mistress, my mistress] *Q1;* mistris,
mistris *Q2.*   27–30.] *Q2; Q1 prints as verse, dividing after* brother, did,
fell, *and* to.   28. his] *Q1;* hir *Q2.*   29. a] *Q1;* such a *Q2.*   and] *Q1;*
that *Q2.*   30. into] *Q1;* in *Q2.*   34–8.] *Q2; Q1 prints as verse, dividing
after* life, plainly, leane, euer, many, *and* to.   34. help] *Q1;* hope *Q2.*
35. sustenance] *Q1;* sust'nance *Q2.*   starved] *Q1;* staru'd *Q2.*   36.
and] *Q2;* that *Q1.*   she is] *Q1;* shee's *Q2.*

23–5.] Cf. *Fortune by Land and Sea*, IV: 'O my Master, my Master, what
shal I do for my poor Master' (Pearson, VI, 423).

32. *repentance . . . late*] Cf. the proverb 'Repentance never comes too
late' (Tilley R80).

36. *lean . . . lath*] proverbial (Tilley L86). This is the earliest use recorded
by Tilley.

38.1.] A type of stage-direction common in Elizabethan and Jacobean
plays; cf. the first part of *If You Know Not Me You Know No Body*: '*Enter
Elizabeth, in her bed*' (Pearson, I, 200) and *The Late Lancashire Witches*:
'*A Bed thrust out, Mrs. Gener. in't*' (Pearson, IV, 249); Bates cites three

Mal. How fare you, Mistress Frankford ?

Anne. Sick, sick, O sick! Give me some air I pray you.   40
   Tell me, O tell me, where's Master Frankford ?
   Will not he deign to see me ere I die ?

Mal. Yes, Mistress Frankford; divers gentlemen,
   Your loving neighbours, with that just request
   Have mov'd and told him of your weak estate,   45
   Who, though with much ado to get belief,
   Examining of the general circumstance,
   Seeing your sorrow and your penitence,
   And hearing therewithal the great desire
   You have to see him ere you left the world,   50
   He gave to us his faith to follow us,
   And sure he will be here immediately.

Anne. You half reviv'd me with those pleasing news.
   Raise me a little higher in my bed.
   Blush I not, brother Acton ? Blush I not, Sir Charles ?   55
   Can you not read my fault writ in my cheek ?
   Is not my crime there ? Tell me, gentlemen.

Sir Cha. Alas, good mistress, sickness hath not left you
   Blood in your face enough to make you blush.

Anne. Then sickness like a friend my fault would hide.   60
   Is my husband come ? My soul but tarries

---

40. air] *Q1; aire. Q2.*   pray you.] *Q1;* pray *Q2.*   41. where's] *Qq;*
where is *Reed.*   42. he] *Q1; not in Q2.*   53. half] *Q1;* haue half *Q2.*
those] *Q1;* the *Q2.*   55. brother Acton] *Q2;* maister Franksord *Q1.*
60.] *Q2; Q1 misassigns this line to Charles.*

---

other similar directions from Heywood's plays. Here, presumably, the
curtains of the inner stage were opened to reveal Mistress Frankford in her
bed, which was probably then drawn forward to the outer stage. Or if, in
accordance with much recent scholarly opinion, there was no true 'inner
stage', the bed would have been 'thrust out' from one of the rear-stage
doors.

45. *mov'd*] taken action.
   estate] condition.
   51. *faith*] promise.
   53. *half*] Q2's 'haue half' makes a better tense sequence, and the 'have'
might easily have been skipped over by the Q1 compositor. But either
version makes a readable line of verse, and Q1's past tense is not impossible.

His arrive and I am fit for Heaven.

Sir Fra. I came to chide you, but my words of hate
Are turn'd to pity and compassionate grief;
I came to rate you, but my brawls, you see,   65
Melt into tears, and I must weep by thee.

Enter FRANKFORD.

Here's Master Frankford now.

Frank. Good morrow, brother; good morrow, gentlemen.
God, that hath laid this cross upon our heads,
Might had He pleas'd have made our cause of meeting   70
On a more fair and a more contented ground;
But He that made us, made us to this woe.

Anne. And is he come? Methinks that voice I know.

Frank. How do you, woman?

Anne. Well, Master Frankford, well; but shall be better   75
I hope within this hour. Will you vouchsafe,
Out of your grace and your humanity,
To take a spotted strumpet by the hand?

Frank. That hand once held my heart in faster bonds
Than now 'tis gripp'd by me. God pardon them   80
That made us first break hold.

Anne.   Amen, amen.
Out of my zeal to Heaven, whither I am now bound,
I was so impudent to wish you here,
And once more beg your pardon. O good man,
And father to my children, pardon me.   85

---

62. and] *Q1;* then *Q2.*   63. *Sir Fra.*] *Q2; Charles Q1.*   66.1.] *Q1;*
after l. 67 Q2.   68. good morrow] *Q1;* morrow *Q2.*   71. and a] *Q1;*
and *Q2.*   79. That] *Q1;* This *Q2.*   82. I am] *Q1;* I'me *Q2.*

---

62. *arrive*] arrival.

63–6.] Q1's attribution is not impossible (unlike that in l. 60 above), but
the speech is much more natural in the mouth of Anne's brother.

65. *rate*] reproach.

brawls] reproaches, chidings. Not in *O.E.D.* in this sense, but compare
brawl, v., 1b, 'to chide, scold, revile', with citations from 1474 to *a.* 1649.

75. *better*] i.e. in Heaven.

Pardon, O pardon me! My fault so heinous is
That if you in this world forgive it not,
Heaven will not clear it in the world to come.
Faintness hath so usurp'd upon my knees
That kneel I cannot; but on my heart's knees   90
My prostrate soul lies thrown down at your feet
To beg your gracious pardon. Pardon, O pardon me!

Frank. As freely from the low depth of my soul
As my Redeemer hath forgiven His death,
I pardon thee. I will shed tears for thee,   95
Pray with thee, and in mere pity
Of thy weak state I'll wish to die with thee.

All. So do we all.

Nich. [*Aside*] So will not I;
I'll sigh and sob, but, by my faith, not die.   100

Sir Fra. O Master Frankford, all the near alliance
I lose by her shall be supply'd in thee.
You are my brother by the nearest way;
Her kindred hath fallen off, but yours doth stay.

Frank. Even as I hope for pardon at that day   105
When the Great Judge of Heaven in scarlet sits,
So be thou pardoned. Though thy rash offence
Divorc'd our bodies, thy repentant tears
Unite our souls.

Sir Cha.   Then comfort, Mistress Frankford;

94. death,] *Q1;* death. *Q2.*   95. thee.] *Collier (1825);* thee, *Q1;* thee; *Q2.*
96–7.] *Q1;* Pray . . . estate, / Ile . . . thee. *Q2.*   97. weak state] *Q1;* weake
estate *Q2.*   99. *Aside*] *Oliphant.*   107. pardoned] *Q1;* pardon'd *Q2.*

86–8. *My . . . come*] a moving plea, but theologically unsound.
93–4.] Cf. *2 Edward IV:*
> *Jane.* Ah, *Shore* ist possible thou canst forgiue me?
> *Shore.* Yes, *Jane,* I do.
> *Jane.* I cannot hope thou wilt.
>   My faults so great, that I cannot expect it.
> *Shore.* Ifaith, I do, as freely from my soule,
>   As at Gods hands I hope to be forgiuen. (Pearson, 1, 182.)
96. *mere*] complete, absolute.
104.] Although she, being about to die, will cease to be my sister, you
are still of my kin.

You see your husband hath forgiven your fall;   110
Then rouse your spirits and cheer your fainting soul.

Susan. How is it with you?

Sir Fra.   How do you feel yourself?

Anne. Not of this world.

Frank. I see you are not, and I weep to see it.

My wife, the mother to my pretty babes,   115
Both those lost names I do restore thee back,
And with this kiss I wed thee once again.

Though thou art wounded in thy honour'd name,
And with that grief upon thy deathbed liest,
Honest in heart, upon my soul, thou diest.   120

Anne. Pardon'd on earth, soul, thou in Heaven art free;
Once more thy wife, dies thus embracing thee.   [*Dies.*]

Frank. New marry'd and new widowed; O, she's dead,

---

112. do you] *Q1;* de'ye *Q2.*   117. again.] *Brooke;* againe, *Q1;* againe: *Q2.*
122. more thy wife, dies] *Qq;* more; thy wife dies *Dodsley;* more thy wife
dies *Collier (1850);* more thy wife dies, *Baskervill.*   *Dies.*] *Reed.*   123.
widowed] *Q1;* widdow'd *Q2.*

117.] Cf. *2 Edward IV:*
        Oh, liuing death! euen in this dying life,
        Yet, ere I go, once, *Matthew* kiss thy wife. (Pearson, I, 183.)
120. *Honest*] chaste.
122.] The line presumably employs 'thy wife' as a squinting construction: 'Once more I am thy wife; thy wife dies thus embracing thee'.
Dodsley's punctuation takes 'Once more' as an appeal for a kiss, Baskervill's suggests that this is her second death, the first being her exile from
her husband; but it seems best to follow the Qq punctuation.
123–4.] Cf. *2 Edward IV:*
        Oh, dying marriage! oh, sweet married death
        Thou graue, which only shouldst part faithful friends,
        Bringst vs togither, and dost ioine our hands. (Pearson, I, 183.)
The famous passage from *Hamlet* joins marriage and death in a different
fashion:
        I thought thy bride-bed to have deck'd, sweet maid,
        And not have strew'd thy grave. (*Ham.,* v. i. 267–8.)
Fletcher and Shirley have a passage much closer to Heywood's in *The
Night-Walker,* I. i:
                A sad wedding,
        Her grave must be her Bridal bed.
                (Beaumont and Fletcher, *Works,* ed. Waller, 1909, VII, 326.)

And a cold grave must be our nuptial bed.

Sir Cha. Sir, be of good comfort, and your heavy sorrow   125
 Part equally amongst us; storms divided
 Abate their force, and with less rage are guided.

Cran. Do, Master Frankford; he that hath least part
 Will find enough to drown one troubled heart.

Sir Fra. Peace with thee, Nan. Brothers and gentlemen,   130
 All we that can plead interest in her grief,
 Bestow upon her body funeral tears.
 Brother, had you with threats and usage bad
 Punish'd her sin, the grief of her offence
 Had not with such true sorrow touch'd her heart.   135

Frank. I see it had not; therefore on her grave
 I will bestow this funeral epitaph,
 Which on her marble tomb shall be engrav'd.
 In golden letters shall these words be fill'd:
 'Here lies she whom her husband's kindness kill'd.'   140

FINIS.

124. our] *Q1;* her *Q2.*   137. I will] *Q1;* Will I *Q2.*   140.] *Q1, but
without inverted commas; Q2 prints the line in italics.*

---

124. our] Q1's reading is certainly more effective.
139.] 'The engraved letters shall be filled in with gold' (Spencer).

The Epilogue

An honest crew, disposed to be merry,
Came to a tavern by and call'd for wine.
The drawer brought it, smiling like a cherry,
And told them it was pleasant, neat, and fine.
    'Taste it', quoth one. He did so. 'Fie!' quoth he,   5
    'This wine was good; now 't runs too near the lee'.

Another sipp'd, to give the wine his due,
And said unto the rest it drunk too flat.
The third said it was old, the fourth too new.
'Nay', quoth the fifth, 'the sharpness likes me not'.   10
    Thus, gentlemen, you see how in one hour
    The wine was new, old, flat, sharp, sweet, and sour.

Unto this wine we do allude our play,
Which some will judge too trivial, some too grave.
You as our guests we entertain this day   15
And bid you welcome to the best we have.
    Excuse us, then; good wine may be disgrac'd
    When every several mouth hath sundry taste.

Text in italics in Qq.   5. one. He] *Qq;* he: one *conj. Daniel.*

2. *by*] nearby.
4. *neat*] pure, unadulterated.
6. *lee*] lees, sediment.
13. *allude*] compare.

The Source of the Sub-plot[1]

Salimbene, and Angelica

A Gentleman of Siena, called Anselmo Salimbene, curteously and gently deliuereth his enemy from death. The condemned party seeing the kinde parte of Salimbene, rendreth into his hands his sister Angelica, with whom he was in loue, which gratitude and curtesie, Salimbene well markinge, moued in Conscience, woulde not abuse hir, but for recompence tooke hir to his VVyfe.

The XXX. Nouell.

(287) In Siena then . . . were two families very rich, noble, and the chiefe of the Citty called the Salimbenes, and Montanines. . . .

(287v) So the huntinge of the wylde Bore defyled the City of Siena, with the bloud of hir owne Citizens, when the Salimbenes and Montanines vppon a daye in an assembled company, incountring vpon a greate & fierce Bore, toke hym by force of men and Beastes. When they had don, as they were banketting and communing of the nimblenesse of their dogs, ech man praising his owne, as hauing done beste, there rose greate debate amongs them, and proceeded so farre, as fondly they began to reuile one another with words, and from taunting termes to earnest blowes, wherwith diuers in that skirmish were hurt on both sides: In the end the Salimbenes had the worsse, and

---

[1] The text of this appendix is a transcription, with omissions, from *The Second Tome of the Palace of Pleasure* . . . by William Painter (1580 ?), Fos. 286r to 307r. In the original the body of the text is in a black-letter typeface, with proper names in roman (and small capitals). This distinction of faces is ignored in my text. I have expanded the contractions of the original (except the ampersand), such contractions being indicated by the use of italic type; but 'ye' and 'yt' are expanded silently. Page-references are inserted in round brackets and omissions indicated by the use of dots. Paragraph divisions, except those on Fos. 287 and 292v, are editorial. I have silently corrected a few obvious misprints.

The transcription was made from the Folger copy and collated with a microfilm of the University of Illinois copy.

one of the principall slayne in the place, which appalled the rest, not
that they were discoraged, but attending time and season of reuenge.
This hatred so strangely kindled betwene both partes, that by lyttle
and lyttle, after many combats and ouerthrowes of eyther side, the
losse lyghted vpon the Montanines, who with their wealth and
rychesse were almost brought to nothing, and thereby the rygour
and Choler of the Salimbenes appeased, none being able to resist
them, and in space of time forgot all iniuries. The Montanines also
that remayned at Siena, liued in quyet, wythoute chalenge or quarell
of their aduersaries, howbeit mutuall talke & haunt of others company vtterly surceased. And to say the truth, there were almost none
to quarell wythall, for the whole Bloude and Name of the Montanines rested in one alone, called Charles the Sonne of Thomas
Montanine, a young man so honest & well brought vp, as any then
in Siena, who had a syster, that for beauty, (288) grace, curtesy and
honesty, was comparable with the best in all Thoscane. This poore
young Gentleman had no great reuenue, for that the patrimonie of
his predecessors was wasted in charges for entertainement of Souldiers
in the time of the hurly burly & debates aforesaid. A good parte also
was confiscate to the Chamber of Siena for trespasses and forfaitures
committed: with the remayne he sustained his family, and indiffer-
ently maintained hys porte soberly within his owne house, keping
his sister in decent & moderate order. The Maiden was called Angelica, a Name of trouth, without offence to other, due to hir. For in
very deede in hir were harbored the vertue of Curtesy and Gentlenesse, & was so wel instructed and nobly brought vp, as they which
loued not the Name or race of hir, could not forbeare to commend
hir, & wyshe theyr owne daughters to be hir lyke. In sutch wise as
one of hir chiefest foes was so sharpely beset with hir vertue and
beauty, as he lost his quiet sleepe, and lust to eate and drinke. His
name was Anselmo Salimbene, who woulde wyllinglye haue made
sute to marry hir, but the discord past, quite mortified his desire, so
soone as he had deuised the plot wythin his brayne and fansie. Notwithstanding it was impossible that the loue so lyuely grauen and
roted in his mind, could easily be defaced. For if once in a day he had
not seene hir, his heart did fele the torments of tosting flames, and
wished that the hunting of the Bore, had neuer decaied a family so
excellent, to the intent he myght haue matched himself with hir,
whome none other could displace out of his remembraunce, that was
one of the rychest Gentlemen and of greatest power in Siena. Now
for that he durst not discouer his amorous griefe to any person, was
the chiefest cause that martired most his hearte, and for the auncient
festred malice of those two families, he despayred foreuer, to gather
either floure or fruict of that affection, presupposing that Angelica

would neuer fixe hir Loue on him, for that his Parents were the cause of the defaite & ouerthrow of the Montanine house. . . .

(288v) During these haps it chaunced that a rich Cittizen of Siena, hauing a ferme adioyning to the Lands of Montanine, desirous to encrease his Patrimony (289), and annexe the same vnto his owne, and knowing that the yong Gentleman wanted many thinges, moued him to sel his inheritaunce, offring hym for it in ready money, a M. Ducates, Charles which of al the wealth and substaunce left him by his auncester, had no more remaynyng but that countrey Ferme, and a Palace in the City (so the rich Italians of ech City, terme their houses,) and with that lytle lyued honestly, and maintained his sister so wel as he could, refused flatly to dispossesse himselfe of the portion, that renewed vnto him the happy memory of those that had ben the chief of all the Common Wealth. The couetous wretch seeing himself frustrate of his pray, conceiued sutch rancor against Mon-tanine, as he purposed by right or wrong to make him not only to forfait the same, but also to lose his lyfe, following the wicked desire of tirannous Iesabell, that made Naboth to be stonned to death, to extort and wrongfully get his vineyard. . . .

This Citizen then purposed to accuse Montanine for offending against the law, bicause otherwise he could not purchase his entent, and the same was easy inough for him to compasse, by reason of his authority and estimation in the Citye: for the Endytemente (289v) and plea was no sooner red & giuen, but a number of post knightes appeared to depose against the poore Gentleman, to bear witnesse that he had trespassed the Lawes of the Countrey, and had sought meanes to introduce the banished, with intent to kyll the gouerners, and to place in state those factions, that were the cause of the Italian troubles. The myserable Gentleman knewe not what to do, ne how to defend himself. There were against him the Moone and the vii. starres, the state of the City, the Proctor and Iudge of the Courte, the wytnesses that gaue euidence, and the law whych condempned him. He was sent to Pryson, sentence was pronounced against him with sutch expedition, as he had no leysure to consider his affayres. . . .

Amongs al the comforts which this pore (290) Siena Gentleman found, although but a curssed Traitor, was thys vnfaithfull and pestiferous Camæleon, who came and offred him al the pleasure and kindnesse he was able to do. But the varlet attended conuenient tyme to make him taste his poyson, and to let him see by effect, how dan-gerous a thing it is to be il neighbored, hoping after the condempna-tion of Montanine he shoulde at pleasure purchase the Lordshippe, after whych with so open mouth he gaped. Ouer whome he had hys wyll: for two or three dayes after the recitall of the endytement, and giuing of the euydence, Charles was condempned, and hys fine sessed at M. Florins to be payed within xv. dayes, vntyl whych time to remaine in Pryson. And for default of sutch payment to loose his heade, bicause he had infringed the Lawes, and broken the Statutes of the Senate. This sentence was very difficult for poore Montanine to digest, who saw all his goodes like to be despoyled and confiscate, complayning specially the fortune of fayre Angelica his sister, whych all the tyme of the imprysonment of hir deare Brother, neuer went out of the house, ne ceased to weepe and lamente the hard fortune whereinto their family was lyke to fall by that new mischaunce. . . .

(290v) Whyle this fayre Damsell of Siena in this sort dyd torment hir self, poore Montanine seeinge that he was brought to the last extremity of his desired hope, as eche man naturally doth seke meanes to prolong his lyfe, knowing that all other help fayled for hys delyuer-aunce except he sold his land, aswel to satisfy the fine, as to preuayle in the rest of his Affaires, sent one of the gailers to that worshipfull vsurer the cause of hys Calamity, to offer him his land for the pryce and sum of a M. Ducates. The pernicious & trayterous villain seeing that Montanine was at his mercy, and stode in the water vp to the very throte, and knew no more what to do, as if already he had try-umphed of hys life and Land so greatly coueted, answeared him in this manner: My friend thou shalt say to Charles Montanine, that not long ago (291) I would willingly haue giuen him a good Summe of Money for his Ferme, but sithens that time I haue imployed my Money to some better profit. . . .

This detestable Villayne hauing sometimes offered M. Ducates to Charles for his Enherytaunce, will now doe so no more, aspiring the totall Ruine of the Montanine Family. Charles aduertised of his minde, and amazed for the Counsels decree, well saw that all thinges contraried hys hope and expectation, and that he must needes dye to satisfie the excessiue and couetous Lust of that Cormerant, whose mallice hee knew to be so vehement, as none durst offer him Money, by reason of the vnhappy desire of this neuer contented Varlet: For which consideration throughly resolued to dye, rather than to leaue hys poore Sister helplesse, and without reliefe, & rather than he would agree to the bargayne tending to his so great losse and dis-aduauntage, and to the Tirannous dealing of the wicked Tormentor of hys Lyfe, seeing also that all meanes to purge and auerre his inno-cency, was taken from him, the finall decree of the Iudges being already passed, he began to dispose himselfe to repentaunce and saluation of his Soule. . . .

(292v) When Charles thus complayned himselfe, and throughly was determined to dy, great pitty it was to see how fayre Angelica did rent hir Face, and teare hir golden Locks, when she saw how im-possible it was to saue hir obstinate brother from the cruel sentence pronounced vpon him, for whom she had imployed all hir wits and (293) fayre speach, to perswade the neerest of hir Kin to make sute. . . . But of one thing I can wel assure you, that if ill fortune had permitted that Charles should haue bin put to death, the gentle damsel also had breathed forth the final gasp of hir sorowful life, yeldinge therewithall the last end of the Montanine race and family. What booteth it to hold processe of long discourse ? Beholde the last day is come deferred by the Iudges, whereupon he must eyther satisfie the fine, or dye the next day after like a rebel & Traytor agaynst the state, without any of his kin making sute or meane for his deliuerance. . . . Angelica accompanied with hir kin, and the maidens dwelling by, that were hir companions, made the ayre to sound with outcries & waymentings, & she hir selfe exclaymed like a woman destraught of Wits, whose plaints the multitude assisted with like eiulations & outcries, wayling the fortune of the yong gentleman, & sorowfull to see the mayden in daunger to fal into some mishap. As these things were thus bewayled, it chaunced about .9. of the clocke at night, that Anselmo Salimbene, he whom we haue sayd to be surprised with the loue of Angelica, returning out of the Countrey, where he had remayned for a certayne time, and passing before the house of his Lady, according to his custome heard the voyce of women & maydens which mourned for Montanine, and therewithall stayd: the chiefest cause of his stay was, for that he saw go forth out of the Pallace of hys Angelica, diuers Women makinge Moane, and Lamentation: Wherefore he demaunded of the neyghbors what noyse that was, & whether any in those Quarters were dead or no. To whom they declared at length, al that which yee haue heard before. Salimbene hearing this story, went home to his house, and being secretly entred into his chamber, began to discourse with himselfe vpon that accident, and fantasying a thousand things in his heade, in the ende thought that Charles should not so be cast away, were he iustly or innocently condempned, and for the only respect of his sister, that (293v) shee might not bee left destitute of the Goods, and Inheritaunce. Thus discoursing diuers things, at length he sayd: I were a very simple person nowe to rest in doubt, sith Fortune is more curious of my felicity than I could wishe, and seeketh the effect of my desires, when least of all I thought vpon them. For behold, Montanine alone is left of all the mortall enimies of our house, whych to morow openly shal lose his head like a rebell and seditious person, vpon whose Auncesters, in him shall I be reuenged, and the quarell betweene our two Families, shall take ende, hauinge no more cause to feare renuing of discorde, by any that can descend from him. And who shall let mee then from inioying hir, whom I doe loue, hir brother being dead, and his goods confiscate to the Seigniory and she without all Maynetenaunce, and

Reliefe, except the ayde of hir onely beauty and curtesie? What mayntenaunce shall she haue, if not by the loue of some honest Gentleman, that for hys pleasure may support hir, & haue pitty vppon the losse of so excellent beauty? Ah Salimbene, what hast thou sayd? Hast thou already forgotten that a Gentleman for that only cause is esteemed aboue al other, whose glorious facts ought to shine before the brightnesse of those that force theymselues to followe vertue?....
(294) And not willing to forget a wrong done vnto me, whereof may I complayne of Montanine? What thinge hath hee euer done agaynst me or mine? And albeit his Predecessors were enimies to our Family, they haue therefore borne the Penaunce, more harde than the sinne deserued. And truely I should be afrayde, that God would suffer me to tumble into some mishap, if seeing one afflicted, I should reioyce in his affliction, and take by his decay an argument of ioy and pleasure. . . . Being assured, that there is no man (except he were dispoyled of all good nature & humanity) specially bearing the loue to Angelica, that I do, but he would be sory to see hir in sutch heauinesse and dispayre, & would attempt to deliuer hir from sutch dolorous griefe. For if I loue hir as I do in deede, must not I likewise loue all that which she earnestly loueth, as him that is nowe in daunger of death for a simple fine of a thousand Florens?.... Vaunt thy selfe then O Angelica, to haue forced a heart of it selfe impregnable, and giuen him a wound which the stoutest Lads, might sooner haue depriued of lyfe, than put him out of the way of his gentle kinde: And (294v) thou Montanine, thinke, that if thou wilt thy selfe, thou winnest to day so hearty a frende, as only death shall seperate the vnion of vs twayne, and of all our posterity. It is I, nay it is I my selfe, that shall excell thee in duety, poynting the way for the wisest, to get honor. . . . After this longe discourse seeing the tyme required dilligence, hee tooke a thousand Ducats, and went to the Treasurer of the fines, deputed by the state, whom he founde in his office, and sayde vnto him: I haue brought you sir, the Thousande Ducates, which Charles Montanine is bounde to pay for his deliueraunce. Tell them, and gieue him an acquittaunce that presently hee may come forth. The Treasorer woulde haue giuen him the rest, that exceeded the Summe of a Thousand Florens: But Salimbene refused the same, and receyuing a letter for his discharge, he sent one of his Seruaunts therewithal to the chiefe Gayler, who seeing that the Summe of his condemnation was payd, immediatly deliuered Montanine out of the Prison where he was fast shut, & fettered with great, & weyghty Giues. Charles thinckinge that some Frier had bin come to confesse him and that they had shewed him some mercy to doe hym to death in Prison, that abroade in open shame of the world he might not deface the Noble house whereof he came, was at the first sight astonned,

but hauing prepared himselfe to die praysed God, & besought him to vouchsafe not to forget him in the sorrowful passage, wherein the stoutest and coragious many times be faynt and inconstaunt. . . . When he was caried out of Pryson, and brought before the Chiefe Gayler, sodaynely his Giues were discharged from his Legges, and euery of the standers by looked merily vppon hym, without speakinge any Woorde that might affray hym. That Curtesie vnlooked for, made hym attende some better thynge, and assured hym of that whych before by any meanes hee durste not thyncke. And hys ex-pec(295)tation was not deceiued. For the Gayler sayde vnto hym: Bee of good Cheare Sir, for beholde the Letters of your discharge, wherefore you may goe at liberty whether you list. . . .

(295v) Montanine, when he was delyuered, forthwyth wente home to hys house, to comfort hir, whom he was more than sure to be in great distresse and heauinesse for his sake, and whych had so mutch neede of comfort as he had, to take his rest. . . . When Angelica was assured that it was hir Brother, sobbes wer layde aside, sighes were cast away, and heauy weepings conuerted into teares of ioy, she went to imbrace and kisse hir Brother, praising GOD for hys dely-uerance, and making accompt that he had ben raised from death to lyfe, considering his stoutnes of minde rather bent to dye than to for-go his Land, for so smal a pryce. . . . Their friends & kinsfolk being departed, & assu(296)red that none of them had payde his ransome, hee was wonderfully astonned, and the greater was his gryef for that he could not tell what hee was, whych withoute requeste, had made so gentle a proofe of his lyberality: if he knew nothing, farre more ignoraunte was his sister, forsomutch as she dyd thinke, that he had changed his mind, and that the horrour of death had made him sel his country inheritance, to hym whych made the first offer to buy the same: but either of them deceyued of their thought went to bed. . . .

And when hee saw the Day begyn to appeare, and that the Morn-yng, the Vauntcurrour of the day, summoned Apollo to harnesse hys Horsse to begynne his course in our Hemisphere, he rose and went to the Chamberlaine or Treasurer, sutch as was deputed for receypt, of the Fines, sessed by the State, whom he saluted, and re-ceyuing lyke salutation, he prayed hym to shewe hym so mutch pleasure as to tell hym the parties name, that was so Lyberall to satysfie his fine due in the Eschequer of the State. To whome the other aunswered: None other hath caused thy delyueraunce (O Mon-tanine) but a certain person of the World, whose Name thou mayst easily gesse, to whome I gaue an acquittance of thyne impryson-mente, but not of the iuste summe, bycause hee gaue me a Thousand Ducates for a Thousand Florens, and woulde not receyue the ouer-plus of the debte, whych I am readye to delyuer thee wyth thyne aquyttaunce. I haue not to doe wyth the Money (sayd Charles) onely I pray you to tell me the name of him that hath don me thys great curtesy, that hereafter I may acknowledge him to be my Friend. It is (sayd the Chamberlayne) Anselmo Salimbene, who is to bee commended and praysed aboue all thy parents and kinne, and came hither very late to bryng the Money, the surplusage whereof, beholde here it (296v) is. God forbid (sayd Montanine) that I should take awaye that, whych so happily was brought hither to rid me out of payne: and so went away wyth his aquittance, his mind charged with a numbre of fansies for the fact don by Salimbene. Being at home at his house, he was long time stayed in a deepe consideration, desirous to know the cause of that gentle parte, proceeding from him whose Parentes and Auncesters were the capitall Enimies of his race. In the end lyke one risyng from a sound sleepe, he called to mynd, that very many times he had seene Anselmo with attentiue Eye and fixed looke to behold Angelica, and in eying hir very louyngly, he passed euery day (before theyr gate) not shewing other countenaunce, but of good wyll, and wyth fryendly gesture, rather than any Ennimies Face, saluting Angelica at all tymes when he met hir. Wherefore Montanine was assured, that the onely loue of Salimbene towards his sister caused that delyueraunce. . . .

Hee called Angelica asyde, and beynge bothe alone together, hee vsed these or sutch lyke Woordes: You knowe deare Si(297)ster, that the higher the fall is, the more daungerous and greater gryefe he feeleth that doth fall from highe than hee that tumbleth downe from place more low and of lesser steepenes. . . .

But one thing alone ought to content vs, that amid so great pouerty, yl luck, ruine and abasement, none is able to lay vnto our charge any thing vnworthy of the nobility & the house, whereof we be descended, our lyfe being conformable to the generositie of our predecessors: whereby it chanceth, that although our poore estate be generally knowne, yet none can affirme, that we haue forligned the vertue of them, which vertuously haue lyued before vs. If so bee wee haue receiued pleasure or benefit of any man, neuer disdained I with al duety to acknowledge a good turne, stil shunning the vyce of ingratytude, to soyle the reputation: wherein hitherto I haue passed my lyfe. Is there anye blot which more spotteth the renoume of man, than not confessing receiued benefites and pleasures perfourmed in our necessity ?. . . . (297v)

It is Anselmo Salimbene, the son of our auncient and capital enimies, that hath shewed himself the very loyall and faithfull fryend of our family, and hath deliuered your brother by payment to the State, the summe of a Thousand Ducats to raunsome the life of him, who thought him to be his moste cruel aduersary. . . .

I can not tel what name to attribute to the deede of Salimbene, and what I ought to call that his curtesy, but this must I needes protest, that the example of his honestie and gentlenes is of sutch force, and so mutch hath vanquished me, as whether I shal dye in payne, or lyue at ease, neuer am I able to exceede his lyberallity. Now my life beyng ingaged for that which he hath don to mee, and hee hauynge delyuered the same from infamous Death, it is in your handes (298) (deare sister) to practize the deuyse imagined in my mind, to the intente that I may be onely bound to you for satisfying the liberalitye of Salimbene, by meanes whereof, you which wepte the death and wayled the lost liberty of your Brother, doe see me free and in safety hauyng none other care but to be acquited of hym, to whome both you and I be dearely bound. Angelica hearyng hir brother speak those words, and knowing that Salimbene was he, that had surpassed all their kinne in Amity and comforte of theyr familye, answered hir brother, sayinge: I woulde neuer haue thought (good Brother) that your deliuerance had come to passe by him whose name euen now you tolde, and that our Ennimyes breaking al remembraunce of Auncient quarels, had care of the health and conseruation of the Montanines. Wherefore if it were in my power I would satisfy the curtesy and gentlenesse of Anselmo. . . . Notwythstanding Brother, consider you wherein my power resteth to ayde & helpe you, and be assured (myne honor saued) I wyll spare nothynge for your content-ment. Sister (sayd Montanine) I haue of long time debated with my self what is to be done, and deuised what myghte be the occasion that moued this young Gentleman to vse so greate kindnesse toward mee, and hauing diligently pondred and waied what I haue seene and knowne, at length I founde that it was the onely force of Loue, which constrained his affection, and altered the auncient hatred that he bare vs, into new loue, that by no meanes can be quenched. . . . (298v)

And syth I am not able *with* goodes of Fortune to satisfie his boun-tye, it is your person which may supply that default, to the intent that you and I may be quytted of the Oblygation, wherein we stand bound vnto him. It behoueth that for the offer and reward of Money whych he hath imployed, we make present of your Beautye, not selling the pryce of your chastity, but delyueryng the same in exchaunge of curtesye, beyng assured for hys gentlenesse and good Nourtoure sake, hee wyll vse you none otherwyse, or vsurpe any greater auth-ority ouer you, than Vertue permitteth in ech gentle and Noble hearte. . . . (299)

At those words Angelica stode so astonned and confused, and so besides hir selfe, like as wee see one distraught of sense that feeleth himself attached with some amaze of the Palsey. In the end recouer-ing hir sprytes, and bee blubbered al with teares, hir stomacke pant-

ing like the Bellowes of a forge, she answeared hir brother in thys
manner: I knowe not louyng Brother by reason of my troubled minde
howe to aunswere your demaund, which seemeth to be both ryght,
and wronge, righte for respect of the bond, not so, in consideration
of the request. But how I proue the same, and what reason I can
alleadge and discouer for that proofe, hearken me so paciently, as I
haue reason to complayne and dispute vpon this chaunce more hard
and difficulte to auoide, than by reply able to be defended, sith that
Lyfe and the hazarding thereof is nothing, in regarde of that which
you wyll haue me to present with too exceeding prodigall Liberality,
and I would to God that Life mighte satisfie the same, than be sure
it should so soone be imployed, as the promise made thereof. . . . (300)

Ah Charles my Brother deare, where hast thou bestowed the Eye
of thy foreseeing mynde, that without prouidence and care of the
same due to honest Dames, and chast Damosels of our Family,
hauyng lost the goods and Fathers inheritance, wilt haue me in like
sort forgoe my Chastity, whych hytherto I haue kept with heedeful
dilygence. Wilte thou deare Brother by the pryce of my virginity,
that Anselmo shall haue greater victorye ouer vs, than he hath gotten by fight of Sword vpon the allied remnaunt of our house ?. . . .
O God why was not I choaked & strangled, so sone as I was taken
forth the secrete imbracements of my mothers Wombe, rather than
to arriue into this mishap, that either must I lose the thing I deeme
most deare, or die *with* the violence of my proper hands ? Come death,
(300v) come, and cut the vnhappy threede of my woefull Lyfe: stope
the pace of teares with thy trenchant Darte that streame outragiously
downe my face, and close the breathing wind of sighes, whych hynder
thee from doing thine office vpon my heart, by suffocation of my lyfe
and it: When she had ended those Words, hir speache dyd faile, and
waxing pale and faint, (sitting vppon hir stoole) she fared as though
that very death had sitten in hir place. Charles thynking that his
sister had bene deade, mated with sorrowe, and desirous to lyue no
longer after hir, seeing he was the cause of that sownyng, fell downe
dead vpon the Ground, mouing neither hand nor foote, as though
the soule had ben departed from the bodye. At the noyse which
Montanine made by reason of hys fall, Angelica reuiued out of sowne,
and seeinge hir Brother in so pytifull plyght, and supposing he had
bene dead for care of hys request, for beyng berieued of hir Brother,
was so moued, as a lyttle thynge would haue made hir do, as Thisbe
dyd, when she viewed Pyramus to be slayne. But conceyuing hope,
she threw hir self vppon hir Brother, cursing hir Fortune, bannyng
the Starres of cruelty, and hir lauish speach, and hir self for hir little
loue to hir brother, who made no refusall to dye to saue his Lande
for reliefe of hir: wher she denyed to yeld hir self to him that loued

hir with so good affection. In the end she applied so many remedies
vnto hir brother, sometimes casting cold water vpon his face, sometimes pinching and rubbing the temples and pulses of his armes and
his mouth with vineger, that she made hym to come agayne: and
seeing that his eyes were open, beholding hir intentiuely with the
countenance of a man half in despayre, she saied vnto him: ...

Be of good cheere, and doe wyth mee and my body what thou list,
giue and presente the same to whom thou pleasest. Wel be thou sure,
that so sone as I shal bee out of thy hands and power, I wyl be called
or esteemed thine (301) no more, and thou shalt haue lesse authority
to stay me from doing the deuises of my fantasie, swearing and pro-
testing by the Almighty GOD, that neuer man shall touch Angelica,
except it be in mariage, and that if he assay to passe any further, I
haue a heart that shall incourage my hands to sacrifice my Life to the
Chastitye of Noble Dames whych had rather dye than liue in slaunder
of dyshonesty. I wyll die a body without defame, and the Mynde
voyde of consent, shall receiue no shame or filth that can soyle or
spot the same....

Wherefore sayd he to Angelica, I was neuer in my Lyfe so desirous
to liue, but that I rather choose to dye, than procure a thinge that
should turne thee to displeasure and griefe, or to hazarde thine honor
and reputation in daunger or peryll of damage, which thou hast euer
knowne, and shouldest haue still perceyued by effect, or more properly to speak, touched with thy finger if that incomparable and rare
curtesy and Lyberality of Salimbene had not prouoked me to requyre
that, which honestly thou canst not gyue, nor I demaunde without
wronge to thee, and preiudice to mine owne estimation and honoure.
But what ? the feare I haue to be deemed ingrate, hath made me forget
thee, and the great honesty of Anselmo maketh me hope, yea and
stedfastly beleue, that thou shalt receiue none other displeasure, but
to be presented vnto him whome at other times we haue thought to
be our mortal ennimy.... (301v)

Angelica knew and confessed that hir brother did but his duetye,
& that she was bound by the same very bond. On the other side, hir
estate and virginall chastity, brake the endeuors of hir duety, and
denyed to doe that whych she esteemed ryght. Neuerthelesse shee
prepared hir self to follow both the one and the other: and by acquit-
ing the duety to hir brother, she ordayned the meane, to discharg
him of that, which he was bound to his benefactor, determinynge
neuerthelesse rather to dye, than shamefully to suffer hir selfe to be
abused, or to make hir lose the floure, which made hir glyster amongs
the maidens of the city, and to deface hir good fame by an acte so
vyllanous....

Anselmo was come home oute of the Countrey, whereof Charles

hauing intelligence, about the second houre of the night, he caused
his sister to make hir ready, & in company of one of their seruaunts
that caried light before them, they came to the lodginge of Salimbene, whose seruaunt seing Montanine so accompanied to knocke at
the Gate, if hee did maruel I leaue for you to think, (302) by reason
of the displeasure and hatred which he knew to bee betwene the two
families, not knowing that which had already passed for the beginning of a final peace of so many controuersies: for which cause so
astonned as he was, he went to tel his maister that Montanine was at
the gate, desirous secretely to talke vnto hym. Salimbene knowing
what company Charles had with him, was not vnwilling to goe downe,
& causing two Torches to be lighted, came to his gate to entertaine
them, & to welcome the brother and the sister, wyth so great curtesie
and friendship as he was surprysed with loue, seeing before his eyes
the sight of hir that burned hys heart incessantly, not discoueryng
as yet the secrets of his thought by making hir to vnderstand the good
wyl he bare hir, & how mutch he was hir seruant. . . .

When they were set downe, and al the seruants gone forth, Charles
began to say to Salimbene, these Words: You may not thinke it
straunge (sir Salimbene) if against the Lawes and Customes of our
Common Wealthe, I at thys tyme of the Nyght doe call you vp, for
knowyng the Bande wherewyth I am bound vnto you, I must for
euer confesse and count my selfe to be your slaue & bondman, you
hauing don a thing in my behalf that deserueth the name of Lord &
maister. . . . (302v) And bicause that I am well assured, that it is
Angelica alone whych hath kindled the flame of desire, and hath
caused you to loue that which your predecessours haue deadly hated,
that same sparke of knowledge, whych our misery could not quench
with all his force, hath made the way, and shewed the path whereby
we shall auoide the name of ingrate and forgetfull persons, and that
same which hath made you lyberall towards me, shalbe bountifully
bestowed vpon you. It is Angelica sir which you see present heere,
who to discharge my band, hath willingly rendred to be your owne,
submittinge hir selfe to your good wyll, for euer to be youres. And I
which am hir brother, and haue receiued that great good wyll of hir,
as in my power to haue hir wyl, do present the same, & leaue hir in
your hands, to vse as you would your owne, praying you to accept
the same, & to consider whose is the gift, and from whence it com-
meth, and how it ought to be regarded. When he had sayd so, Montanine rose vp, and without further talke, went home vnto his house.
If Anselmo were abashed at the Montanines arriuall, and astonned
at the Oration of Charles, his sodain departure was more to be mar-
uelled at, & therwithal to see the effect of a thing which he neuer
hoped, nor thought vpon. He was exceding glad & ioyfull to see him-

self in the company of hir, whome he desired aboue al things of the
world, but sory to see hir heauy and sorrowful for sutch chaunce.
He supposed hir being ther, to procede rather of the yong mans good
(303) and gentle Nature, than of the Maidens will and lykynge. For
whych cause taking hir by the hand, and holding hir betwene hys
armes, he vsed these or sutch lyke words: Gentlewoman, if euer I
had felt and knowne with what Wing the variety and lyghtnesse of
worldly thynges do flye, and the gaynes of inconstant fortune, at this
present I haue seene one of the most manifest profes which seemeth
to me so straunge, as almost I dare not beeleue what I see before myne
Eyes. I know well that it is for you, and for the seruice that I beare
you, that I haue broken the effect of that hatred, whych by inheritaunce I haue receiued against your House, and for that deuotion
haue deliuered your Brother. But I see that Fortune wyll not let mee
to haue the vpper hand, to bee the Conquerer of hir sodaine pangs.
But you your self shall see, and euery man shall know that my heart
is none other than noble, and my deuises tend, but to the exploit of all
vertue and Gentlenesse: wherefore I pray you (sayd he kissing hir
louingly) be not sad, and doubt not that your seruaunt is any other
now, hauing you in his power, than he was when he durst not dys-
couer the ardent Loue that vexed him, and held him in feeble state, ful
of desire & thought you also may bee sure, that he hath not had the
better hande ouer me, ne yet for his curtesy hath obteined victory,
nor you for obeying him. For sith that you be myne, and for sutch
yelded and giuen to me, I wyl keepe you, as hir whome I loue and
esteme aboue al things of the World, makyng you my Companion
and the onely mistresse of my goodes, heart, and wyll. Thinke not
that I am the Fryend of Fortune, and practise pleasure alone without
vertue. It is modesty which commaundeth me, & honesty is the guide
of my conceipts. Assure you then, & repose your comfort on mee:
for none other than Angelica Montanine, shall be the wyfe of Anselmo Salimbene: and during my life, I wyll bee the Fryend, the de-
fender and supporter of your house. At these good Newes, the drousie
and wandryng Spirite of the fayre Siena mayd awaked, who endyng
hir teares and appeasing hir sorrow, rose vp, & made a very lowe
reuerence vnto hir curteous fryend, thanking hym for hys greate and
incomparable liberalitye, promising all (303v) seruice, duetie, and
Amitye, that a Gentlewoman ought to beare vnto him, whom God
hath reserued for hir Spouse and husband. . . .

Glossarial Index to the Commentary

This index lists words, phrases, and names which have required elucidation in the Commentary. It is neither a concordance nor a complete list of annotations. Words are normally cited in simple form (i.e., nouns in the singular, verbs in the infinitive), whatever the form in the text. Phrases are normally cited under more than one key word. When more than one line-reference is given, the word has been used in more than one sense. An asterisk before a word or a reference indicates that the meaning is not covered, or is only partly covered, by O.E.D., or that a date given by O.E.D. is corrected.

A, *prep.*, ii. 44
abject, *sb.*, xiii. 104
abound, iii. 108
abroad, v. 16, xi. 21
acquittance, xiv. 95
action, xiii. 38
admiration, xiv. 97
*afford, Prol. 5
against, i. 46
*alacrity, xi. 42
alliance, vi. 33
allude, Epil. 13
ally, *sb.*, vii. 68
and, xiii. 36
angel, i. 96
answer, *vb*, xii. 8
appeal, stay an, x. 21
——, sue an, vii. 59, ix. 70
applausive, x. 32
appoint, xi. 67
apprehend, vi. 1
apprehension, xiii. 91
approve, i. 27
arrive, *sb.*, xvii. 62
at once, iv. 14, xiv. 131
atone, xvii. 4
attach, *sb.*, iii. 94
attend, viii. 26

Balance, x. 102
balk, *vb*, viii. 115

balls, hale these, vi. 15
band sides, iv. 48
base, *adj.*, vii. 84
bastardy, stripe of, xiii. 125
bead-roll, vii. 37
beard, before your, viii. 33
Bedlam, vi. 55
before your beard, viii. 33
beholding, vi. 88
bells, Milan, iii. 18
bewray, vi. 149
blab, *sb.*, vi. 165
——, *vb*, xiii. 3
bodkin, xv. 7
bond, vii. 32
boot, *sb.*, iv. 101
booted, iv. 21
booty you play, viii. 185
bosom, xi. 101
*brawl, *sb.*, xvii. 65
breath, x. 35
bride-lace, i. 83
*brief, in, iv. 47
bring him on his way to horse, vi. 65
—— it to an execution, vii. 29
broker, ix. 53
but, i. 25
by, xiii. 167, xvi. 7
by circumstance, viii. 87

117